URBANISATION AND THE GOVERNMENT OF MIGRATION

URBANISATION
AND THE
GOVERNMENT OF
MIGRATION

*The Inter-relation of Urban and
Rural Life in Zambia*

by

HELMUTH HEISLER

Foreword by
R. MANSELL PROTHERO

With an Appendix on some Migration Histories by
M. G. MARWICK

ST. MARTIN'S PRESS
NEW YORK   ·

TO KAROLINE AND LEWIS HEISLER

CONTENTS

FOREWORD

There is an extensive literature on population mobility in tropical Africa, and particularly on what is described as labour migration. In the latter especially, but in other forms of migration also, economic factors have been shown to be of paramount importance in influencing peoples' decisions to move. Other factors of a political and behavioural character are generally of lesser influence. Differentials in the location and exploitation of resources have resulted in the concentration of more advanced economic developments in limited areas. These islands of more precocious economic advancement, associated with agriculture and in the case of mining and industry with the growth of towns, are set in vast seas of limited development where economies still retain a strong subsistence element. The former have acted as magnets of attraction for peoples from the latter. Those under pressure, real or felt, move to the greater economic and social opportunities that seem to offer themselves. These apparent opportunities for betterment have not proved real for all, and migrants in Africa as in other parts of the world in the past and at the present have found themselves frustrated.

Some labour migration has been closely controlled, particularly to the mines of South Africa. In general much of the labour migration has been of a spontaneous nature, subject to only limited control, and has been influenced by the free play of market forces. Or thus it might seem to be, and certainly was in the case of massive seasonal movements of labour which occurred in West Africa more in the earlier decades of the present century than is the case at the present time. Relatively little specific attention has been paid to the influence on the movement of people in Africa of government measures of a direct and indirect nature. It is in this respect that Dr. Heisler's work on *Urbanisation and the Government of Migration* is an unusual and important contribution to the study of population mobility.

Zambia, in which the study is located, must be the best documented of African countries in respect of labour migration, both into, within and from the country, from the work of Godfrey Wilson in the 1930s to that of Clyde Mitchell and others in the 1950s and 1960s. The earlier economic developments along 'the line of rail' and the somewhat later development of the Copperbelt had labour needs and provided job opportunities for those from economically backward western, eastern and nothern parts of the country. The greater part of the study directed to these movements, in the home areas but even more in the destination areas of migrants, has been undertaken by social anthropologists. While by no means restricted in approach and taking due recognition of economic factors, their work has tended inevitably to concentrate more on socio-cultural aspects. Direct consideration of political and administrative factors in migration processes and patterns and their relationship to processes of urbanisation has been limited. This gap has now been filled by Dr. Heisler.

His study of urbanisation and the government of migration is rightly balanced in the consideration it gives to the interrelation of urban and rural life in Zambia. The majority of migration studies have tended to concentrate on either the rural or the urban ends of what is in effect a continuum. In Zambia government measures in both rural and urban areas have exercised important influences on the development of migration and consequent urbanisation, at different times and in different circumstances encouraging and inhibiting. People have responded to these in complex fashion. This book traces these complexities over time from early colonialism at the turn of the century through to political independence in the last decade. One may not agree in some respects with the political viewpoints from which Dr. Heisler has examined and interpreted these changes. One may not wholly subscribe to some of his conclusions, for example his concept of mass migration. Nonetheless the pioneer nature of this work makes it of major importance and it is thus to be commended. Though circumstances were and are different in other parts of Africa from those in Zambia we must hope that this book will provide the impetus for studies of a comparable nature to be undertaken elsewhere.

Liverpool   R. MANSELL PROTHERO

PREFACE

Labour mobility, as much as mineral wealth, was a prerequisite for the establishment of capitalism and the creation of wealth in Central Africa. It brought in its train the dislocation of tribes and enables the creation of an urban-capitalist society which determines the form of the Republic of Zambia.

While the rural areas were the heart of the country in 1900, the position had been well and truly reversed by 1970. The social problems of the country were first approached by considering the pre-capitalist societies as the main concern of Government, many of whose officials deplored the necessity to allow the centres of capitalism to suck in from these tribes their most virile men. Slowly, the approach to social problems and policy swung around to conceiving the pre-capitalist societies as the periphery and satellites of the capitalist-urban society which would propel the country into the twentieth century. While social continuity was the essence of social concern in the first phase of imperialism and capitalism, the Ten-Year Development Plan of 1947 symbolised the displacement of this focus by greater concern with standards of living and relationships in the urban-capitalist organisation. Money and cash fail to indicate adequately the concentration of organised economic power in colonial Zambia. Capitalism is thus used in preference to refer to the overwhelming domination of the life of the country by a few huge mining companies which were long controlled from London, Johannesburg and New York.

Within the public rules, practices and attitudes which are here termed the government of migration will be found a mirror of the modernisation of Zambia. The interest of this study extends to the contribution of the government of migration to modernisation itself which, at the empirical level, is approached in three ways. One of these is an examination of the rural scene, and in Chapter II there is a review of the sequential societal structures of the country and the peasant economies, while in Chapter V the rural pressures which influenced the mobility of women are evaluated. In Chapters III and IV, the second approach is an account of the institutions of the labour market and the meaning of the change from recruiting wage labour in villages to recruiting it at the gates of places of work. Thirdly, in Chapters VI and VII the interaction between the government of migration and urbanisation is considered in relation to the sequence of three forms of urbanisation: Labour Camps, Towns for Africans and African Towns.

From this attempt to mirror reality, in Tables 8, 9 and 10 there is an attempt to epitomise the more important elements in the institutions of the peasantry, the labour market and urbanisation. Though generalisation of these models to other countries in Africa would be fraught with difficulty, because of their divergent historical experiences, it may be found that such models are required as baselines for comparative studies of population mobility in Africa.

To my mind this study affirms the validity of the observation by John Stuart Mill that 'the occupation of teaching a branch of knowledge . . . is a help rather than an impediment to the systematic cultivation of the subject itself.' For questions about the evolution of their society put to me by students at the

Oppenheimer College of Social Service, Lusaka, in the early 1960s could not then be answered, and prompted the explorations of which this study is a product. Professor Paul Halmos then provided me with a work situation at University College, Cardiff, which was as conducive to research as to teaching. These two activities reinforced each other in a way which permitted me to pursue research on Africa seriously for the first time – a situation, alas, less common in British universities than is often presumed. Polytechnics are concerned that research and teaching should be combined by academic staff because academic activity can be improved in this way, and so my transfer to the Lanchester Polytechnic provided an appropriate environment to prepare the manuscript of this study.

I am indebted to the Government of Zambia for access to whatever documents in the official archives my inclinations indicated might prove of interest. With the aid of this data the parameters of this study were identified – though this resource has been more obviously employed in the parallel study of estates and classes which formed my doctoral thesis. Of equal importance as a resource have been numerous conversations with former colleagues in the civil service of Zambia and acquaintances in the European community, many of whom encountered the country in the 1930s and recalled the people and issues of the time. Social attitudes constitute the presumptions of many social policies which are but weakly illuminated in archival data and I was indeed fortunate that these attitudes were thrown up and crystallised in these meetings and unrestricted conversations. It is with diffidence that I touch upon changes in the 1970s which can only be inadequately analysed by those who do not live in Zambia; to explain with the aid of documents alone the swift changes of the 1970s will in itself scarcely allow one to observe their nuances. The paucity of information subsequent to the publication of the 1969 census provides another inhibition to an up-to-the-moment comment, but I have not hesitated to point to the more obvious trends.

The Foreword by Dr. R. Mansell Prothero (Reader in Geography and Director, African Mobility Research Project, University of Liverpool) and the Appendix by Professor Max Marwick (Professor of Sociology, University of Stirling) call for my grateful acknowledgement. Dr. Prothero's long-standing connection with the investigation of African population mobility enables him to place in a comparative context studies of the population of Zambia. Professor Marwick has studied some people of the Eastern Province of Zambia (1965) and in so doing enquired into their experiences of migration. While the craft of the social scientist is in the main inferior to that of the novelist in evoking the atmosphere of situations and endowing their characters with flesh and blood, human experience can, by means of case studies, be brought to life for those who tire of the neutral prose of social analysis. Professor Marwick's Appendix, composed of a few brief cases of individual migration, introduces a little colour which, added to my account, helps to reinforce some of its meaning. My final debt is to Jill and our boys who have made my task lighter by means of their interest and tolerance whenever I have ignored them in favour of my curiosity about Zambia.

Coventry   HELMUTH HEISLER
1973

CHAPTER I
OVER-URBANISATION

URBAN ORIGINS

To explain how and why the towns of Zambia* were formed is the task of this enquiry. Three perspectives will be used to illuminate their growth. One of these concerns the motivations of men and women. The several ways they interpreted their situations in the rural and urban areas not only influenced their propensity to migrate but in addition helped to form distinct patterns of migration. Another perspective is concerned with the economic demand for the services of male migrants in the workplaces around which towns mushroomed. These were some distance from their birthplaces. Thus the nature of the foreign and domestic labour markets affected both the distribution of migrants and their economic conditions at industrial-urban centres. And thirdly we examine the conditions and interests which initially opposed the building of towns and were then reversed. In particular, it will be shown that the Provincial Administration blocked induced urban growth until it was challenged if not superseded in importance by functional civil servants in 1945-6, when it became policy to stabilise the urban population of Zambia. The rural exodus provoked much disquiet in the ranks of the Provincial Administration who perceived their colonial duty to be the generation of a 'civilised' society out of the bush and primitive technologies of pre-contact Zambia. These civil servants in the main did not believe that urbanisation was the right path towards 'civilisation'. For this reason they believed that migration, which supplied the manpower for urbanisation, should be checked.

Before contact was made with Europeans there were but a few large stockaded settlements in the present Fort Jameson District, among the Ila-Tonga people in the Southern Province, and Kasama District. Following contact these were disbanded into small villages, which were the common pre-contact

* The constitutional history of Zambia began in 1899 with the proclamation of the Barotseland-North-Western Rhodesia Order in Council. In the following year the North-Eastern Rhodesia Order in Council formed a parallel territory north of the Zambesi and present day Rhodesia. In 1911 the two territories were amalgamated into Northern Rhodesia. Throughout these early years the territories were administered by the British South Africa Company which ceased to discharge this duty in 1924 when the Northern Rhodesia Order in Council proclaimed the territory to be a British Protectorate. By this Order the British Government assumed the direct administration of Northern Rhodesia. This lasted until 24 October 1964 when sovereignty was transferred to the people and Republic of Zambia.

settlements (1944 Native Locations: 5; Kay 1967: 9, 38-9). Small villages had long been popular because large ones were difficult to defend, unless the defenders were strong and militant, and because the soil was so poor that it could rarely support large concentrations of people. With the introduction of *Pax Britannica*, the military need for large stockaded settlements vanished.

Large settlements in modern Zambia owe their origin to British Imperialism which sanctioned the migration of Europeans into Central Africa. Preliterate peoples would be raised out of their barbarism and it was believed that Britain would be strengthened by this very same expansion overseas. Cecil Rhodes who founded modern Zambia perceived imperialism as the outstanding instance of the government of migration. 'My cherished idea', he declared, 'is a solution to *the social problem*, i.e. in order to save 40,000,000 inhabitants of the United Kingdom from bloody civil war, we colonial statesmen must provide new lands to settle the surplus population, to provide new markets for the goods produced in the factories and mines. The Empire . . . is a bread and butter question. If you want to avoid civil war you must become imperialists' (Lenin 1968: 74). It is not surprising that the British South Africa Company, founded by Rhodes to exploit Central Africa, and the effective government of modern Zambia between 1895 and 1924, should let it be known at an extraordinary meeting in January 1918 that 'it was an association formed for the purpose of gain'.

Not only did Rhodes wish to solve the social problem of Britain but he wished, by occupying Central Africa, to forestall any advance by Boers from South Africa who might wish to annex the region. For these twin motives in imperial policy Central Africa must be settled by British who would only come if it were for their profit. The bait was the mineral wealth owned by the British South Africa Company. But this would remain idle under the bush if there were no labourers to dig and transport it. The density of African population was low and insufficient to supply the labour demands of mines from the resources of immediately adjacent tribes. In order to reduce the 'disproportion' between capital accumulation and consumption in Britain, imperialism in Zambia created a 'migrant labour system' (Wilson 1941: 18). The settlements of these migrant labourers were the origin of the contemporary African Towns. Placed in a comparative perspective, 'This sudden juxtaposition of twentieth-century cities and extremely primitive cultures (virtually stone-age in their organisation and technology) give rise in some respects to a sharper rural-urban contrast than can be found anywhere else in the world' (Davis and Golden 1954: 20).

By the extension of political and economic frontiers towns were inaugurated in land-locked Zambia. Priority in time must be accorded to the towns founded as administrative centres for the territorial Governments. Fort Jameson, in the present Eastern Province, was the first and controlled access to Zambia through the Eastern Gateway. Immediately following the Ngoni Rebellion in 1898 it was laid out as a capital for North-Eastern Rhodesia. When North-Eastern Rhodesia was split off from British East Africa, Fort Jameson became its capital. From Malawi, through Fort Jameson, were conveyed the best aspects of British Imperialism: preference for Africans; discrimination against Europeans, especially those whose mother tongue was not English; and the Indian Civil Service tradition of impartial lawgiving. The pressures which tugged the evolving social systems of Zambia in the direction of making them resemble those of East Africa entered Zambia through Fort Jameson.

But Livingstone, on the Zambesi River and boundary with Rhodesia, sat astride the Southern Gateway and the pressure of South Africa. Europeans entered Zambia through this Gateway in pursuit of their own interests. For long Livingstone competed with Fort Jameson and, in the end, Fort Jameson won the battle for political dominance in colonial Zambia whereas Livingstone keeps economic control. Symbolically, the economic life of colonial Zambia came to be dictated through Livingstone and the political life of the country through Fort Jameson. On 24 October 1964 Fort Jameson won when British handed over the state of Zambia to Africans who commenced measures to bring the economic forces, inspired by South Africa, and filtered through Livingstone, under Zambian control. When Ian Smith and Rhodesia unilaterally declared independence from Britain on 11 November 1965, Zambia, to protect her autonomy, began to reopen the Eastern Gateway to East Africa. But on this occasion it was directly to the north of Fort Jameson, with a number of consequences for new urban growth which have still to be assessed.

At the 'Old Drift' outside Livingstone a settlement of roughnecks and bar keepers began in 1898. Livingstone was founded in 1905 when the railway arrived from Bulawayo in the south and the people moved from the 'Old Drift' into the town. Railway traffic, the transit of African labour to Rhodesia and South Africa, the tourist trade of the Victoria Falls, and cattle dealing, occupied the town until 1907. Then the capital of North-Western Rhodesia was moved from Kalomo, a few miles to the north, to Livingstone. In the previous year, from Livingstone, the European voice was heard in the first regular newspaper published in the country and with the seat of Government also in Livingstone this town became the centre of European influence. When the railway had pushed just north of Broken Hill and, from there, a road had been made with Tanzania and North-Eastern Rhodesia the two northern Rhodesias were amalgamated in 1911 and Livingstone became the capital of Northern Rhodesia. The capital moved to Lusaka in 1935, partly to escape from some of the influence of Europeans in Livingstone.

In 1902 lead and zinc, which could be mined at low cost, were discovered at Broken Hill and in 1904 the Rhodesia Broken Hill Development Company was formed. The commencement of mining at Broken Hill in 1904 provided the incentive to extend the economic frontier of European South Africa to the north of Bulawayo. To bring supplies of machinery, men and food to the mine and export minerals, the railway to Broken Hill was completed in 1906. Broken Hill became the headquarters of the railways in Zambia, of the Central African Road Services, the largest road passenger and haulage service in Zambia, and of the Central Province. The substitution of motor for porter services which was completed by 1927 in the Luapula and Northern Provinces, with the exception of Chiengi station on Lake Mweru, completed the next important official communication link for the country.

Between Livingstone and Broken Hill to the north a ribbon development of settlements grew up around the railway halts. By chance they passed through some of the best commercial farming areas in Zambia and attracted Afrikaner and British farmers. These halts distributed the produce of these farmers and sold them supplies. Not far south of Lusaka, the first annual agricultural show was held at Kafue in 1910. Settlement began on a permanent basis in the farming areas around Lusaka in 1905, following the arrival of the railway; but the first private building was not erected there until 1908; and in 1911 Lusaka was described as still very much a sleepy farming village, whose situation on a limestone plateau made drainage expensive.

When the British South Africa Company handed over control of the country to the British Government, while retaining free access to the mineral wealth of the country, a new policy for exploiting this wealth was devised. From this dates the inception of the Copperbelt and the largest population concentration in Zambia. The British South Africa Company declared itself ready to lease mineral rights only to those companies whose resources were large enough to guarantee to undertake costly exploration and the capital investment for mining. Active exploration followed, at first based on Ndola, officially founded in 1924. Ndola, which was reached by the railway in 1909, became the commercial centre of the Copperbelt and the headquarters of the Copperbelt Province. Mining settlements sprang up and in 1928 the old Nkana Township was established. Alongside this, in 1935 the handsomely laid out town of Kitwe began official life. In 1929 the Roan Antelope Copper Mine began production and developed residential facilities for European employees at the garden town of Luanshya. Thus between 1924 and 1930 the most important settlements on the Copperbelt were born.

Minute administration centres around the Bomas of Abercorn, Mongu, Fort Rosebery and Feira were and are the remaining outstanding population concentrations in Zambia. When the large settlements along the line of rail began the remaining population of the hinterland was thinly distributed, with densities below five persons to the square mile, in tiny hamlets which rarely contained more than thirty people.

PUBLIC POLICIES

Increasing numbers of Africans relinquished their traditional pursuits and came forward to fill the many jobs in the new settlements on the political and economic frontiers of Europe. Should the public attitude towards these events be total indifference? Or should the public authorities steer changes in such a way that the European entrepreneurs and shareholders were completely satisfied? Shortsighted as imperialism in Central Africa happened to be in so many respects, it is to the credit of the imperialists that, in spite of the inclination to reap the rewards available from the outrageous exploitation of labour, a middle path between the interests of capitalism and the African people was sought. The same framework of attitudes which moulded British Imperialism specified the public response to the issues raised by the migration of Africans to work in large settlements. Indeed, the government of migration was the most determined effort to promote the welfare of Africans in colonial Zambia. To encourage *industrialisation without urbanisation* was the wish of public policy during the first phase of the government of migration.

One perspective on the government of migration is to gauge its contribution to induced development – the raising of standards of living and the increase in the effective choices available to people as a result of public policy. For conceptual purposes induced development may be divided into community development, services, and community organisation compartments. Most often induced development is conceived as the supply of social and economic services to form the social overhead capital of schools, roads, credit organisation and the like without which subsequent and desired changes are impossible. Less often induced development − in the form of community development − is concerned with morale. Community development is thus concerned with the socio-psychological adjustment of people's attitudes to give them the will to make the most of the opportunities created for them by the supply of social overhead capital.

But a resource which tends to be neglected in programmes of induced development is relational and arises from the state of community organisation. The quality and form of social relationships may serve or impede development; particular states of community organisation block or facilitate specified changes. For instance, mining and smelting in mid-eighteenth-century England was arrested by the absence of large settlements in the neighbourhoods of many mines. A particular state of community organisation became the goal for the government of migration in Zambia. This goal aimed at a balanced sexual ratio in the rural peasant societies and a shortage of women in the large settlements. All this absorbed more attention, over a longer period, than did community development or extension services programmes after the Second World War; the government of migration was the prime obsession of the colonial government. Nowadays, by contrast, the African government of Zambia tackles the causes of rural exodus and community disorganisation through community development and service programmes, rather than by directly regulating community organisation in the manner of its colonial predecessor.

Progress through community development and service programmes are the innovation of this century. But ever since recorded history governments have been aware that community organisation and prosperity are related and so it is of little wonder that the colonial Government should have singled this out as its first priority. Impetus to this was added by imperial policy in the British dependencies between the two world wars. This was outlined in 1922 by Lord Lugard in *The Dual Mandate in British Tropical Africa*, which became the bible of British colonial administration. This was an expansion of ideas and obligations contained in Article 22 of the Covenant of the League of Nations concluded in 1919. *The Dual Mandate* makes no mention of community development and allows little part for rural extension services, because it was believed that British dependencies would develop according to the activities of western capitalism as well as the capacities inherent in peasant societies. Private enterprise and the state of community organisation would, in combination, make Africa 'civilised'. Rural depopulation was a wound which sapped the strength of rural community organisation. Lest this be irreparably disrupted the careful government of the migration required for industrialisation was imperative.

The reconciliation of opposites was the task of the Dual Mandate. Due regard for humanity and self-interest are often incompatible. Britain as an imperial power 'opened' her dependencies to the ravages of capitalism, in part by ensuring that the labour demands of industry were satisfied. As the Deputy Administrator of what is now Zambia remarked in 1898, 'the export of labour to Mashonaland is one of the obvious directions in which we can contribute to the development and prosperity of Rhodesia' (Kuczynski 1949: 439). Only this could stir the African peoples out of the slumber and decadence which enwrapped them and which stultified their progress, according to Victorian and Edwardian opinion; only the 'open door' would repay the money and hopes invested in mines, railways and plantations. It mattered little where an African was employed if he was to be purged of his history and habits, but there were insufficient Africans to meet all the demands for labour in Southern Africa. Should Mashonaland (in present-day Rhodesia) become the favoured target for development by African labour? Tension between this objective and that of promoting economic expansion everywhere, of making the door truly 'open', appeared when the South Africa Inter-Colonial Conference held at Bloemfontein in 1903 decided that 'all British possessions in South, Central and East Africa should be an open field for labour recruiting, and that all natives should be allowed to choose their own spheres of work.' The freedom of labourers to select their own employers, the needs of industries increasingly identified with the prosperities of different countries, and the concern of governments to promote the interests of their own countries, from then on tussled to influence the distribution of African labourers.

Yet there was no reason why African societies and institutions should become no more than pale imitations of Europe. Unlike the capitalists, Lugard and many other colonial servants believed that inherent in African institutions was an ability to develop in desirable yet non-European ways. It was the task of the colonial service to nurture this capacity for African evolution and protect it from those pressures of capitalism which would turn African dependencies into Western satellites. Quite opposed, these 'Open Door' and 'Self-Determination' principles of colonial policy motivated the contradictory results of the government of migration. Contemporary Africa is as much obsessed with this question, posed by neocolonialism, as was the colonial service. Hence the practical measures taken in pursuit of 'Self-Determination' have contemporary relevance. Having once unleashed the radical and capitalist forces of the 'Open Door', could the conservative interests in 'Self-Development' – with governmental prompting – override the social problems of capitalism and trace an African path to development?

Government played its part in increasing the supply of labour: it provided, through the poll tax, an added incentive for tribesmen to seek wage employment. After 1905 it was no longer possible for tribesmen to pay their taxes in kind and this added a pressure to their lives to induce them to earn cash which must in part be used to pay taxes. This served the twofold purpose of the 'Open Door'. First, it aided the establishment of capitalist enterprise by ensuring the availability of the labour factor of production. Secondly, it partly paid for the attainment of law and order without which capitalism would feel insecure. Until the Colonial Development and Welfare Act of 1940 the government of a dependency was obliged to pay for itself and any social overhead capital from its own local resources. The poll tax paid by Africans in Zambia made a vital, though diminishing, contribution to this: whereas in 1936 ordinary income tax paid by Europeans provided 26 per cent of the revenue of government, the revenue derived from the taxation of Africans was 13 per cent of the total (1938 Colonial 145: 111, 129). Without the encouragement of migration the ability of the Government to initiate the prerequisites for development would have been seriously impaired.

A new look at migration policies accompanied the beginning of large scale copper production. This created the danger that all the Africans in Southern Africa would be decanted from their villages into the industrial areas. By the later 1920s the colonial Government wished to avoid any accusation of impinging on the freedom of the individual through the direction of labour, though this apprehension was temporarily suspended during the Second World War. Much more important, the prospect of a rural vacuum faced the Government when it allowed the 'Open Door' to be implemented in the form of the Casual Labour System. How were villagers to be fed, housed and controlled in the cramped industrial camps? What future was there for African 'Self-Determination' if tribesmen became townsmen and wage earners?

'Stabilisation' was the name given by the local Government to its efforts to control migration. Without this 'stabilisation' of the peasant systems their 'Self-Determination' was impossible. The issues involved in 'stabilisation' cannot be understood without a closer examination of 'Self-Determination', in particular the question of what population and what kind of society was to be encouraged to chart its own destiny. To a large degree the colonial service was manned by refugees from the overcrowding, squalor and bitterness of the First Industrial Revolution; colonial service was an alternative to the self-discipline of suburbia and provided a more leisurely, idealised, rural existence where the fellowship of trust and not the oppressiveness of inequitable contracts regulated social relationships (Glass 1968; Furse 1962; Heussler 1963). A second source of the aversion of the colonial service to urbanisation was the belief that Europe and Africa were destined to be culturally separate and that the most worthwhile resources of Africa inhered in her traditional institutions. Through the instrument of 'native administration' these would be reformed and evolved to the point where the protection and guidance of the colonial power could be dispensed with (Lugard 1965; Lee 1967). But urban life in Africa offered no similar resource and hope, according to many colonial servants who had adopted their profession to avoid this kind of life in Britain.

In November 1935 the colonial service was first called upon to safeguard the 'Self-Determination' of the peasant systems. Rioting had occurred on the Copperbelt of Zambia, and a Royal Commission made a report. It observed that a choice between urban and rural 'stabilisation' was necessary to evolve measures which would prevent further discontent. The question whether urbanisation should be encouraged and what services should be provided for an urbanised population on the Copperbelt was considered by the Native Industrial Labour Advisory Board, which was set up after the riots. In its first report, the Board advised 'that there is a gradual tendency towards stabilisation of labour in industrial areas and that no general steps are necessary or desirable to encourage or discourage this tendency at present.' While the 'Open Door' committed the colonial service to permit industrialisation it did not bind it to build an urban society.

The government of migration was essentially 'a policy of retarding stabilisation' (25.1.1944 SEC/LAB/71). The actual arguments used in its favour were twofold. First, in the event of a slump there would be a major African employment problem. This would mean that a colonial government, denied generous aid by the metropolitan power, would be faced with an unemployed, urban population which would be dependent on it for relief. If they lost touch with peasant life the unemployed Africans would not be able to return to the peasant systems to sustain themselves, as they did in the 1931 slump. As long as there were no social security arrangements *in* the industrial society, the peasant systems must be kept viable. Secondly, and more positively, the peasant systems could not advance without the injection of wealth from industrialisation by means of remittance and money brought back by returning migrant labourers. As labour was their major economic asset the 'Self-Determination' of the peasant systems depended on their ownership of the workers and families employed on the Copperbelt and along the line of rail, which split Zambia into east and west.

Government was accused of adopting a policy of *laissez-faire* in this matter. In fact its policy was more positive. The colonial service appreciated that a degree of urbanisation was occurring; that a steadily increasing number of Africans were tending to spend their lives in the towns; and that there was an increasing juvenile population which either had never been in the rural areas or had never been there since infancy. It was realised that the system of migratory labour under the Casual Labour System was very wasteful of energy and manpower. These problems would be made more acute if urbanisation were encouraged by providing amenities in the urban areas. It was better that every facility should be given to labourers in the large settlements to return at frequent intervals to their villages.

The objects of the government of migration were to avoid accelerating the process of urbanisation 'to the detriment of the rural community which was constantly being drained of the cream of its adult male population and to keep workers in touch with their tribal life as long as possible' (25.1.1944 SEC/LAB/71). Several employers were in favour of workers returning to their villages to rest every eighteen months or so. Underground mineworkers especially appeared to deteriorate after this length of time. In pursuance of this policy the government encouraged voluntary savings schemes and transport bonus schemes, and sought to foster cheap and rapid transport. Rest camps on labour routes were also provided.

The distinct social control and welfare objectives of 'stabilisation' will now be apparent. Urban unrest would mark the poverty of the peasant systems and their divorce from the urban settlements along the line of rail. Social control was indeed a precondition for the success of both the 'Open Door' and 'Self-Determination' policies and so its instruments had long and wide-ranging implications. When in 1935 the Royal Comission criticised the government for losing contact with the workers on the Copperbelt two social control solutions competed for adoption. Local government institutions suitable for an urban society and Africans could be introduced. Inevitably this would entail the copying of British practices and the denial of 'Self-Determination' through uniquely African institutions. Though the government baulked at this solution it agreed to build African townships with urban governments for the tiny handful of middle-class Africans indispensable to an industrial society. To do more would have alienated the majority of industrial workers from their peasant obligations.

But the reduction of unemployment in the cash economy remained the key objective of social control. By extending certain features of the government of the peasant systems into the urban areas, such as native courts and councils of tribal elders (Epstein 1953, 1958), it was hoped that there would be a visible reminder to the worker that he was no more than a temporary proletarian and that his future remained wrapped up with that of his village. Recognition of the settlements along the line of rail as administrative units which were different in kind from those which pertained in the peasant systems was denied. Yet the administrative authorities of the peasant system, Native Authorities, were not to be entrusted with the direct control of civic affairs in these camps. This would have acknowledged the permanency of cash employment for their inhabitants. Moreover, it would do violence to the theory of native administration, with its desire to give every tribe its own Native Authority. To put a homogeneous Native Authority in charge of a heterogeneous industrial population would violate the first principles of native administration. This would also have the effect of stealing the population of other Native Authorities and so countenancing the redistribution of population. For this reason, until the early 1960s, the Provincial Administration ascribed the residents of the densely populated Copperbelt to the rural Native Authorities from which they or their parents originated. The result was that this élite cadre of the colonial service recognised as its inhabitants only the peoples who had been in the Copperbelt before colonisation; the *de jure* population of the Copperbelt, on this assumption, was about one twentieth of its *de facto* population. As an urban area was a place to settle, the large settlements on the Copperbelt were more appropriately termed 'industrial areas'.

The rationality of the government of migration was a social theory based on the following model of desirable economic relations and social action. Zambia was composed of consumer and producer areas, which corresponded to the peasant systems and 'industrial areas' respectively. Workers should commute from their consumer dormitories to the factory. This was the only source of considerable wealth. Wealth would be distributed and spent in the consumer areas after the workers returned home from work. Between shifts men would rest in their consumer dormitories because the management of the factory refused to increase the cost of production by providing more than camping facilities on the factory precincts. Only in the consumer areas could a wholesome family life be enjoyed. After all, the object of production was to increase consumption and welfare, and on this the progress to 'Self-Determination' would depend. Industry and the 'industrial areas' must be a servant and not the master of the consumer society. It was considered morally wrong to grant any selfish autonomy to those who were idle and not public spirited enough regularly to undertake the arduous and long treks from the producer areas to their consumer wives and children resident in the peasant systems.

OVER-URBANISATION

This fear of urbanisation, as distinct from industrialisation, was not peculiar to public policies in Zambia. Many other African countries devised measures to deal with the unwanted flood to the towns in the 1960s (Hance 1970: 277-9). By urbanisation three things are indicated: the movement of people from rural to urban areas and the increase in the proportion of the population of Zambia who live in urban areas; the transformation of one kind of urban social system into another; and the unique resources of urban systems which distinguish them from rural systems (Tables 8, 9, and 10). Rapid urbanisation became an important reproach on the modernisation of the Third World. As such it was developed into the theory of over-urbanisation for which a scientific status, belief that it reflected observable and measurable realities, was claimed (Davis and Golden 1954; Hauser 1963).

Without disagreeing with the theory of over-urbanisation at this point, it is necessary to register two ways in which the present study differs from methods most commonly employed in the study of over-urbanisation. First, very often over-urbanisation has been investigated by comparing similar aspects of industrialisation and urbanisation among a range of countries so that statistical norms for these features, in developed and underdeveloped areas, could be calculated. It has proved convenient to include only large towns, with populations in excess of 100,000 for example, as indices of urbanisation. This disregards not only much urbanisation in Zambia, where it is vigorous in much smaller centres, but also the discontinuities with previous conditions occasioned by industrialisation, urbanisation and political change (Epstein 1967: 276). The effects of these discontinuities must be understood as part of the comprehension of over-urbanisation in Zambia. Secondly, some aspects of urbanisation are not universal and are specific to certain regions or countries (Roth and Wittich 1968: 1215) and the very abstract approach to over-urbanisation will overlook these particulars. What is attempted, therefore – recognising the importance for a country of small-scale urbanisation and the uniqueness of its own urbanisation experiences and forms – is a developmental examination of the context of urbanisation in one country, Zambia.

The logic of the theory of over-urbanisation, in social science and public policies, begins with rural poverty. Rural poverty pushes people out of rural areas and has three consequences. First, this migration is premature because people enter towns where there are no jobs for them. Rather than expel their unemployed, the towns provide scarce facilities for them in order to persuade them not to become a nuisance and in order to improve their welfare which is low by urban standards. To pay for this the towns become parasitic and gobble up resources which would have been better diverted to investment in production and the desolate rural areas. Urban unemployment and parasitic towns are two signs of over-urbanisation. Secondly, the rural exodus makes rural poverty worse. Young adults are in the majority among those who quit rural societies, and their absence disorganises the only known ways of rural production and relationships. Thirdly, the solution is to return parasitic townsfolk to rural societies, prop them up, and cut towns down to viable proportions. Reinforcing this debatable economic and social logic is a belief that dense settlements and overcrowding detract from the quality of life and that sparse populations and unblemished nature are desirable.

Although the theory of over-urbanisation lays claim to be part of the science of cities, and pretends to avoid the inaccurate interpretations inherent in public policies supposedly grounded on social myths, the theory shares the same defects as past public policy in Zambia. Essentially, over-urbanisation theory and public policies generally are concerned with connections between industrialisation and urbanisation, which are presumed to be one way. This prejudgement leads to the dominant interest of city scientists and policy makers: whether the economy can support urbanisation. Thus the possibility of urbanisation supporting economic development is excluded more often that not from both over-urbanisation theory and public policy making. It is of interest that, in the single study of this connection in the development of Zambia, it was concluded that the relationship is 'ambiguous' (Barber 1967: 107–119). Part of the task of Chapter VIII will be to revaluate over-urbanisation in the light of the Zambian experience and the present attempt to explore the possibility of two-way relationships between urbanisation and economic change.

SYSTEMS

By means of a developmental approach the interrelations of industrialisation and urbanisation will be examined. Development reveals a discontinuity between a point of reference and a succeeding social existence. Social systems and social action systems are the kinds of developments which will be examined (Table 8). Rules, roles and relations interlocked in a distinctive pattern of pressure are the essence of a social system; the meanings and motivations a group or person obtains from interpreting a social situation form the corresponding essence of a social action system. When contact with Europeans was initiated, there was one type of social action system available to Africans; several coexist today. Thus social action systems develop, in this study, by the increase in the behavioural choices available to people. The relative differentiation and complexity of social systems is a measure of their development.

This outlook on social development in Zambia concerns the creation, transformation, and partial dissolution of systems which are to be regarded as open technically. If raw social resources enter a system and it emits certain social products as a result it is open; if nothing enters or leaves it is closed. Discontinuity between a system and its successor occurs when the inflow of resources to a system changes. The decisions of Government and the copper mining companies to stabilise the urban population in the 1940s was a point of discontinuity which profoundly affected the supply of resources to the urban system. Political, economic and personal decisions thus constituted the prime inputs into systems and their metamorphoses in Zambia.

Chapters II and V deal with changes in social action systems. The changing economic and social situations of rural men and women are described in these chapters to account for differences in their propensity to go to the towns. From these differences in migration propensity types of potential wage earners and women can be distinguished (Table 9). Deprivation and geographical opportunity will be shown to account for much of the rural exodus.

Africans were involved in industrialisation through their participation in the labour market. Chapter III describes the first system whereby the labours of tribesmen and the organisation of capitalism were combined. These Africans were often most unwilling workers while this system prevailed. In consequence they tried to change the system and adapt it to suit their own needs. But though this received support from employers this adaptation was opposed by the local Government. Chapter IV will detail this and changes in the labour market.

In the early years of this century Zambian Africans were considered to be a species of *homo economicus* who required the barest of board and lodging while employed by industry. To the extent that Africans reciprocated this view and were anxious to leave their employment and return to their villages at the earliest opportunity this seemed to make sense. In Chapter VI this situation is described and with this the limited interest in improving the urban environment. Chapter VII outlines the manner in which *homo sociologus* emerged in the social mind and legitimated the concentration of the appurtenances of 'civilisation' around the employees and dependents of industry. In consequence, Labour Camps were replaced by Towns.

As a result of the transformation of the labour market into the Casual Labour System and the abolition of Labour Camps all kinds of changes were set in motion. These affected rural as much as urban life. Thus the modernisation of Zambia is bound up with the history of migration whose course and repercussions are summarised in the final chapter. In this some elements in the connection between industrialisation and urbanisation in Zambia will be laid bare to enable a judgement of the question whether Zambia is overurbanised.

CHAPTER II
ORIGINS AND SUPPLY OF LABOUR

The rural origins and motivations of town dwellers varied over time and accorded with a sequence of societal structures. From two interpretations of societal structures and their capacity to innovate, two views about the potentiality of man have entered into the theory of development in Central Africa and elsewhere. On the one hand there is the pessimistic theory of dualism (Lewin 1945; Boeke 1953; Sadie 1960; Berg 1961; Bezy 1963:77; Taylor 1963:224; Baldwin 1966:41) which recognises subsocietal structures, which cannot mix for their mutual advantage any better than can oil and water, as the predominant structures of the Third World. Concepts such as the dual economy and the backward sloping supply curve of labour, which postulates limited and restricted *per capita* output of labour due to constant wants, are versions of this pessimism common to many studies of the Third World as well as Central Africa. But the peculiar Central African version of the pessimistic outlook for progress derived from the meanings attached to the notion of 'detribalisation', which was the symptom of harm incurred by African peoples as a result of their contact with modern societies. 'Detribalisation' was the consequence of the growth of a labour market and urbanisation and meant that Europeans believed that African tribal institutions were smashed, that Africans in the capitalist system lived unhappily in a kind of anomic limbo until they became 'westernised' and thereby incorporated into the capitalist system. To sustain the notion of 'detribalisation' the pessimists were committed to assume that the preindustrial systems of Central Africa were autonomous and brittle and beyond the reach of help from other systems.

But the fact that voluntary and widespread rural response to the growth of the capitalist system did not occur points to similarities in the motivations of the inhabitants of pre-industrial and capitalist systems. This provides a basis for the optimistic theory of the heterogeneous society (Goodfellow 1939; Trapnell & Clothier 1937; Trapnell 1943; Lewis 1953; Barber 1961:174; Miracle and Fetter 1970; Heisler 1972) in which the complementarities and respective specialisations of a number of subsocietal structures is seen to increase welfare. The rationality of man is a basis of the optimism that welfare in any state of technology tends to be maximised. Not only were native agricultural practices adapted to pre-industrial conditions but as a result of their rationality, in the words of a government officer, 'a high degree of development within the limits imposed by the general cultural level of the people resulted' (Winterbottom 1945:38). The pessimists detected only two possibilities, two systems: the dual economy cum dual society. But Table 6 suggests that there are differences in the autonomies of the respective rural systems, wide differences in their responses to industrialisation, and that a plurality of systems is indeed coterminous in contemporary Zambia. Perhaps there is a measure of truth in the pessimists' view that social and economic man are in conflict and that in those rural societies where there is least material progress the presence of social man is most in evidence. But Table 6 reveals the ubiquity of economic man, even if his presence was less marked in some societies. However social man need not be less rational than economic man and may simply attach more importance to welfare measured according to social inputs. Consequently the pessimists' conception of the dual system must be replaced: the capitalist and preindustrial systems sit on the poles of a continuum; in between the optimists identify emerging peasant systems, which are semi-independent of the industrial economy. Reference to Table 9 reveals the contemporary scene with a plurality of open systems; eliminate the peasant systems from this table and the position at the beginning of this century, and the picture currently in the minds of pessimists, is represented.

Abstracted from their historical and contemporary contexts, pessimists and optimists argue as if one or other has the monopoly of truth about human progress. In reality each point of view is valid as long as it does no more than refer to the historical and empirical context in which it arises and is not used as a basis for generalisation to all contexts. The first section of this chapter develops this argument by taking an overview of the development of the dual society into a linked heterogeneous society. This is the necessary preliminary to more detailed accounts of the origins of townspeople and the nature of the labour force which are influenced by impressions of the growing reality of a heterogeneous society.

SOCIETAL STRUCTURES

In the first decade of this century less than 5 per cent of the population lived within 20 miles of the line of rail and its halts — the nuclei of urban growth — where 40 per cent of the population of the whole country live today. Local supplies of labour were soon exhausted because of the growth of the money economy around this railway and men from distant rural societies were persuaded to migrate to it. Eventually over 120 alien rural societies contributed to the needs for wage labour in Zambia. This gave rise to the migrant labour system whose recruitment and casual forms will be described in Chapters III and IV. Contemporary Zambia has been fashioned by the interrelations of rural and urban life involved in this migration between the railway line and the villages. Three distinct patterns of interrelationships may be discerned and are termed the successive societal structures of Zambia.

Classical dualism (Boeke 1953) describes the essence of the first post-contact societal structure. While this lasted, some rural peoples were unwilling to undertake wage employment and a measure of indirect compulsion to make them migrate was introduced. It is true that before contact with Europeans, a few of these people engaged in trading links which terminated at the Indian Ocean, and thereby appreciated the advantages of commerce, but this was a rare experience for most whose welfare depended on the self-sufficiency of their villages. Though rational the logic of their value systems was communal and not capitalist. From 1905 onwards, however, they were obliged to undertake some wage labour every year to meet their tax liabilities which were payable in cash and no longer in kind. Had wages been higher this might have been unnecessary or more palatable. But the need to raise wages was obviated by the Recruited Labour System which, from 1905 when it was regulated more closely by Government, eliminated competition among recruiters. Initially the political coercion of the poll tax induced migrants to work for as short a time as possible in industrial centres. From this pattern of behaviour the image of the target worker, who worked for industry for highly specific purposes and only for short periods of time, was formed. Effectively, wage workers behaved like tribesmen when pressed into the service of industry. For instance, they did not bring their womenfolk to the labour camps, which were largely male reserves composed of men who tried to remain in constant touch with their villages of origin. As long as classical dualism persisted, the pre-contact forms of rural social organisation continued and rural people made the least possible contribution to industrialisation.

Between the two World Wars this dualism was supplanted by a heterogeneous society. In contrast to its dualistic predecessor, a variety of systems then emerged in Zambia (Heisler 1970, 1972). Though Barotseland continued in its traditional political organisation and production of a variegated income from local supplies of meat, fish and crops in the neighbouring Southern Province, a peasantry dependent upon cash cropping, a social phenomenon of this century, suddenly appeared. A similar peasant development occurred in the Eastern Province where, nevertheless, the habit of wage labour, particularly in Rhodesia, was formed. Traditional life in the Luapula and Northern Provinces was shatteringly undermined by the widespread institutionalisation of casual and voluntary migrant labour as the principal mode of involvement in the money economy. The major innovation of the heterogeneous society was the attachment of much of rural life to the margin of the money economy and its social attributes (Wilson 1942; Merle Davis 1967). Conceptually, this achievement may be depicted as the collapse of the tribes and their replacement by peasantries involved in industrialisation through the sale of produce and their willing labour services.

Along with the increase in number the nature of the systems changed in the heterogeneous society. Once, the binary semi-autonomous systems were practically closed in the classical dualistic society, split neatly into pre-industrial and industrial elements. Then the sole rural input into the industrial-urban system was unwilling men who were in time returned to their tribal birthplace. Later, much more interaction between the now open peasant and industrial-urban systems occurred in the heterogeneous society. Migrants stayed for ever longer periods in the industrial centres, and by 1951 two-fifths of the men on the Copperbelt had lived for ten years or more in urban areas; before the Second World War up to one-fifth of the wage earnings in cash or kind were remitted to the peasant systems; there was incessant coming and going by relatives on errands and visits between the open systems; many brought their wives to the urban centres, so that by 1948 two-fifths of the married men employed on the copper mines actually lived with their wives. In consequence the values and appurtenances of the industrial-urban system were varyingly diffused among a number of peasant systems in different stages of modernisation. Instead of two competing systems itching to become separate societies there were now several which were increasingly integrated. All of these were scalable along a single continuum of 'civilisation' which represented the axis of centre-periphery relations in Zambia. Such a continuum is hardly apposite for the analysis of the classical dualistic society.

It seems likely that this progression towards the removal of inter-system differentiation began to be reversed and a dualistic society, Mark II, re-emerged in the 1960s. Unlike the first, this second dualistic society is strongly motivated by capitalist values and has witnessed the progression of industrialisation and the competition of interest groups – sometimes in the guise of 'tribalism' and its economic aspirations – in the towns. But gaps between the peasant and urban systems are growing. Remittances to peasant societies from men in urban areas were below 4 per cent of their wages in 1960. *Per capita* income differences of peasant and urban peoples widened quickly. In terms of money values, urban incomes were two-and-a-half times larger than estimated *per capita* peasant incomes in 1954, three-and-a-half times greater in 1964, but seven times greater in 1970 – and the gap continues to widen. The majority of women in peasant systems married to men resident in the urban areas have by now joined them, and so the migrant flow to reunite separated families – the central process of the heterogeneous society – seems to have ceased. An autonomous urban system capable of generating its own population, concerned to improve their welfare as an alternative to urban disorder, now exists. Alongside these changes are signs of increased travel between peasant systems, and of increasing rural wage employment. Once familial ties united the dualistic society Mark I and then the heterogeneous society. Now it would appear that in the dualistic society Mark II the industrial-urban and peasant systems will be combined mainly by the concern of a single and shared Government (Second National Development Plan 1971).

PEASANT PROVINCES

A variety of responses to similar innovations and opportunities occurred among the pre-capitalist systems of Zambia. Cassava provides a clear instance of this. When the Luapula peoples relinquished the cultivation of uncertain grain crops, by means of shifting cultivation, and turned to the production of more dependable and regular crops of cassava, certain consequences followed. Not only did these people stop moving from place to place as frequently as shifting cultivators, and therefore built the best rural houses to be seen in Zambia, but they ceased to practise the agro-economic rituals and other sacred practices which the uncertainties of grain crops once seemed to demand of them. Yet though the peoples of the valley areas of Feira and Gwembe know about cassava and continue to suffer from fairly regular crop failures, they do not grow cassava. The response of the Kaonde people to a similar plight is to walk to the neighbouring Luvale and buy cassava from them, sometimes by bartering their own labour for this, rather than grow cassava themselves.

One reason for the adoption of an advantageous innovation is the existence of egalitarian values and relationships (White 1961). But egalitarianism is a commodity which is unevenly distributed among rural peoples and hence it must not be anticipated that there have been identical rural responses to the presence of capitalism in Central Africa. This in turn means that Table 9 must be considered as a continuum along which rural peoples are dispersed. Though they are now out of the pre-capitalist system they do not cluster in one place on this continuum. Several kinds of peasant systems, displaying different responses to capitalism, co-exist, and it is the task of this section to distinguish one kind from another.

Somewhere between the pre-capitalist and capitalist systems, taking on elements of both, reside the rural systems of contemporary Zambia. In spite of their differences they have a number of features in common and in order to facilitate their easy designation and symbolise their key characteristics they will be called peasant societies or provinces. In Table 9 a summary of their prime characteristics is arranged. In a pre-industrial society around the beginning of this century, organisation at the societal level centred on the tribe or clan; whereas in a peasant society territorial organisation during the colonial era became focused on the *Boma* — the local administrative centre of the representatives of the Central Government. Since Independence there has been a tendency to extend this form of grass roots identification to the settlement which accommodates the headquarters of a province — a *Boma* is the head of a District, a Province is a collection of Districts. The appointment of a politician — a provincial minister — over the civil servants, to superintend the life of a province has increasingly made provincial life important as a means of communication with the central Government and allocating public resources (Heisler 1965). Resettlement schemes, and the locations of cash markets which began to emerge in the 1950s (Rotberg 1963), also reflect the reorientation away from the tribe and clan towards the decentralised agents of the Central Government. Valuation of money as a means of exchange and unit of account is present in a peasant system; whereas a pre-capitalist system often regarded money, in the same way as jewellery is regarded in a capitalist system, as a store of value. Nevertheless interest in consumption, as opposed to production in capitalism, is almost as characteristic of a peasant as of a pre-capitalist system. But this takes different forms in a peasant system where the utility of the products of capitalism in the form of trousers, dresses, radios, sewing machines and bicycles have long been appreciated and are widely owned.

A couple of measures of the transition to peasant life must suffice. One measure is rural orientated and concerns the marketing of food. Whereas in 1945 some 20 per cent of the rural families sold food by 1963 this had risen to 30 per cent — receipts were £4 10s in 1945 and £13 per family in 1963 (Makings 1966: 238). However only one in four of these families used a plough, which is perhaps 'a fair indication of the number of producers moving into commercial agriculture' (Makings 1966: 232). Does this mean that the 70 per cent of families who did not sell food were not peasants because they had no money income? An industrial-urban oriented answer is no: these families were attached to the fringes of capitalism by the sale of the labour services of their adults, who would live apart from their families for long spells for this very purpose. Excluding the two-fifths of the urban males who were unlikely to return to the villages, derived from a calculation of the Rhodes-Livingstone Institute for Social Research in the 1950s, it would seem that on average in 1963 one in every two of all rural families had a member who was either employed or actively seeking employment mainly for cash. Thus at least half the rural families were in some way actively involved in the affairs of capitalism. As for the remainder, if this does not include the 30 per cent with cash incomes from sales of food, it must be recalled that it was most unlikely that there was an able-bodied male in the country who had not at some time laboured for money, and *pari passu* for some period every family would have experienced a cash income from the sale of labour. It is possible to obtain an idea of the relative importance of peasant sales of food and labour from a study of the most prosperous farmers, the Plateau Tonga, which was executed in the late 1940s: this tells us that in a year of good harvests the income from maize sales represented about half the gross cash income; the rest was derived from the sale of subsidiary crops, livestock, trading and wage labour (Colson 1958: 72). Reference to Table 5, columns 4 to 6, will reveal that the peasant systems astride the line of rail obtain a greater proportion of their income from agriculture than do the peasant systems in the hinterland. Thus those peasant systems along the line of rail conform more closely to the classical concept of a peasantry than do those further away, who tend to sell their labour and scarcely any food.

Sex and land formed the major strains in the peasant systems and profoundly influenced their interaction with the capitalist and urban systems. Table 5 reveals the sex situation in column 3. Apart from the Copperbelt and Central Province peasant societies, there was a severe dearth of men. On the assumption that polygyny was unpopular in Zambia, a fact borne out by the 1969 census, that the matrilineal institutions of the people on the whole favoured one to one relationships between men and women, that rural poverty and urban overcrowding discouraged the burden of a second wife, then it may be inferred that the disproportion between the sexes in the peasant systems was a source of tension. This could be resolved by the return of men from the towns, where the shortage of women was acute, to the villages. Otherwise sex-starved and deserted women would leave their villages and migrate to the towns where men were easy to come by in the beerhalls. An index of strain is compiled by ranking the provinces so that the one with the greatest shortage of men is 1. It then follows that the Eastern Province is 1, Barotseland 2, Northern Province 3, North Western Province 4, Southern Province 5, Luapula Province 6, (and with an excess of males) Central Province 7, and the peasant societies of the Copperbelt Province 8. The surplus of men in the Copperbelt and Central Province peasant societies is partly influenced by the extension of peri-urban areas and the presence of men rejected by nearby towns who eke out an existence until they perceive employment in the towns. Another factor which contributes to this surplus of men in the villages close to the towns was the desertion of their women attracted by the pleasures of towns within easy access.

The paradox about land in Zambia is that per capita it is in ample supply but the facts of the distribution of population and suitable land indicates that it is in short supply. Columns 1 and 2 of Table 5 reveal that the density of the rural population doubled between 1937 and 1963, but it is clear that by world standards the population per square mile, which was established at 10 between 1963 and 1969, is very low. Yet there is a problem. For instance, in the Serenje Plateau of the Central Province it was reported that there were 1.8 times as many people as the land could bear without declining yield and irreparable damage (Peters 1950); and the Ngoni area of the Eastern Province carried 3.6 times as many people as was desirable to maintain production levels, given the means of production extant (Priestley and Greening 1956). It seems that the critical capacity of land to carry people without deterioration is reached at 10 persons per square mile on the plateaux of Central and Northern Zambia and around 25 to the square mile on the plateau of the east. This must be considered in relation to the population of the rural areas of which virtually two thirds are uninhabited. It is possible to identify 12 population regions in rural Zambia which absorb only 12 per cent of the area but in 1963 contained 47.3 per cent of the rural population. The overall density of these regions was 37 persons to the square mile (Kay 1967[a] : 20-21), a figure which considerably exceeds the critical densities just indicated. In as much as per capita income depends on cultivation it may be expected that every addition to the workforce of cultivators will produce less than the cultivator who began the work immediately before him.

Land is still available in great quantities, away from the better roads and often in the Kingdom of the Fly and on inhospitable hills, and given the change in the technology of production the critical capacity of this vast deserted area could be raised (Allan 1965). Every agricultural technology determines a different critical capacity of the land to support human existence and the majority of peasants have not yet adopted the technology of commercial farmers. This is highly important because individual access to land provides the greatest measure of social security available in the country.

Until the early 1960s there were three sound reasons why a labourer should ultimately return to a village. Before Independence came to the country in 1964, it was practically impossible for an African to own land or property in a town and when, on retirement, he found himself without an adequate cash income and no longer able to afford to rent a home he was compelled to leave town. What home ownership schemes were operated by local authorities and mining companies after 1950 appealed to a mere seventy-eight owner-occupier Africans by 1964. When a man returned to his village he found his only tangible personal wealth: land. By law this could not be alienated and sold in his absence without his assent and it was the duty of headman to protect the cultivation rights of an absentee from a village. Some 94 per cent of the land in Zambia is disposable in this way. But a man returned to more than land in his village. What little capital he had acquired while away, such goodwill as he had accumulated by judicious generosity on periodic holidays spent in his village, would enable him to re-enter the stream of village life and secure his welfare in old age.

As there is no authority to protect it there is no communal land and individual land tenure is the mode, though registered titles are rare. The Land Tenure Officer reported that 'an individual is free to cultivate any land not subject to rights over it already established by a previous individual; he may acquire as much land as he likes this way; he is free to transfer it to another whether by loan or outright gift; inheritance of land thus acquired is now common; transfers for cash considerations are now beginning to emerge as a result' of the spread of commercial agriculture. The only participation of a headman or chief 'in the acquisition of land is to provide information as to whether or not existing land rights are already enjoyed by an individual in a piece of land which another wishes to acquire'. There is a slight difference between access to land in authoritarian and egalitarian peasant systems. It is unrestricted in the latter save for the considerations already stated, but in an authoritarian system with a centralised authority there is a conception of a peasant area and unit occupying a territory. Here persons seeking land must not only be accepted by the local authority but must in turn accept the rule of this authority (White 1958 and 1963). For those persons who are prepared to live away from the peasant townships and on the fringes of their markets land and subsistence remains available and it remains the policy, first laid down in 1947, that peasants should control 94 per cent of the land in Zambia.

To return to the problem of identifying types of peasant systems, it has been noted that the sex ratios of those systems along the line of rail are more normal than is general in those peasant systems in the Hinterland and that on the whole the systems with the most unbalanced sex ratios are in the Hinterland. A prosperous indigenous economy based on land is highly correlated with conditions conducive to family life. That this is so can be determined through an understanding of rates of migration to the towns, so Table 6 has been constructed to supply pertinent information. Table 6 is derived from the 1960 Demographic Sample Survey of the eight main towns and the 1963 census of Africans in Zambia. Peasant systems, here assumed to be discrete provinces each of which is homogeneous in its domestic conditions, determined the pushes experienced by migrants. Table 6 reveals the effect of these pushes as well as the pulls exerted by the capitalist and urban systems. It deals with the rate and not the incidence of migration from each province. With the information at hand it is impossible to delineate the migration pattern of each Zambian province more accurately, the first report of the 1969 census – the most recent information available when this matter was studied in 1971 – was no more informative. The best information about migration patterns and peasant systems is probably the semiquantitative picture obtained from the 'circumstantial evidence' of Table 6.

Three measures of migration are contained in Table 6. The first to be mentioned concerns sex ratios which, it has been argued, provide clues to migration patterns (Census 1964: 11; Prothero 1968: 257; Harries Jones 1965: 132; Lorimer, Brass, Van de Walle: 300). According to this approach balanced sex ratios indicate zero migration. From differences in the sex ratios of town and country, such as 90 males to 100 females in the country and 110 males to 100 females in town, it has been inferred that abnormal positions prevail in both town and country and people will circulate to redress these imbalances. Unfortunately, it has been realised recently that by themselves sex ratios may be misleading as to the volume of migration, if similar proportions of males and females enter a particular migration stream (Mitchell 1969: 48-49). This has occasioned the second measure of migration used in Table 6. To illustrate, the fairly high migration from the Central Province would not have been revealed by a study of sex ratios alone. To overcome this in part and provide clues as to the movement of women in Zambia of whom it was written 'No information was available' in the 1963 Census (Prothero 1968: 257) which is here employed for the very purpose of providing information about female migrants – the proportion of each sex category who were adult is presented in columns 1 and 2.

Rough emigration rates emerge from this information and comparison between each province becomes possible. It is presumed that the North-Western Province with 52 per cent of its females of adult years has experienced less female outmigration than the Northern Province where only 41 per cent of all females are adults. This may be the soundest evidence of outmigration from the rural areas available even though it does not express the volume of outmigrants as a proportion. It is superior, with the information available for Zambia, to the measure proposed by Southall (1961: 169). He has constructed an emigration rate by subtracting from the total population of a tribe recorded by census in a country the numbers of that tribe resident in its home district. A similar exercise for each province would remain defective, perhaps for the reason that Southall's measure as used in East Africa may be defective, because many Zambians live outside their country and would thereby be excluded from the Southall emigration rate which would underreport the scale of outmigration. The Southall method however, can be adapted to depict urban inmigration and is employed for this purpose in Table 6, columns 4 to 6.

In order to minimise the distortion occasioned by the rural to rural migration of Africans resident in the rural areas who were born outside Zambia, aliens are excluded from Table 6, columns 1 to 3. Zambia forms part of an international labour market which shrinks a little with each step in the course of political change: independence to former colonial possessions; Unilateral Declaration of Independence by Rhodesia, etc. Nevertheless, many Zambians continue to live outside their own country and more than 40,000 were employed in Rhodesia when the Unilateral Declaration of Independence was announced. Part of the Rhodesian sanction against Zambia is to swell the unemployed in Zambia by repatriates from Rhodesia. Column 7 represents only those rural outmigrants who were enumerated as resident in the main towns of Zambia in 1960. Barotseland was an important supplier of labour to the Rand in South Africa until 1965, the Southern and Eastern Provinces to Rhodesia, and the Luapula to the Copperbelt in the Congo and, therefore, this precludes any attempt to depend solely upon column 7 for information about the proportions of the sexes who left the rural areas in each province. Foreign-born Africans resident in the main towns are naturally omitted from columns 4 to 7.

By means of migration characteristics a rough distinction between peasant societies was once to be observed. Two adaptive and one rigid type of peasant society, defined by responses to the spread of capitalism, each with its own distinct migrational concomitants, once had *prima facie* claims to recognition. Peasants may acquire cash by commercial farming or fishing. When this form of adaption to capitalism occurs 'the rate of labour migration drops' (Mitchell 1959: 24, 34). The other adaptive peasant system is organised in such a way that it has a labour surplus or underemployment when all the men are in the villages and it still retains enough female and male labour to maintain production and subsistence levels while some men are absent in the towns (Watson 1958, 1959; Van Velsen 1961). Labour migration is the means by which this form of adaptive peasantry responds to the opportunities of capitalism.

By contrast, a state of full employment in a peasant system prior to migration makes it rigid. As a result of the absence of males, essential tasks cannot be completed, production falls, and famine periods lengthen and become more frequent. Rigid systems of this kind seem to be the majority of those which supply long term migrants in Central and South Africa, but this is not obviously so with respect to East Africa. From these distinctions it should be possible to predict trends, such as that adaptive systems will in the future supply migrants who continue to circulate between town and country, whereas those rigid systems whose production arrangements are not viable and which experience declining levels of living, will increasingly send their men on one-way journeys to towns. Not only do these rigid systems find difficulty in surviving but they are the principal suppliers of the stabilised urban population. Inasmuch as the social and theoretical pessimists witnessed only rigid systems their simple dichotomy was fundamentally correct.

None of the reports of the Central, Southern and Luapula Provinces substantiate the generalisation that cash cropping reduces the rate of labour migration to levels which are 'relatively lower than in the provinces in which agricultural production is a less profitable alternative'. This conclusion was anticipated by reports on the Lenje, close to Broken Hill in the Central Province, and on the Eastern Province. These will be considered in turn. 'The contrast between the situation of a tribe such as the Lenje which has a market for produce open to it, and that normal among the other tribes is most marked. Only 23 per cent of the Lenje taxpayers are away in the European centres at any one time; and, as many Lenje women are away also, the disproportion of the rural population is relatively slight. . . . They have an effective choice between the sale of their labour and the sale of their grain, their hens, their caterpillars and their fish' (Wilson 1941: 69). Here we have an instance of a comparatively low rate of emigration of males coexisting at a time when 'many . . . women are away also'. The situation in the Eastern Province also helps refute the proposition concerning the relation between the elasticity of the supply of labour and prosperous agriculture. Three-quarters of the official 'Peasant Farmers' in Zambia 'prosper' in this province where 'the rate of migration is, in fact, greatest in Petauke and Fort Jameson Districts where agricultural progress has been most marked' (Kay 1967[b] : 98).

To what extent will adaptive systems participate in the circulation of labour? This question must be considered for each kind of adaptive system and with respect to the rates at which peasants leave and return to such a system.

(a) *Cash-cropping adaptive systems*: 'As a tentative generalisation, it would appear that in the areas in which agricultural production for markets can be carried out successfully the absence of male labour for wage employment is relatively lower than in the provinces in which agricultural production is a less profitable alternative' (Barber 1961: 76). Unfortunately the preceding paragraph contradicts this generalisation which must be further tested by examination of the migration history of cash-cropping provinces. Cash-cropping has been of note in the Luapula, Eastern, Southern and Central Provinces.

The Luapula 'valley in fact is a desirable place to live, materially' (Cunnison 1959: 29) it was reported for the later 1940s, and in consequence the proportion of labourers from the valley on the Copper Mines between 1940 and 1950 'has declined, very probably because of the development of a fishing industry on the Luapula which provides an alternative source of income' (Mitchell 1956: 112). But today the Luapula remains adaptive primarily through labour migration – the impact of commercial fishing in the 1940s was no more than an interlude in this characteristic which has often been remarked since the beginning of this century. Similarly among the Plateau Tonga, a numerous peasantry in the Southern Province, 'the shift to cash-cropping apparently occurred between 1925 and 1930. Labour migration continued to exist, but it has played a minor role in Tonga life. Over the years there has been a steady decline in the length of time that men spend in employment, and an increase in the number of men who have never been away to work' (Colson 1958: 66) was the situation reported for the late 1940s. Turning to a parish in the Central Province we learn that 64 per cent of the males were away at work in 1960 'due partly to increased employment opportunities on the mines and in industry and partly to the poor economic situation existing at home. . . . Yet by 1963 there appeared to be a distinct drop in the proportion of men absent. . . . One reason for this could have been the increased opportunities existing at home for earning cash' (Long 1968: 32). Consistency in the evidence of these three provinces in respect of adaptive cash cropping systems is lacking and weakens the explanatory utility of this concept.

From reports of the Lenje, the Petauke and Fort Jameson Districts it is discovered that in some zones where cash-cropping has progressed there is a high rate of outmigration by both men and women. This is the meaning in Table 6 of columns 1 and 2. This fact would have been concealed had column 3 been used as the principal guide to this information, as has often been recommended. If the provinces are ranked by their comparative proportional contributions to migration as in Table 6:1, 1 may be designated to show the province with the greatest proportional contribution and 8 the province with the least; the comparative contributions of the provinces to the supply of labour will appear from this. Columns 1 and 2 combined reveal that the so called cash-cropping provinces occupy the following ranking: Copperbelt 8; Central Province 5; Eastern Province 3; Southern Province 3; Luapula Province 2. This challenges the utility of the notion of cash-cropping provinces as a distinct system which restricts the supply of labour. Similarly column 1 yields the following ranking for male migrants: Copperbelt 8; Central Province 6; Southern Province 4; Luapula Province 3; and Eastern Province 2. It is possible that some of the 44,000 unemployed who had been pushed into the rural areas in 1963 were resident on the Copperbelt and inflated the proportion of adult males shown in Column 1. Only the Northern Province made a greater contribution to migration than the so called cash-cropping provinces, apart from the Copperbelt.

Cash cropping is thus just one of several variables which affect migration. Ease of communications is obviously one of these which affects the migration of women in particular: the Luapula is in daily contact with what the Belgians called Elizabethville in the Congo and the copperbelt in that region; the Central and Southern Provinces are on the line of rail and adjacent to a string of townships; and the people from the Eastern Province have been accustomed to travelling to Rhodesia via Malawi as much as by the line of rail, though U.D.I. by Rhodesia has altered this pattern and directed more of them to the line of rail. A survey of main towns in 1960 revealed that their geographical position had an important bearing on the source of their African population. Towns on the Copperbelt derived 34 per cent of their population from people born in the province; the corresponding figures for main towns in the Central and Southern Provinces were 48 per cent and 37 per cent respectively.

(b) *Labour migration adaptive systems*: It may be that cash-cropping systems remain viable because the pressures on their resources are relieved by the exodus of men and women in their prime, but it is not clear that these migrants will return in middle age, though the relative prosperity of these systems is certainly an attraction and there are indications that their social structures readily reabsorb migrants, or were able to some twenty odd years ago when they were studied closely. There is perhaps more certainty that systems which adapt to the exchange economy through labour migration are more likely to experience a higher rate of complete circulation than cash-cropping systems when they remain viable. The economic viability of labour migration adaptive systems, it would seem, does not depend on curtailing outmigration, for this would lead to poverty, but on securing the return of migrants.

It is possible to present indirect evidence of the fortunes of two tribes which have adapted by labour migration and make inferences from this about the return of migrants. In the Fort Jameson District of the Eastern Province live the Cewa whose consanguineal organisation 'is well adapted to a high labour migration rate'. If there was increasing poverty among these people this might be reflected in an increase in their rate of labour migration but in 1962 only 2 per cent more Cewa men were away than in 1951. Furthermore, compared to the whole Eastern Province average percentages of men and women in the total sex categories, fewer Cewa were absent than was the norm for their province. It would seem that there is a high rate of complete circulation among the Cewa. Secondly, among the Mabwe of the Abercorn District in the Northern Province it is predicted that disaster will result when there are more than two women for every man in the villages (Watson 1958), but in this case the rate of migration is about the provincial average. As the sex ratio of the rural area of Abercorn District was 77 in 1963 it would seem that there remains a fair margin of safety. But this had dropped from around 91 males to every 100 females in 1951. However, this difference may be due in part to two definitions of adult: in 1951 an adult was probably eighteen years or more whereas in 1962 it was taken as 22 years or more. Though the Mambwe are like the Cewa in requiring complete circulation as a guarantee of their economic viability, they require a lower rate of complete circulation in order to maintain viability.

The distinction between the kinds of adaptive tribes breaks down when, as seems to be the case in the Eastern Province, tribes participate in both cash cropping and a high rate of labour migration, with women tending to remain in the villages. But the Luapula seems to be a case of an adaptive labour migratory peasantry, whose peculiar feature is that women circulate almost as much as men. So there may be conceptual merit in the distinction between kinds of adaptive peasantries.

The proposition that rigid systems will tend to send their men on one-way journeys to the towns is a long term prediction based upon observation of the effects of absolute and relative deprivation upon rural peoples: absolute material deprivation, starvation, will compel people to move in the hope that at some point in their journey they will find subsistence; relative deprivation is occasioned by the envy which results from comparison between the levels of living in a rural area and the podgy, well-dressed, coca-cola-drinking townspeople. As Read observed, 'what we refer to nowadays as the "African's love of Adventure" ... is part of his traditional urge to seek a new and more propitious environment when impoverished soils and successive bad seasons made him leave his village home. . . . The gulf between urban and rural standards makes for a profound malaise in the village' (1942).

If these observations explain the motivations underlying the rates of migration from rigid tribes how do they apply to the North-Western Province, Barotseland and the Northern Province, which contain the majority of the rigid systems in Zambia? One instantly notes in Table 6, colums 1 and 2 that the provinces in the Western Hinterland send a smaller proportion of their adults to the towns than the Northern Province. All these provinces experience absolute deprivation (Richards 1939; White 1959; Gluckman 1967), but in Barotseland this is a phenomenon which has occurred since the 1940s. Barotseland and the North-Western Province, however, may not experience relative deprivation to the same degree as the Northern Province and this may account for the differential migration records of these provinces, which are equally penalised by poor communications and remoteness from the towns. For instance, not until 1961 did nationalism sweep into Barotseland, whereas the Northern Province showed its hostility to colonialism as soon as any other province — and there are grounds for supposing that the Watch Tower activities in this province until 1935 sometimes put it beyond the close control of the Provincial Administration and marked the early immersion of this province in the affairs of a wider world. Rigid systems which only experience absolute deprivation are likely to attract some of their absentees when they have accumulated a little capital in middle age, whereas those rigid systems stricken by the malaise of relative deprivation, which erodes the quality of traditional life after which so many migrants hanker, tend to send their men on one-way journeys. In the latter kind of system more women will follow the men to towns.

The distinction between those adaptive systems which rely mainly on the export of labour and those which concentrate on food production is no longer always useful in the ways asserted by many field studies. It would perhaps be more accurate now to write about adaptive systems in general and then note that the distribution of opportunities, such as easy access to towns and cash-cropping, influence the rate of outmigration. With regard to rigid systems a distinction between those which experience mainly absolute deprivation and those which in addition experience relative deprivation is useful only temporarily. The pace of change in the 1970s is such that it is unlikely that relative deprivation should not come to them all.

Man has frequently considered the connection between his welfare and his environment, a relation between resources and the number of people. At times he has attributed his abundance to a kind providence and at other times he has bemoaned his pittance and the barren nature from which this issued. In our contemporary jargon we speak of over-population and under-population to express similar connections because we have realised that though nature may be a constant, man is a variable whose numbers directly affect his wellbeing. Over-urbanisation is a variant on this idea and expresses the presence of too many people in towns. A corresponding expression of over-ruralisation is not only required for general scientific purposes but for the specific task of succinctly stating the present condition of the peasant systems of Zambia.

Under the pressures of the endogenous land, technology, culture and motivation – which in symbiosis form nature and a resource which cannot be increased easily in the short run – it seems that the peasants in Zambia will adjust to nature by receiving less and less each year. Nature, in the meaning used here, and the social mind between them determine that there are too many people in the rural areas.

There are three aspects to the deterioration of nature. One is that health services from the 1940s onwards have contributed to a higher rate of survival and increased rural population and this, in conjunction with intrarural migration, has placed too much pressure on limited plots of land. A congestion of peasants around waterholes, a railway and new roads made in the 1940s and onwards, squeeze life out of land which is never allowed to recover. The second aspect is the deterioration in the technology of cultivation practised by the majority of peasants. Audrey Richards (1939) has recorded how the shortage of fit and able men in rural areas means that many essential production tasks are not done and less satisfactory substitute measures are tried with the result that there is a fall in *per capita* output. The third aspect is linked to this and shows that for the moment it is irreversible: though the increase in population now means that more labour is available it is incapable of raising *per capita* productivity. Zambian peasants scarcely know how to work harder and produce more. Both the major works on economic institutions in Zambia testify that under-employment is a myth: Barber writes of 'quasi-full employment' (1961) and Baldwin concludes that 'disguised unemployment does not appear to be a condition generally characterising the subsistence economy in Northern Rhodesia' (1966: 170). The marginal product of adult male labour is above zero but falling.

To turn to the social mind which helps to determine that rural life is second best for many peasants, one must first note that the returns from wage labour nowadays buy food as well as consumer durables for many peasants. Rising expectations make this a necessity and as rural nature in itself is not sufficiently opulent to keep peasant families entirely by itself they look towards the towns for release from rural deprivations. Mass migration has been a symptom of overpopulation and without it the low levels of rural incomes represented in Table 5 would have been even lower. The social mind in the rural areas determines that rural existence and levels of living are intolerable and pushes peasants out of their villages.

TYPES OF WAGE-EARNERS

A chronological glance away from systems to the men who made them reveals a variety of motivations, which are summarised in Table 8. In this section these changing responses of rural men to capitalism, urbanism, and their rural systems are characterised. Implicit in this is a form of determinism: these men were captives of these systems and acquired their social personalities from the pressures placed by these systems upon them. Originally only one kind of wage-earner existed, but now two or more coexist. Whereas Traditional Man and Exploited Man have disappeared, Permanent Target-Workers, Temporary Target-

Worker and Industrial Man mingle in the modern towns of Zambia. Indirectly, each kind of wage earner has a different commitment to urbanisation: Traditional Man had none; the Permanent Target-Worker often enjoyed his brief life in a town but was happy to return to his village; the Temporary Target-Worker would like to finish his most active working life in a town, but if a disaster such as unemployment hits him he will seek shelter in a village; but an Industrial Man either has no will to find refuge like a Temporary Target-Worker or else he has no village to go to because he was born in a town.

Traditional Man. Traditional or Pre-capitalist Man is a member of a pre-capitalist society. When European colonialism and capitalism were introduced into Central Africa, Traditional Man inhabited the bush and was not motivated like the Western Man, rational in his world view and largely economically motivated, whom he encountered. His mind was then guided by custom, the supreme importance of a moral and relational community, and by advancement through ways other than economic profit. Political authority was then the most highly prized commodity; today this successfully competes in importance with the accumulation of wealth as the desirable property of a successful man. Compared to West and East Africa, there are few rich Africans in Zambia, but most adults aspire to be chiefs, headmen, or more modern leaders. Within the framework of a small-scale pre-capitalist system, in which goals might seem unalterable, various means by which these ends could be attained were and are possible. Wage labour was often regarded by the rural African as another means by which his fortune and that of his rural society might prosper. European clothes, for instance, might earn him more esteem within a pre-capitalist society and were evidently more useful and available than bark cloth from a diminishing number of trees. To the ethnocentric Western Man, willingness to engage in wage labour displays economic rationality, but to an African it might simply depict a new activity by which statuses prescribed by pre-capitalist societies could be achieved.

Money was interpreted as an equivalent of some other valuable and was not accepted as an independent standard of value through which other items could be equated (Colson 1962: 611-16). Among the Bemba, encapsulated by the traditional system, bark cloths were replaced by calico cloths and x bark cloths came to be equated with y calico cloths. Subsequently a money value was set on calico cloths and *mpango* (matrilineal bride wealth) could be paid in money as long as this equated with the number of calico cloths previously paid for this purpose (Richards 1939: 210). In this way *mpango* is indirectly valued in terms of bark cloths. Similarly, among the Gwembe Tonga, who are comparatively more involved in the capitalist economy, bridewealth and damages are commonly quoted in goats irrespective of the items in fact transferred. The goat was arbitrarily valued at 10 shillings, a price which was stable for a long while and independent of the price which might be paid for a goat. Hence a bride wealth of fifteen goats might be paid in money or a cow valued at £7 10s (Colson 1960: 37). In this way the valuation of bark cloths and goats suffused that of money. As Colson nicely put it, 'when the average Tonga is involved in the external system he tends to adhere to the pattern of the internal'; for most rural economic activities there was no market value as it is understood in capitalist systems (Deane 1953: 123-30). Although it was not a medium of exchange cash was used as a unit of account and in a way not dissimilar from that of the Middle Ages in Europe, when money units were sometimes employed to measure obligations and not necessarily to make payments. To make one's social arrangements work better, albeit with traditional meaning, seems to be the case of the most economically advanced peasant system in Zambia today (Colson 1967: 92-111) and therefore of rural systems in general.

Exploited Man. It may be found that the supply price of Africans differed partly according to the degree of authority and egalitarianism in a rural system and that the more authoritarian of these systems, because their means and goals were less adaptable in response to exogenous economic change, exacted the highest supply price for their marketable labour services. For a while, following the expansion of the South Africa economy in the 1880s, some rural systems in Zambia supplied a greater proportion of their labour forces than others to capitalist enterprises, and this was sufficient to satisfy the demand for wage labour.

When the Central African demand for labour grew to exceed this supply, following the suppression of the three uprisings north and south of the Zambesi in the 1890s, at a time when the profitability of enterprises was precarious, wage levels were pegged low. How to overcome the resistance to low-paid labour migration which arose from the relatively high value some rural peoples placed on their wage labour services was a problem the Colonial Administration resolved by exploitation through taxation: against their will Africans from rural systems, with supply prices above the prevailing wage levels, were forced to work by the need to pay taxes in the decade before the First World War. To overcome the subsidiary problems of inertia in the supply of labour, ignorance of work opportunities and geographical isolation, labour recruiters received semi-official encouragement. Recruitment was the alternative to slavery as a means to satisfy labour demands in Southern Africa. The problem which confronted the colonial administration was that as long as wage levels did not rise, traditional goals continued to be most advantageously pursued by traditional means. In the absence of spontaneous volition, as long as they felt exploited and nothing more, Africans would work the minimum periods necessary in order to meet the tax demands of the administration and after this would return to their villages. Huge turnover rates, periods of service averaging two or three months at the best, were the responses to this form of politically engineered exploitation.

Permanent Target-Worker. Some kind of profound shock was experienced by the rural Africans when they were thus driven to work – our modern idiom might speak of culture shock or cognitive dissonance – and their goals might be displaced (Heisler 1971b). When this occurred they were no longer oriented to the ends of their rural systems alone and they began to be geared to those of urban-capitalist systems. This attitudinal change was manifest in the habit of working for wages for longer and longer periods to acquire an income which would buy consumer durables, valued for their utility as much as the prestige they brought their owners; it would also pay for the annual poll tax.

At this stage in economic evolution, Major Orde Browne was Labour Adviser to the British Secretary of State for the Colonies, and discovered the model of the target-worker. This model is identical to that here described as the Permanent Target-Worker. When the planned purchase of consumer durables was completed in the towns, where they were cheaper than in the countryside, the

Permanent Target-Workers had accomplished their missions and would transport their new trophies back to the villages. There they and their possessions were instantly absorbed, often with the conferment of new and more satisfying status. In his classic analysis of this worker Wilson wrote that 'circulation of population is the keystone to the unstable arch of the Northern Rhodesia economy' (Wilson 1941: 38). The economic life of a Permanent Target-Worker was alternation between the practice of subsistence peasantry and that of wage earning. By means of the circulation of labour the frontiers of rural systems were extended to include the social spaces occupied by their absentee members in the industrial-urban centres and so wage employment became a means to serve their social goals.

Temporary Target-Workers. The patterns of the Permanent Target-Worker continues among rural peoples such as the Mambwe into the present (Watson 1958). But this tends to be the exception and a profound sense of deprivation converts Permanent Target-Workers into Temporary Target-Workers. This is because most indigenous economies deteriorated and it became increasingly difficult for families to obtain subsistence in the villages while males acquired capital in the towns. Town earnings were then consumed for subsistence rather than capital purposes and increasingly rational and economic rural people were driven to make one-way journeys to towns, where even spells of unemployment were to be preferred to increasing rural poverty. Deprivation was the state by which the African responded to these external facts. On the one hand he was hungry and looked for food and other necessities; on the other hand he was impressed with the greater ease and comfort of the urban African. It is a paradox that after the revival of the Mining Industry from the depression in the early 1930s up till 1957 the Zambian employers complained of a shortage of labour, although the value of output grew at a somewhat slower pace than the volume of those in search of work. This is testimony of the pressures that pushed Africans out of rural areas and their transfer of hope to the capitalist economy in place of their indigenous systems.

But this does not wholly explain how those hungry people interpreted their situation, for they maintained some links with their villages of origin. Industry and commerce did not shoulder to any significant degree responsibility for the social security of their African workers, who had to do this entirely by themselves by remaining in touch with their villages. For this purpose they would periodically quit work 'to make their social security payments' in their villages pending their retirement. Ostensibly many Temporary Target-Workers behaved like Permanent Target-Workers, but from desperate economic calculation and not from any sense of primary loyalty to their systems of origin. These are the men who tend to drift and hang about towns even when unemployed.

Industrial Man. It was estimated that if an African had spent ten years or more away from his rural society, his return was improbable. On the basis of this conclusion it seemed that in the 1950s two-fifths of the population of the Copperbelt had irrevocably become Industrial Men who were totally dependent on the capitalist economy for their livelihood. Since then pension arrangements by employers have increased their coverage and for the unestablished, low-grade wage-earners a National Provident Fund was established in 1966, so the number of Industrial Men who know no other way of life apart from that of the industrial-urban centres is on the increase.

TODAY'S WORKFORCE

Having examined the origins and supply of labour theoretically and historically, it is now possible to appreciate the present labour scene. This is achieved in Table 7, which is largely based on the census of Europeans and employers of 1961, the census of Africans in 1963, and the first census of all the population in 1969 – only the first report of the latter was at hand when Table 7 was compiled. Both the 1963 and the 1969 censuses express reservations about the reliability of their information concerning the economic characteristics of the people investigated, and Table 7 is accordingly nothing better than an approximation. Reading between the lines of the 1963 and 1969 censuses the impression that they erred in enumerating the same particular characteristics has been formed. Perhaps they both undercounted the number of subsistence farmers. If this is indeed so the comparability of information for 1963 and 1969 which is attempted in Table 7 is enhanced and a more accurate impression of rapid change is produced.

A number of comments on the components of Table 7 will clarify their meaning. The assets of the heterogeneous society of Zambia are shown as its total population and all those who work. A distinction between dependents and non-dependents in the total population is implied: those under fifteen and more than forty-four years of age are considered dependents, though of course a few go to work. The law prohibits the employment of youngsters and, in a country where the life expectancy at birth is forty-seven years, as reported in the 1969 census, it seems reasonable to expect persons around this age to drop out of the workforce.

Though those workers with incomes mainly in the form of cash are definitely within the orbit of the capitalist system, some workers who receive an income in kind, free board and lodging, also operate within it. But the majority who receive incomes in kind work within the peasant systems. Included in the available workforce are those who are self-employed, employees, employers, unpaid full-time helpers, and those without work who have actively searched for wage employment not long before enumeration. Interpolation of information for women proved necessary as the 1963 census contained no information about the employment of women and so, to illustrate, it was assumed that in 1963 the proportion of women unavailable to the workforce was the same as in 1969, whereas it was probably higher. Housewives, students, the sick and disabled, and a few retired persons are excluded from the available workforce which is composed of Africans aged more than fourteen years.

On the right hand side of Table 7 attention is given to workers in direct relation to the capitalist system. Only those with incomes mainly in cash are counted among the employed. As for the unemployed, their importance is imputed to be their portion of the total available workforce and not merely those employed mainly for cash rewards in the capitalist system, as is customary in economic literature. It is high time that the practice of calculating unemployment in relation to capitalist systems alone is discontinued in the Third World. The very origin of this practice stems from the pessimistic and dubious habits of thought, already criticised here, which follows Boeke in conjuring with the simple dichotomy of dual systems. From this naivety it has been reasoned that there is no real alternative to employment for cash available to workpeople. In a heterogeneous society such as Zambia this is not true of the majority of townsfolk, apart from those few born in the towns. While they live in towns the landrights of most townfolk are preserved so that access to cultivation remains a matter of will. Moreover, as Barber has shown, it has been customary for Africans to maximise their income by combining the subsistence produce of village families with cash earned by men in towns. For these reasons – the presence of a heterogeneous society and the maximisation of family incomes – it cannot be presumed, when a person is shown as unemployed and seeking a cash income, that he does not have access to a subsistence income. Hence the definition of proletarian, provided by Marx – viz. the person most exposed to the vicissitudes of a market for wage labour and totally dependent upon it for livelihood – cannot be applied to the African wage-earner in Zambia. Even wage-earners have access to subsistence income and their unemployment as wage-earners is therefore represented in relation to the combined subsistence and cash incomes available to them. In recognition of a heterogeneous society unemployment has been reckoned as the proportion of persons in the total available labour force who do not want to rely only on incomes in kind and therefore seek work paid for in cash. Of course this is to examine the objective situation by itself; today there are an increasing number of urban-born and middle-class Africans who do not know how to shift out of the capitalist system, even if they had the will, but they are a minority. Though this is a justification of a specific calculation it must not obscure the complex reality of changes in modes of livelihood and different positions, in relation to geography and kinds of incomes, which are discernible in the workforce.

More substantively, Table 7 provides evidence of the spread of the heterogeneous society and with this the growth of the capitalist system and its increasingly large margin here described as the peasant system. This can be analysed by examining the various kinds of incomes of the workforce. To take the situation of the peasant system first, the workforce must be considered in relation to overall population changes. If the statistics are reliable, 22 per cent more Africans were employed in peasant systems in 1969 than in 1963, whereas the gross population of these same systems had only increased by 3 per cent. Fewer dependents and a greater use of all manpower in the peasant systems are thus revealed. This may not be a matter for congratulation because it may reveal the inability of the peasant systems to support as many dependents as hitherto. It may also reflect the distinct possibility that the one time dependents of the peasant system have left them and migrated to the capitalist and urban systems. A similar qualification must temper pleasure at the fact that the proportion of persons largely employed for cash income was 33 per cent greater in 1969 than in 1963 because this must be judged in relation to the 264 per cent increase in those seeking paid employment during these years. But whether it is safe to assume that the latter did not have easy access to subsistence incomes as is presumed in the censuses is doubtful. What this information does reveal is a vast increase in the proportion of persons in the peasant systems for whom either a larger slice of their family income is obtainable in the form of cash or for whom this has become desirable. The characteristic income of peasant families today is maximised by mixing the production of food and fishing for domestic consumption with occasional wage labour. As the 1969 census took place in September, the slack period in agriculture, many who were described as unemployed would have been classified in seasonal employment at another time of year.

Two migration characteristics of people in peasant systems can be identified. One is the classic case of migration to a town and eventual but delayed return to a village family; another is migration from one rural area to another in search of irregular employment, usually by the Government, local authorities or commercial farmers. The overall distances involved in the latter migration are often much shorter than in the case of rural—urban migration. The importance of short-term migration for seasonal employment is that it is an indicator of the increasing autonomy of the peasant systems. Like the towns, they are connected to the capitalist system but less than formerly, by diminishing contribution to it through long term migration. Involvement in capitalism without becoming townsmen has become more of a reality to many peasants.

But the sheer scale of the peasant systems in Zambia has declined, while the scale of the urban system has exploded. In 1963 the urban African population was only 18 per cent of the total African population of the country; the corresponding figure for 1969 was 30 per cent, which indicates a growth in the urban population of 102 per cent between 1963 and 1969. Corresponding to this population explosion, the number of Africans employed for cash in the towns increased by 25 per cent and the unemployment of their men simultaneously increased by 27 per cent. It would appear that the displacement of peasant expectations occasioned by Independence in 1964 has created a situation where the bachelors and married men without their wives employed in the towns have brought rural women and children out of the villages to stay with them in the towns. A large increase in the numbers of townspeople directly dependent on the employed townspeople has been the result.

Were this the complete picture of a self-contained, autonomous, urban system this would be cause for grave concern from any welfare consideration. But, from the perspective of the heterogeneous society, this is less serious because the proportion of urban men unemployed in 1963 and 1969 was the same. What this means, though, is that a large number of townsmen now have little incentive to return to the peasant societies until they retire to their parcels of land. Put in another way, for half a century the urban employed would make frequent, often yearly, trips back to their villages and families, but much of this contact is now unnecessary because family life in the towns is possible for the majority of townsmen. Alongside the peasant income, which is the maximisation of subsistence production with a cash supplement, there is the spread of an urban-type income dependent solely upon urban employment, because urban wives and children are ill-placed to engage in subsistence production.

But the numbers of urban-type incomes must not be exaggerated for two reasons. One is that since Independence there has been an unprecedented growth of periurban areas which are like dormitory villages hanging on to the outskirts of towns. Observation indicates that a substantial proportion of urbanisation during the past decade has been of this nature, but the 1969 census deliberately avoids the problem of carefully defining urban areas and so avoids the identification of these satellite settlements. Men can live in these settlements and journey each day to work in town while women develop a trade in brewing beer, entertainment or the sale of agricultural produce from their own nearby gardens (Kay 1960; Bettison and Rigby 1961). This means that mixed subsistence-cash family incomes are still important to many classified as living in urban districts.

The other reason why dependence on urban-type incomes must not be exaggerated is because when they are unfit to continue to work in towns many men return to take up cultivation in peasant societies. As pensions are not widespread, these people initially employ their cash savings to put a galvanised roof on a village house and perhaps buy a plough and oxen, and they consume most of their own produce. As they are no longer able to sell their labour services, their meagre cash income is derived from the sale of fish or maize.

Finally, the cash earnings of women are a startling new fact revealed by the 1969 census. One reason is that the nationalist turmoil of the 1960s did much to smash the conservation of women, and of men's attitudes towards women, and so their cultural lag behind men in adjusting to capitalism seems to be on the point of vanishing. Another reason is that the European population of Zambia dropped by 57 per cent between 1961 and 1969 and so at last the occupational positions of European clerks could be filled by African women as well as men. Thirdly, since the break-up of the Federation of Rhodesia and Nyasaland the capitalist economy has become more differentiated and somewhat less reliant on mineral production. In consequence secondary and tertiary economic activities have emerged to help make Zambia more independent of Rhodesian and South African supplies of manufactured goods and services, and one effect of this has been to expand the employment opportunities of African women. Fourthly, the educational system has shown more consideration for the education of girls in recent years and hence they are increasingly qualified to compete with their male counterparts for cash employment. Thus while about 7,000 African women were employed for cash in 1963, by 1969 30,187 relied on this kind of income and 178,504 women searched for wage employment. This means that of all the women aged more than 14 years 18 per cent wanted to be involved in the capitalist economy, even though they lived in peasant systems; and, correspondingly, 19 per cent wanted to earn their own living in towns.

Substantial numbers of women are at last involved in a workforce which increasingly seeks a money reward. Many more people are totally dependent upon money incomes during the best part of their working lives. And few families in peasant societies do not receive an important part of their incomes in the form of cash. Were it not for the initiation of wage labour and migration, as well as the growth of towns, this would be otherwise.

CHAPTER III
THE RECRUITED LABOUR SYSTEM

Industrial expansion in Southern Africa preceded the urbanisation of Zambia, hence the urbanisation of Zambia relied upon many men already called into the service of modern industry. Men attached to rural life had to be uprooted before they could be attached, however temporarily, to an urban centre. By the transformation of labour into a commodity disposable in a market to various bidders, in return for which workers were given the ability to purchase goods which they could not produce through their own efforts, the pre-condition for urbanisation became satisfied. In this preliminary phase of industrialisation the institutions of the Recruited Labour System were of paramount importance in the formation of modern Central Africa. Labour recruitment was a device to connect the suppliers with the users of labour, but not by marketing labour to the highest bidder. This will become clear after an outline of the growth of industrialisation, public policy, and the arrangements and functions of the recruitment of labour in villages in preference to engaging them at the gates of the workplaces owned by Europeans.

LABOUR DEMAND

Labour migration in Zambia cannot be understood outside the context of economic changes throughout Southern Africa because Zambia was in no sense a closed economy, self-sufficient and in control of its own destiny. Before 1926 the major impetus for the migration of Zambians to work for wages came from economic activities beyond the borders of the country. From 1926 until the 1960s, about one-third of able-bodied Zambian males continued to be employed outside their own country.

Africans left Zambia 'to seek work in Cape Colony and the coastal areas of South Africa before the Rhodesias were occupied by Europeans' (1938 Colonial 145: 29). But this was altered by the discovery in the interior of the Witwatersrand gold reef in 1886, followed by the boom in Kaffirs on the London Stock Market in 1888-9. Before the arrival of the second gold boom in 1895-6 the Rand employed 10,000 labourers to produce a quarter of the world's gold. A general labour shortage was then experienced in South Africa, where it had proved necessary to import Indian coolies into Natal as far back as 1860, and the deficiency was compensated by imports of workers from countries to the north. So most Zambians stopped travelling to Cape Town and the shores of the Indian Ocean, and were content with the shorter journey to the Rand in search of wage employment. By 1889 many Zambians had already visited the Rand and returned to their villages (Hole 1926: 213).

Belief that the El Dorado of the Rand golf reef ran north into present day Rhodesia was the magnet which drew the Pioneer Column of European settlers into that country and inaugurated its economic development in 1890. Only £21,000 worth of gold had been extracted by 1898, and it is doubtful if this was on account of the labour shortages alleged by the pioneer settlers. Optimism revived in the following year with gold production worth £126,000, and this marked the beginning of the real labour shortage which threatened productivity, the value of which had shot up to £3,580,000 by 1914. By the turn of the century it was estimated that 15,000 to 20,000 labourers were required in Rhodesia where local supplies were grossly inadequate, and native police resorted to force to make Rhodesian Africans work for wages in 1895 (Hickman 1960: 63). No more success met the attempt to convert Rhodesian chiefs into recruiting agents for the gold mines because this earned an immediate rebuke from the Imperial Government in 1899. The position in Rhodesia was that by 1901 more than 99 per cent of the Mashonaland police and 90 per cent of the mine labourers came from Zambia and Malawi. Police recruitment from the north started with the enlistment of 150 Ngoni from the east of Zambia in 1897 and continued with the further enlistment of 500 in the following year; in the same year Barotse from the west of Zambia went to work in the Rhodesian mines for the first time. It was intended that the Paramount Chief of the Barotse should recruit labour for Rhodesia commencing in 1899, because the British South African Company was jealous that so many fine Barotse went further south to work on the Rand mines, but the Paramount Chief showed no enthusiasm to keep his end of the bargain. A recession set in with the commencement of the Boer War in 1899 and disappeared between 1905 and 1908. As the shortage of labour faded, fewer foreigners were engaged, and by 1904 two-thirds of the labourers on the mines in Rhodesia were Rhodesians. It is possible that shortages of local workers were created because of the strong competitive strength of experienced foreigners and there is evidence that during recessions when foreigners were not re-engaged or repatriated, as in the early 1920s and early 1930s in Zambia and Rhodesia, permanent proportionate displacement of foreign workers occurred in these countries.

Once the Pioneer Column had terminated their march at Salisbury in 1890 Rhodes and his adventurers controlled the mineral wealth of the Rand and Rhodesia. In this same year Rhodes attempted to include Katanga in his regime, but he was foiled by the recognition by Britain in the previous year of the boundaries of the Congo Free State, which incorporated Katanga. A geological survey of 1891 revealed the mineral potential of Katanga which remained inaccessible to Europe until the railway line from South Africa linked up with the Congolese railway at Elisabethville in the heart of Katanga in 1910. At last the means for economic development were available and copper output, starting in 1911, sprang to 20,000 tons by 1918. Katangese labour contributed little to this phase of Congolese industrialisation and until the later 1920s Zambian labour was indispensable: the Zambian share of the labour force of the *Union Minière du Haut-Katanga* dropped from 56 per cent in 1921 to 0.7 per cent in 1931 due to Zambian public policy. Most of the early Zambian migrants to the Katangan mines were from the Luapula and to a lesser extent the Bemba peoples.

So rapidly did Zambians respond to the economic development of foreign countries that by 1921 one quarter of the able-bodied Zambians worked outside their own country (Kuczynski 1949: 452). This proportion was in the neighbourhood of 50,000 men, of whom more than 31,000 lived in Rhodesia, maybe 11,000 in Katanga, 2,000 in Tanzania, the bulk of the remaining 6,000 in South Africa, and a handful, whose movement from Zambia dates from around 1890 when the warlike Ngoni first took their slaves with them to work in the coffee plantations (Johnson 1906: 162), in the plantations of Malawi. At the time the Zambian money economy was so underdeveloped that perhaps no more than 35,000 were engaged in wage employment in the territory, but this estimate is based on indirect evidence. It is a measure of the pace by which the habit of wage earning spread among Zambians that by 1921 around 42 per cent of all able-bodied Zambian males were engaged in this activity induced by the external and mainly recent industrial expansions here outlined. But this proportion was shortly to swell by the explosion of domestic demand.

When completed in 1909 and linked with the Congolese railway system, the Zambian railway, which stretched south to Livingstone on the Zambesi and from there on to Cape Town, opened the country to economic development. Not only did this make possible the easier flow of wage earners but it reduced the need for porters and freed them for industrial employment. Agricultural settlement by Europeans was greatly stimulated along the line of rail and this raised the number of agricultural labourers to 16,000 in the 1920s; railway construction gave employment to several thousand temporary and some 3,000 permanent employees, about the same number of Africans as were in government employment. Indisputably, the greatest contribution of the railway was to make possible the growth of the mining industry. Low cost copper production in Zambia first needed the railway, then the revival of world demand for copper in 1923, and next the largest prospecting operation ever undertaken until that time in Africa in what is now the Copperbelt Province. It was established that the cost of producing ore was considerably lower than in Katanga. A construction boom in mine shafts and housing for mine employees quickly followed and the number of men directly employed on the mines trebled between 1927 and 1930 to 30,000. All spheres of domestic employment were influenced by this and the numbers employed for wages in Zambia almost doubled to 79,000 between 1927 and 1931.

FORCED LABOUR?

Compared to French practices (Skinner 1965) those adopted by the Central African Administration to persuade Africans to look for wage employment were mild. Judged by British culture it can hardly be contended that Africans were compelled to enter into industrial slavery. The grounds for this opinion arise from practices in regard to taxation, the sale of African produce, the roles of government officers and chiefs. Undoubtedly these practices made the 'open door' a reality, but usually by indirect means.

The treatment of the Ngoni constitutes a notable exception to this in that it involved resort to force to compel this offshoot of the Zulu people of South Africa to work. As a protest against an attempt to obtain a fraudulent concession of land by European interests, the Ngoni were aroused and then quelled by a punitive expedition from Malawi in 1898. This was the single noteworthy resort to force to bring Zambia under foreign control. The mineral resources of the country occupied by the Ngoni may have been largely illusory but the human resources were real. Ngoni men could fight for slaves, for dependents, for cattle and for glory; they could carry loads from Tete and prepare to work in the North Charterland's mines; or they could migrate to Southern Rhodesia to work there: but they could not do all these things simultaneously. The fight to destroy the Ngoni army was as much one to secure a labour supply for European capital investment as it was to secure law and order. In this not only the Ngoni were involved because there was a shortage of labour in Malawi, and Ngoni raids had prevented labourers reaching that country (Barnes 1954: 102) from the Luapula and other areas of Zambia. As a result the Ngoni become one of the foremost peoples among those young men who travelled long distances to work.

Taxation is the best known of the stimulants to migrate to work but in its implementation, in contrast to the intention of the local Administrations, it was not entirely concerned with the labour supply. The poll tax began to be collected in North-Eastern Rhodesia in 1900 and in North-Western Rhodesia in 1904. It was intended primarily to pay for the administration of these territories (Gann 1958: 77-9; Buell 1928: 241) and not merely to alleviate the labour shortage to the south. Only the Ila and the Western Lunda, who disliked work in Rhodesia, resisted paying the tax. Nevertheless it had the consequence of compelling men to work to meet tax liabilities. The local Administration originally wished to make the poll tax double what was eventually imposed (Gann 1958: 80), but the influence of Westminster reduced the power of the poll tax as a stimulant. More crucial was the decision in 1905 that this tax must be paid in cash and not in kind; hence it could not be paid from indigenous resources. Westminster and the local Administration differed in their notion of what the poll tax was to effect, the local Administration being inclined to employ it more as an economic than as a fiscal measure. At Kasempa in 1909, for instance, the tax was doubled partly to increase the supply of labour to the nearby mine, which suffered from an acute labour shortage.

Less clarity in objective was revealed in the regulation of trading. Many Africans sought wage employment to free themselves from the burden of debt they contracted with European owned stores. It is uncertain whether store-keepers, who often doubled as labour recruiters, deliberately enticed Africans into debt to encourage them to take wage employment. Perhaps they were just greedy for custom, for in 1912 the Administration imposed some restriction on the liberal credit they frequently extended to Africans. The other and more deliberate device used by traders to encourage the labour flow was the purchase of food from other territories to deprive Africans of local markets and thereby induce them to become wage earners. In this they were encouraged by the local Administration which in 1905 exhorted them not to interfere with labour supplies by buying local grain (Gann 1958: 124, 157).

When the Administration of North Eastern Rhodesia was first confronted by a shortage of porters for its activities it is known to have burnt huts to impress men into its own service. Individual government officers also helped labour recruiters by all means short of force. This was mainly a phenomenon of the

1890s and by 1910 it was rare. However, their discretion in this matter was curbed in 1926 when they were instructed that, while they might not assist labour agents to find recruits, they must give the best possible service to those Africans who had already decided to work. This assistance was to take the form of advice concerning labour routes and conditions of employment. If Africans had complaints about recruitment or their conditions of employment they were encouraged to present their grievances to the nearest District Officer. This superseded all previous instructions on this matter (1926 District Circular 15). In 1903 and 1933, years of depression, officials wished to provide employment in lieu of taxation, but Westminster forbade this, although it might have been in the interests of the Africans concerned. In this manner the Administration was protected from the criticism that it forced Africans to work or exerted undue pressure upon them. But the continuing severity of the depression made the Government relent, and in 1935 14,626 man months were worked to liquidate tax arrears by work for the Central Government (Hailey 1938: 620). At the same time these policies declared that though wage employment was desirable for Africans this was to take place under humane conditions which the Administration was prepared to regulate.

Chiefs and headmen made no more than a small contribution to the recruitment of labour. For a chief or headman to act as an agent for a labour recruiter would remind his people and abolitionists in England that recruitment was the chronological and immediate successor to slavery and that chiefs and headmen had once procured slaves for itinerant slave merchants. A chief or headman who actively assisted a labour recruiter stood to lose the respect of his people and his office. One of the minor themes in the twentieth-century history of Zambia, perhaps the first part of this theme, was involved in the attempt to bureaucratise customary leadership and force it into assuming an intercalary, foremanlike position between its followers and the representatives of Britain among whom the District Officers were most demanding. Officially the customary leaders were forbidden to be recruiters, and in practice they did little to discharge the obligations which the acceptance of gifts had placed upon them according to certain recruiting agents.

The local Government drifted as much as planned its way into a policy regarding the connections between chiefs and labour. Eventually it exacted a more positive contribution to the labour flow from the chiefs of the authoritarian societies by abolishing customary labour services. This was most important among the Bemba and Barotse, but had less meaning for the majority of smaller tribes which tended to be more egalitarian in character and less given to uphold chiefly offices. This followed the *Administration of Natives Proclamation* of 1916 whereby an unsuccessful attempt was made to compel villagers to obey the orders of chiefs in respect of customary unpaid labour and the recruitment of paid labour for Government Service was undertaken. This was contrary to the drift in policy whereby it was made known that men were not to be tied to their villages, which they would be if they were obliged to undertake customary duties. It was this issue which led the Administration to persuade the Barotse to commute serfs in 1905, though the Administration was not then strong enough to alter the relationships of free men and chiefs. This becomes clear from the manner of the demise of unpaid labour for chiefs (*mulasa*) which once took priority over other business in the life of an African. The first step in the evolution of a general policy about unpaid labour came in 1927 when District Officers were instructed to refrain from instituting, or encouraging chiefs to institute, prosecutions for the non-performance of unpaid labour (1927 District Circular 8). But in disregard of this instruction several Africans were convicted and fined for failing to perform unpaid labour for chiefs. The matter was taken to the High Court which reversed these convictions in favour of the policy proposed in 1927. Coincidentally the *Memorandum on Native Policy in East Africa* was published and in paragraph 12(ii) this expressed the wish of the British Government that compulsory labour for tribal and public services should be abolished as a regular due. This memorandum applied to Zambia, as well as to other countries, and added its support to the 1927 policy and the decision of the High Court that this was proper. Then in 1930 the 1927 policy was reiterated in even more positive tones, and the right of chiefs to enforce *mulasa* was taken from them (1930 District Circular 14). All this reflected a situation where customary rights and duties had been so far eroded that men would migrate to the line of rail to work rather than perform unpaid labour in the villages. Hence the only sanction left to the chief was to prosecute these defaulters on the ground that they had disregarded customary law. Even the Paramount Chief of the Barotse was unable to secure the twelve days annual unpaid labour substituted for slavery in 1906. A large number of men were pressed into service during the First World War by the Administration, but only several hundred were drafted during the Second World War. The closest approach to unpaid labour which operated in the early 1960s was the use of prison labour, often tax defaulters, for work around *Bomas* and Native Authority Headquarters. Much of this took place in Barotseland and Bembaland, which once had the strongest traditions of unpaid labour.

RECRUITMENT

Rhodesia was not alone in facing a critical labour shortage at the turn of the century and the British South Africa Company gave thought to recruiting Asian labour and importing this into Central Africa. Instead it was decided to solve the problem by imposing taxation on Africans in Zambia and recruiting them for employment in Rhodesia. As the Chartered Company had been reprimanded for trying to persuade chiefs to become labour recruiters in 1899 European recruiters were employed. For a while the conditions of recruitment were most unsatisfactory as the following official assessment in 1899 explains. The Barotse resisted recruitment for Rhodesia and 'object to being taken down in a mob by an agent. Being improperly fed on the journey, some of them run away, some die *en route*, and only a certain percentage arrive at Bulawayo, where . . . they often wait a month to recruit their health before they are fit to work. Those who desert return to their kraals, and prejudice their brothers and friends against going down' (Kuczynski 1949: 440).

The solution was for a recruiter to interview prospective workers in the villages, check their health and then offer them a contract on behalf of an employer. Malawi in the early 1890s required a government officer to witness a contract and in time its discharge to guarantee fair play for Africans engaged for plantation work, but undoubtedly until this century this kind of formality was not regularly observed elsewhere. Wages would be agreed in the contract and the recruiter would undertake to supply food and shelter to and from the place of employment. Then the recruited Africans would be shepherded on foot, until the advent of the railway, to his place of employment. For those engaged for Rhodesia from Eastern Zambia 12 months was the usual contract and 6 months was the corresponding contract for Western Zambia. It was initially agreed that Zambians recruited for Katanga should be repatriated in 7 months, but in the 1920s a three-year contract was evolved. Increasingly, recruiters were not permitted to operate without licence from the Administration which might impose a quota on the numbers recruited from any district. Better treatment for Africans was secured by these rules. Though supervision was introduced in 1899 in Zambia it was not until 1904-5 that labour regulations, covering the conduct of recruiters, were formulated.

But it was not until 1911 when R. W. Yule was placed in charge of recruitment for the Katanga mines that properly organised and inspected recruiting began, under the most explicit regulations and conditions (1938 Colonial 145: 30). It is recorded that no complaint was ever made about Yule's operations. Between 1900 and 1913 Zambians were recruited by the Witswatersrand Native Labour Association for employment on the Rand, but in the latter year this licence was withdrawn because of the phenomenal death rate of Zambians on the Rand. From this year on recruitment north of the 22nd Parallel was prohibited, but this did not prevent many casual workers from making their way to South Africa where they were mainly employed as house and store boys in Johannesburg.

With the introduction of labour regulations the number of labour recruiters was severely reduced in order to maintain standards and eliminate abuses. The Rhodesia Native Labour Bureau was the principal agency which operated in Zambia and was established by the British South Africa Company in 1903 to organise a better supply of labour to Rhodesia. Agents were immediately stationed in Western Zambia, but it quickly seemed that domestic economic expansion would absorb most of the labour in Eastern Zambia and the Kafue District. As initially established the Bureau was too weak to discharge its purpose because of its inadequate resources financed by the British South Africa Company and by voluntary subscriptions. For this reason the Rhodesian Native Labour Bureau was reconstituted in 1906 and financed by a state tax on all employers in Rhodesia. Even so the Bureau was not very active in Zambia until around 1912, by which time it had establihsed a chain of agencies and depots throughout the territory. Zambians objected to that aspect of the contract with the Bureau which prevented them choosing their prospective employers. By the later 1920s the activities of the Bureau in Zambia had considerably diminished.

There was considerable national rivalry between countries, manifest in the activities of recruiting agencies, for control over labour supplies before the well known international labour agreements in Central Africa which date from 1936. By 1901-2 the Rhodesians, who saw Zambia and Rhodesia as part of a unitary political field conveniently separated only for administrative purposes, decided that the Witswatersrand Native Labour Association should enter into another agreement by which it would be understood that Rhodesia should have first call on Zambian labour and the Rand would take what was left over. Despite this Zambians showed a preference to work on the Rand and an official report in 1905 declared that the practice of the Witswatersrand Native Labour Bureau moving their recruits through Rhodesia was 'detrimental to Rhodesian industries because it is calculated to spread discontent among the natives of Southern Rhodesia' (Kuczynski 1949: 441). Rhodesian pressure led to the suspension of recruitment for the Rand in Western Zambia in 1907 because the Rhodesians did not want their employees to know about the better contracts and conditions for employment to their south. An attempt to make the Witswatersrand Native Labour Association ship their recruits down the east coast, bypassing Rhodesia, followed. It was with alacrity that the Rhodesians seized upon the high death rate in the Rand as a pretext to stop South African recruiting labour from north of the 22nd Parallel in 1913, but in so doing they chose to overlook a similarly high death rate in Katanga, which suggests that rivalry as much as humanitarianism prompted the 1913 decision.

An equally outstanding piece of competition occurred when in 1929 the government of Zambia advised Katanga that Zambian industry must have first call on domestic manpower and hence recruitment from Zambia must be terminated. By 1931 only the skilled Zambians continued to be employed on the Katangan mines and then the main body of unrecruited Zambians in Katanga were casual labourers employed principally as domestic servants, a few as market gardeners, in Elizabethville and Jadotville.

Complementary to this decision of 1929 the mining companies in Zambia, at the instigation of their government, formed the Native Labour Association for the purpose of recruiting for their own needs without competition between individual mines. It rapidly got under way and in the period between April 1930 and the end of that year, recruited 10,500 men in Zambia. In the same year 2,000 so-called aliens were recruited from the Rhodesian mines, where they had obtained training and experience, to work on the Zambian mines. It was popularly thought that this marked the beginning of the rise in the efficiency of mining in Zambia, which has been attributed to the skill and adaptability of foreigners. But it is a mistaken impression that Zambians were more backward than the Africans of other countries, because most of these 2,000 skilled recruits were born in Malawi and Zambia and should properly be regarded as repatriates. This denigratory and popular opinion also overlooked the vital contribution made by Zambians to the first decades of mining in Rhodesia and Katanga.

The individual recruiter had to overcome prejudices against his employers and preference for other employers. For example, despite good conditions of service, good wages, and fair treatment by recruiters, employment on the Rand led to grumbling about the shortage of women and the colour bar experienced there. Good conditions on the Rand were in part due to the concentration of management into a few well-run organisations, in contrast to Rhodesia, where there was a proliferation of employers of recruited labour, which deterred many potential recruits who would have no choice but to work for bad employers if they were directed to them under the terms of their contract. Undoubtedly many employers in Rhodesia were skinflints and cruel, but complaints against colour discrimination were absent from Katanga, and Africans indicated that this was one of the attractions of the province. However, a death rate of 117.7 per

1000 in the Katangan mines in 1914 undoubtedly made many would-be recruits think carefully before risking their lives.

Besides better conditions for Africans recruitment had other intentions. Low wages, ignorance of employment opportunities, and atrocious communications kept many men locked up in their villages. It was the prime purpose of labour recruitment to tap new sources of labour. By 1912 the Rhodesian Native Labour Bureau had become obsessed with Zambia because it 'is the only field where fresh supplies of labour can be recruited' left in Southern Africa. All other resources having been exploited and emptied, it became necessary and urgent for the Bureau to concentrate and confine its operations there. This reservoir must have been huge by the standards of the time because in the 1920s the Bureau's agents were still exploring remote areas of the country with success. It would have served little purpose to tax those Zambians isolated in terms of information and geography from centres of employment; it was the function of recruitment to break down this inertial resistance.

It is plain that employers and the local Government disagreed about the permanency of the Recruited Labour System. Like the Congo Government, that of Zambia wanted Zambians to be properly cared for and eventually returned to their villages. Licensed recruitment seemed the ideal measure for this because the recruiter did not discharge his responsibility for a worker until he was returned to the village from which he was recruited at the end of his contract. Permanent recruitment arrangements appealed to the local Government as the way in which all labour should be engaged.

But the Rhodesian Native Labour Bureau saw its task as temporary due to a secondary yet major consequence of recruitment. Recruitment was expensive, costing between £6 and £7 for each recruit, and these costs would be saved if men voluntarily went to work under their own arrangements. From the first it was observed that once recruitment had taken place in a village, when the first recruits had returned with the good news, others were likely to migrate on their own, and the erstwhile recruits often decided to make a second trip independently. Some crude statistics seem to confirm this: between 1911 and 1920-5 the number of casual workers who entered Rhodesia doubled but the share of recruited workers among those Zambians who emigrated to Rhodesia dropped from 38 per cent in 1911 to 31 per cent in 1920-5. The Rhodesian Bureau confidently hoped that its activities would be temporary and merely a prelude to a Casual Labour System. This contrasted with the plans of the Katangan and Rand recruitment agencies who were aware that only through recruitment would the fittest men become available for their mines. The willingness of the Rhodesian Native Labour Bureau to be fairly unselective in its recruitment, engaging what were known as second-class labourers who had been rejected for mining on the Rand and in Katanga, accounts for these differences in policies.

Under the instigation of the local Government, a Native Labour Association was founded in 1929 to serve the needs of Zambian industry. In a way this marked the close of the Recruited Labour System which had incorporated tribesmen ignorant of capitalism into the labour market of Southern Africa. The Native Labour Association was not concerned to discover new and inexperienced sources of labour in the hinterland but concentrated its efforts on the areas of densest population with an established record of labour migration. If the nationalism of a colonial regime — an unusual phenomenon — was concerned to close the territorial frontiers to Zambians thinking of leaving, especially to the Congo, it was equally necessary that they be acquainted with the opportunities within the Copperbelt of their own country. But they must not be left to discover this for themselves and casually move to the Mines because they might then be reluctant to return to their village hearths. Permanent recruitment of Zambians for Zambian industry would resolve this problem. Thus the purpose of recruitment to induct tribesmen into capitalism stopped being important in 1929 to the local Government, which became more concerned that through recruitment arrangements the complete circulation of labour from and back to their villages should be achieved.

LOW WAGES

Yet another function of the Recruited Labour System was to peg the level of wages below the mark which would have ensued from the free interaction of the pressures of the supply and demand for labour without the interference of the government of migration. In consequence of the low level of wages the demand for labour was able to rise above what it would otherwise have been, more men were taken into service than would have been the case under *laissez-faire* arrangements, and greater numbers were induced to make contact with urban life than would have been the case under a free enterprise system.

To establish the first proposition that low wages enabled the demand for labour to increase, from which the quickening of urbanisation in Zambia derived, it will suffice to indicate that Zambians were responsive to differences in the levels of wages and that the Recruited Labour System mitigated pressures to increase wage levels. If Zambians were readily responsive to wage differences their services could have been enlisted, without recourse to the Recruited Labour System, simply by raising their reward from wage employment, but this would have hindered industrial expansion and put a number of firms out of business. It was more rewarding to the commercially created British South Africa Company, which dominated the single political field of Central Africa until 1923, to reflect the viewpoint of the business community and try to stabilise wages while ensuring a more adequate labour flow by the activity of its own recruitment agency and thus feather the nests of European employers and in so doing prepare for the day when the Chartered Company could liquidate its public administration obligations in Central Africa, which sorely strained its purse.

Two extracts from official sources show clearly the elasticity of the supply of labour in response to differences in wages. Before 1926 in Zambia 'a native who wished to earn a wage in excess of something very low indeed — say 5s. a month with food — had to seek work outside the territory' where almost invariably wages were higher (1941 Copperbelt Disturbances: 7-8). A year or so later the inhabitants of the Northern Province of Zambia 'walk 300 miles or more to find employment at sixpence a day rather than be content with twopence nearer home, whether it be northward to the sisal plantations of Tanganyika Territory, westward to the Katanga, or southward to the mines at Bwana Mkubwa or

Broken Hill' in Zambia (Kuczynski 1949: 454). From this it appears that natural economic forces if left to themselves would have ensured a fairly adequate supply of labour for the more profitable industries. But this would have brought to a standstill the activities of many less profitable European enterprises who relied upon the salesmanship of recruiters.

The wages of gold miners on the Rand were the highest available to Zambians and stood at about 3 guineas per month throughout the duration of the Recruited Labour System. 'Well-paid congenial employment' was to be had in Katanga, according to an official report of 1931. Of all foreign mining employment that in Rhodesia paid the least. But for the thousands of 'casuals' who were not in the peak of health, as was required by mining, the plantations of Tanzania and Malawi beckoned in competition with domestic service in Katanga, Rhodesia and South Africa. Though many worked on farms in Rhodesia, this was regarded as little better than a modern form of serfdom, but at 30 shillings a month it was to be preferred to most employment in Zambia until the mining industry expanded its operations. The absence of one-third of the potential Zambian labour force from Zambia is not only testimony to the foreign employment opportunities but to the higher wages paid by foreign employers. Though there were appreciable differences in the wages of African workers the level of wages was lower than it would have been in the absence of the Recruited Labour System.

'What an abundance of rain and grass was to New Zealand mutton, what plenty of cheap grazing land was to Australian wool, what the fertile prairie areas were to Canadian wheat, cheap labour was to South African mining and industrial enterprise' (Kiewet 1941: 96). This was equally true of Zambia and the remainder of Southern Africa. Cheap labour became abundant for seven reasons, several of which arose from labour recruitment.

One reason for this was that the imposition of a cash poll tax from 1905 onwards obliged subsistence cultivators to earn money and thus encouraged the labour flow without forcing up wages. The second reason, the burden of indebtedness and the absence of local markets for grains, has already been noted as securing a similar result. A powerful and third factor was the granting to the Rhodesian Native Labour Bureau in 1903 of the monopoly of much recruitment, in place of the unscrupulous activities and competition of a horde of greedy touts. By this decision the incentive of the major recruiters and the businesses they served in Rhodesia to raise wages was eliminated. There is no doubt that the lack of competition between Rhodesian employers for Zambian labour held wages steady.

The most general, and fourth, factor which held wages steady during economic expansion was labour recruitment. This stimulated the labour supply to grow at a faster rate than the demands of industry, and thus the value of the individual units of labour decreased. This should be considered in conjunction with a fifth factor: the inefficiency and wasteful use of labour. Many employers were undercapitalised, rapacious, poor managers, and could not afford higher wages in their semicapitalist lives on ranches, plantations and stores in particular. Too many workers for the work to be done were employed by these Europeans, many of whom would have become bankrupt had they been compelled to raise wages. This meant that a limited amount for wages was spread over too many workmen (Saffery 1943: 27; 1944 Native Locations: 6). Overemployment, which within the capitalist system is another term for disguised unemployment, was the root of production inefficiency in Southern Africa at least until the depression of the 1930s. It prevented wages from rising until the time came when a more rational use of labour could be made and production could no longer be expanded by the better deployment of existing labour inputs. This incentive to raise wages, to increase productivity by the employment of additional labour inputs which would only be obtained by higher wages, became visible in the 1940s. Sixth, a local and institutional factor which helped to keep down wages concerned organisation. The 1929 plans and legislation for introducing indirect rule into the rural areas of Zambia made forced tribal labour and progression to democratic local self-government incompatible. Hence many men were freed from tribal duties and released to work in modern industry and thus cheapened the value of labour. The seventh reason for cheap labour was that neither casual workers, who on average spent only a month or two with an employer, nor recruited workers were able to combine and demand higher wages. Their lack of commitment to regular employment was thus a factor which adversely affected their welfare.

One of the functions of the Recruited Labour System was to contribute to the prevalence of cheap labour. But more important still, recruitment articulated workers and employers who would not have been matched in any other way. The level of wages was immaterial to many a tribesman who did not know what wages or wage employment meant; nor was the level of taxation of concern to a tribesman for whom capitalism belonged to a universe undreamt of until revealed by the white labour recruiter who walked into an unknown village. Though recruitment deprived labourers of their bargaining power with Rhodesian employers this was offset by the knowledge and fact that there was now some certainty that wages would actually be paid and the individual would not be misused. Labour recruitment, seen in its best complexion, served as the indispensable alternative to industrial slavery in the inauguration of capitalism in Central Africa.

CHAPTER IV
THE CASUAL LABOUR SYSTEM

MASS MIGRATION

As the Recruited Labour System faded it was replaced by the Casual Labour System and its personnel who led the mass migration of peasants to the capitalist-urban systems. In studies of Africa this mass migration has passed unnoticed. Circular migration in contrast to mass migration is the theme of this literature. This suggests that migration in Southern Africa should be analysed in terms of the centrifugal pressures which force peasants out of their villages and the centripetal pressures which later expel them from the towns and return them to their villages (Mitchell 1959). This version of push-and-pull theory conveys the impression that the sets of pressures are such that migrants usually return to their birthplaces and indeed the 'circulation of population' is represented as the pattern of migration in Central Africa (Wilson 1941: 38; Mitchell 1961: 244). 'Certainly the outstanding feature of the contemporary system of employment is the pattern of relatively temporary employment of native workers who migrate to their places of employment and then return to their villages. Like many migratory movements, this transfer of workers is compounded of many elements of "push" and "pull" ... The variant in the African scene is the temporary character of much labour migration, and the rather specific character of economic goals.' When these limited goals have been satisfied the worker leaves his wage employment and removes his savings and himself back to his village (Moore 1964: 296). In this seminal overview of migration in sub-Saharan Africa the pattern of migration is represented as being both short-term and involving a circulation of population.

There is no hint of longer absences from villages nor of a transfer of families to the urban systems in the regional studies of migration *per se*. But the importance of the Casual Labour System was that it arose because migrants no longer wished to be shunted around in conformity with their brief contracts and the desire of Government to keep them incorporated in peasant systems. They much preferred to do as their own inclinations dictated and so many preferred to fend for themselves rather than accept the security of a recruited labour contract. An important feature of casual labour was a disinclination to leave the towns and return to villages at regular intervals. This disposition was contrary to that described in the studies which claim that circulation and short-term migration were the mode. A second feature of mass migration is that it involved people who had nowhere to go but moved in hope rather than in response to actual job opportunities as was the case during the Recruited Labour System. As hopes and wants rose, peasants often left their villages in numbers which exceeded those of the jobs which awaited them. A third aspect of mass migration and the Casual Labour System was that, in contrast to the circulation pattern associated with the Recruited Labour System, many wives and children accompanied their men to the urban system, especially once the Labour Camps were replaced by Towns for Africans.

Tables 1 and 2 present evidence for the growth of mass migration following the onset of the Casual Labour System. The pace of growth in the Zambian capitalist system was closely regulated by the activity of the Copper Mining Industry, which is represented in Table 1 column 1 by its production. On this depended the expansion of wage employment. A comparison of columns 1, 2 and 3 of this table reveals a broad correspondence between the production of copper and the numbers of European and African wage-earners up to 1951. Column 4 of the same table establishes the mass migration thesis: the pace at which Africans in the main towns multiplied appreciably exceeded that at which copper production and capitalist jobs increased. As most of the increases in the urban population was due to inmigration – seven tenths of the total in 1960 – it is concluded that the majority migrated in hope rather than certainty of work and security. But this was not only a movement of men, as was the typical population of the Recruited Labour System and Labour Camps. Following the beginning of the Casual Labour System, an increasing proportion of this flood of peasants arriving in the towns were the families of casual labourers.

Capitalist incomes were such that by themselves their levels would hardly have occasioned mass migration. In the later 1920s the copper industry raised its money wages slightly to induce the fittest Africans to journey to the Copperbelt in preference to the Congo and the Rand. But then the basic minimum rates dropped a little and remained static until 1940 when, following the first strike by African mine employees, a riot, loss of life, and a commission of enquiry, the wages of Africans employed by the copper mines were raised. But the effect of this seemed to be nullified by the steep rise in the cost of living which began during the Second World War and continued into the postwar years to such a degree that a body of Europeans formed the 'opinion that the cost of living of the majority of African employees' in all trades 'has increased to a greater extent than their cash wages' (1947 Interim Cost of Living: 6). While it is true that the wages of the copper-mining industry led the rest in Central Africa and determined their relative levels, it must be remembered that there was a delay in time between an award on the Copper Mines and a corresponding adjustment on, say, the railways. Though the copper mine employees kept pace more or less with the cost of living during the 1940s it is less certain that this was the case in other sectors, hence this European opinion may have been well founded. With regard to the African employees of the copper mines a time series of real earnings is available and expressed in pounds per annum: 1937 £21; 1940 £17; 1949 £25; 1953 £51; 1954 £49; 1958 £71; 1960 £89 (Baldwin 1966: 90). Partly from this, an impression has formed that during the 1930s and 1940s no real increase in the incomes of African employees of the capitalist system occurred. Therefore no additional monetary inducement was responsible for resuscitating the Casual Labour System so quickly after it had been strangled, shortly after its birth, by the great depression of the early 1930s.

Though this study broadly accepts the thesis that peasants participated in dual systems by maximising and joining subsistence and money incomes the evidence which has just been reviewed calls for modification of this thesis. Central to the Barber thesis of family income maximisation is what has here been described as the Permanent Target-Worker who was always keen to return to his village in the shortest possible time. Undoubtedly this character was the source of what is now the myth of the typical migrant as being male and away only for a short while. But mass migration of women and children involved the renunciation of subsistence income. These families of Temporary Target-Workers became dependent upon a single income from wage labour. The question arises why these peasants came to the urban system before the 1950s. It has already been shown that real incomes from wage employment did not become more attractive, and indeed, as will be revealed in Chapter VII, the fact that these were geared to the needs of bachelors and peasants and not family men imposed tremendous burdens on urban family life. But Chapter VI will explain that the towns were grim places for family life at least until the 1950s. On these grounds it seems necessary to explain mass migration largely in terms of pushes from peasant societies until the 1950s. The rising horizon of expectations caused wants to outstrip the needs determined by rural socialisation and the only way peasants could resolve this dilemma was through mass migration founded on hope. However, average monthly incomes were increasingly maximised as Temporary Target-Workers tended to work more months in each year than did the Permanent Target-Workers.

Thus conventional push and pull analysis conceived in terms of the influence of the margin of a level of income does not explain mass migration by temporary target proletarians. Brinley Thomas in his seminal work on migration persuades us to think of push and pull explanations in conjunction with the motivations of rational economic man sensitive to marginal differences in the incomes of two systems (1954). According to Thomas people will be motivated solely by these objective and marginal facts of an historically located situation. When in another phase of history the income margins alter, *homo economicus* will adopt other more appropriate behaviour which may avoid migration. In this sense, push and pull theory is in itself an inadequate explanation of mass migration. When the Recruited Labour System prevailed, men left their villages in response to known opportunities for wage employment, in a way not dissimilar to the transatlantic migrants studied by Thomas; with the advent of the Casual Labour System peasants increasingly fled from their villages, far in excess of the numbers that could be employed, but determined to compensate for the loss of a subsistence element in their family income by working more months at an average income. Economists frequently assert that every man has his price and that Africans remained attached to peasant systems because wage levels were too low. Hence they have been tempted to explain mass migration in terms of a rise in wage levels which induced peasants to desert their villages, on the ground that glaring discrepancies between the combined subsistence and wage incomes of families *vis-à-vis* the incomes available from higher wages became appreciated. But this denies the fact that wage levels remained constant for half a century. It was the possibility of increasing family incomes by continuous wage employment at constant wages that provided the economic pull. Marginal analysis is of little utility in explaining this phenomenon. The pressure of rising expectations linked with the possibility of increasing annual earnings at constant wages persuaded many to migrate.

This chapter is devoted to the influence of public policy on the Casual Labour System. The concern of the Government should come as no surprise because the 'exodus from the countryside and the rapid growth of towns all over Africa pose some of the most acute economic and social problems for governments, both in their rural and urban development programmes' (1963 Report: 178). What is less commonly known is that the scale of mass migration and its repercussions would have been greater but for the government of migration. This was most effective with regard to women, until the 1950s, according to the evidence marshalled in Chapter V. But mass migration has been with us since the 1930s and it is time that the focus of our interest in this should alter: 'instead of asking why people move' we should adopt 'a more realistic view of migration', appropriate to advanced industrial societies, and 'postulate a "norm" of high gross migration and then examine the factors that impede this movement' (Richmond 1967: 269). This is precisely the present intention.

WELFARE OF MIGRANTS

Public concern with the welfare of migrants not only led to some improvement in this condition but justified action to interrupt their movements. Just as much as the creation of viable rural societies, the personal welfare of migrant labour was an objective of the government of migration. The health of Zambians in foreign labour camps gave rise to some controls. These slowed down the peasant exodus while most sick men returned to their villages. From the 1950s onwards the improved health of the towns became a positive inducement to depart permanently from the malnutrition, malaria, sleeping sickness and other infections of the villages. To the migrants who had lived in the relatively clean barracks of the Labour Camps, health became a consideration in persuading them to make a final and one-way journey to towns with their families.

Recruitment for the Rand mines in South Africa was forbidden in 1913 (Robinson 1933: 136) and permitted once more, to a more limited extent, under the terms of an agreement reached in September 1936 between the Government of Northern Rhodesia and that of South Africa. The pretext for this agreement was the improved health situation on the mines in South Africa. By 1937 the mortality of Zambians employed on the Rand mines had fallen from 60 per 1000 in 1912 to 10.2 per 1000 (1938 Colonial 150: 56). This was tolerable compared with the 1927 mortality rates of Zambian miners of 38 at Roan Antelope and 16.5 per 1000 at the other Zambian mines (Kuczynski 1949: 510); and the 1931 rates of 39 per 1000 at Nkana, 17 per 1000 at Roan, 24 per 1000 at Nchanga and 12.3 per 1000 at Broken Hill in Zambia (Coulter 1933: 66). However by 1939 mortality was down to 4.7 per 1000 at Roan Antelope and 6.3 per 1000 at the other Zambian mines (Kuczynski 1949; 510). This drop and that on the Rand mines, which was first noticeable in 1937, was due to the use of anti-pneumonia sulphonamide drugs. This improvement of 1937 persuaded the Government of Northern Rhodesia to permit recruitment for the Rand on a larger scale than had been envisaged in September 1936 (1940 Colonial Report: 23-24).

Whereas the health of Zambians on the Rand mines improved considerably and dispelled concern, the ill-health and widespread scurvy of the compounds in Rhodesia and the sisal plantations of Tanganyika continued to cause anxiety in the late 1930s (1938 Colonial 150: 50-1). For instance, in the mines of Rhodesia the relatively high mortality rate of Zambians was 13.7 per 1000 in 1938 after dropping from 65 per 1000 in 1912 (Kuczynski 1949: 514). In addition, the employers of Zambians were often not too scrupulous in observing their contractual obligations. It was clearly desirable to provide more effective safeguards to the arrangements by which Zambians were employed in Rhodesia (Hailey 1940-2: 278). The need to station a Zambian official in Rhodesia for these purposes was recognised as early as 1930, but this appointment had to await the strengthening of the public finances, almost shattered by the depression, and the Tripartite Migrant Labour Agreement of August 1936. Eventually, in conjunction with the Malawi government, a Zambian representative was also posted in Johannesburg. Another safeguard for Zambians recruited for work outside their country was their need to undergo medical examination and accept appropriate care.

Officials believed that the return from wage employment to the villages would be more likely if the return journey was made easier. Personal hardship would also be reduced and so free transport was made a condition of recruitment from the inception of its regulation. Zambians reported that one attraction of serving a contract with the Witwatersrand Native Labour Association (Wenela) was the ease of the journey to and from South Africa. When recruits in Kalabo in Barotseland were asked to list 'five bad things about the mines', less than one per cent of those interviewed complained about the journey. This contrasts strongly with the complaint familiar to a District Officer who was concerned about the conditions of independent, casual workers in the large towns: 'but my home is very far' (Armor 1962). Easy transport was one feature of the Wenela contract which led to the habit of doing as many as six short contracts with the Rand mines, punctuated by leaves of not more than eight months duration (Armor 1962).

These conditions for recruited labour were increasingly atypical. Many Africans were reported by the Rhodesia *Labour Committee of Enquiry* in 1921 to prefer freelance to recruited migration. Transport difficulties did not deter casual workers from leaving their villages, though these same difficulties seem to have delayed their return. Official sentiment in 1939 was that their hardship made it imperative that food at reasonable prices and rest camps should be provided along the bleak labour routes (1939 Provincial Commissioners: 16-17).

The paths trodden by casual workers did not always follow roads and sometimes went across country for hundreds of miles with nearby people being scarcely aware of their existence (Bradley 1943: 52). If the paths of the Eastern Province were harsh another route between Mulobezi and Mongu in Barotseland was certainly vicious. 'All along the path, at every stream and pan, settlements of Mawika and Angola have sprung up, and these people batten upon the returning travellers, who are enticed into villages by promises of beer and women and then fleeced of both cash and goods . . . That the term "Prostitute's Path" is no exaggeration is well illustrated by the fact that in 1940 in the five Mawiko villages at the Sonso river there were 97 women to 41 men and only 33 children' (Philpott 1945). Between 4,000 and 6,000 migrants passed along this route each month in 1940, which is testimony to the scale of migration by casual labourers because it was something of the order of five times that permitted to the labour contractors who operated in the areas from which the migrants originated. By 1942 Government rest camps had been established along this route in pursuance of the Migrant Labour Agreement of August 1936. The monthly average numbers who used these camps in 1944 varied from 1536 at Mulobezi to 390 at Lui in Barotseland. Food depots and dispensaries were also established along all the main labour routes and persuaded many travellers to stay in rest camps rather than the villages which supplied food (Saffery 1943: 32). With the extension of recruiting operations in Barotseland, Wenela established its own superior route facilities and passed along this some 5,000 recruits from the Protectorate in 1959, as well as 2,300 Angolans recruited across the Kalabo border (Armor 1962), a third of the time taken by casual workers.

Prior to the advent of the public bus or lorry in the Eastern Hinterland a labour route might take two months to walk. It was the length of the route rather than whether it crossed international boundaries that determined the frequency with which a migrant labourer was likely to journey home to his village of origin (1938 Colonial 150: 47). The rapid expansion, as public works, of feeder roads to the railway in the late 1940s and the concomitant expansion of lorry and bus services opened up the hinterland and reduced the trend towards its depopulation (Niddrie 1954).

CAPITALIST SUPPORT FOR CASUAL LABOUR

If the Government tried to improve the lot of casual workers this did not signify that it approved of the Casual Labour System as did the copper mining companies whom it benefited. They welcomed the abolition of the Recruited Labour System in part because during the 1930s when this was finally replaced, there was an abundance of labour which no longer had to be induced to go to work. Hence there was no reason why the mining companies should incur the cost of agency recruitment. Secondly, the Casual Labour System was approved because it lengthened the average continuous service of each African employee. During the 1920s the average length of service of labourers was as low as four months, which was wasteful by any industrial standards, and the companies were unable to increase this by their own efforts. They were delighted to learn in 1931 that their problem had been resolved at no cost to themselves. In this year it was learned that the average duration of employment by the casual worker engaged on a monthly basis was nine to ten months as compared with the six months of a recruited labourer (1935 ILO: 39). Continual recruitment was therefore inefficient from the point of view of industrial production. Undoubtedly, too, there was a feeling by the copper companies that they were better judges of potential workers than an intermediate recruitment agency motivated by the prospect of its commission and perhaps inclined to provide a marginal number of workers who were not as suitable as the companies would have liked. The important factor, however, was the belief that the productivity of the casual and relatively stabilised workers would be higher than that of recruited workmen. Once men wanted to work, and did not have to be politically exploited, there came to be better discipline at work, fewer accidents, fewer men deserting their posts, and an all-round better return due to lengthening industrial experience and training.

The copper-mining companies naturally took the attitude that the Government should do nothing to diminish the volume of casual labourers. To the companies it seemed self-evident that though there were sufficient migrants to fill the vacant jobs many of these were qualitatively unsuitable employees, physically weak, and any decrease in their numbers would likewise decrease the opportunities for careful selection.

When in early 1935 the mining companies experienced a shortage of suitable labour they did not wish to revert to recruiting to compensate for this and instead howled, seemingly in the midst of plenty, that there was a gross shortage of suitable labour about. For instance, the manager of the revived Native Labour Association, now employed by the Zambian mining companies on an emergency and standby basis, declared that in his experience about 60 per cent of the ordinary labourers who offered their services were unfit for heavy work (1936 Chairman NILAB: 10). Only one third of the casual migrants who applied for work at Nkana in 1935 were accepted, though the proportions at Luanshya and Mufulira were higher. At least half of the labourers on the Copperbelt were reckoned to be unsuitable for mine work (1936 Sub-Committee NILAB: 4). It may be noted that the situation improved in the case of the Rhokana Corporation at Nkana-Kitwe, where between July 1941 and June 1942 of the 7,800 who applied for work only 19 per cent were rejected as unfit (Saffery 1943: 26). But at this time the exigencies of the war had led employers to tolerate lower physical standards among their workmen with a consequent impact on the figures of unemployable casual workers. All this is evidence that the growth of the Casual Labour System and mass migration, while denuding the villages of their able-bodied and adult males, did not correspondingly increase the cash incomes of many of those involved, nor did it properly resolve the difficulties of the mining companies in obtaining adequate supplies of fit workers. While the stoppage of domestic recruitment created new difficulties for the mining companies after 1931 it did not outweigh the benefits believed to be derived from the employment of casual labourers.

Commercial agriculture was the only industry in Zambia to rely on the domestic recruitment of labour at its village source after 1931. This was the task of the Agricultural Development Society, which recruited labourers from remote areas such as Kasama and Barotseland and transported them by air to Lusaka (Hailey 1957: 409). From Lusaka they were redistributed along the commercial farming areas adjacent to the line of rail. These arrangements, as well as the issue of recruiting licences to individual farmers by the Labour Department, fell into disuse in the late 1950s when the Government intensified its opposition to the movement of peasants to wage employment at a time when large scale unemployment was a source of unrest in the urban areas (1962 CCTA: 88-9). The conditions of farm workers were even worse than those of domestic servants employed by Indians and meant that European farmers were able to engage only those rejected by the other spheres of cash employment. Rural recruitment by European farmers was among the dwindling number of peasants who had little knowledge of industrial conditions. After 1950 agriculture was the only major industry to look to recruitment as an alternative to raising wages.

GOVERNMENT OPPOSITION TO CASUAL LABOUR

When the economy began to revive in the mid 1930s, the Northern Rhodesia Government wanted to reintroduce recruited labour for all industries. In 1935 there were riots on the Copperbelt and Government officers believed that the rate of rejection of applicants as unfit, as well as the general shortage of jobs, contributed to the unrest (1935 Evidence I: 159); simultaneously, in the same year the Committee on Emigrant Labour in Malawi directed general attention to the effects upon peasant systems of their depopulation. All the neighbouring Governments were profoundly impressed by the report which observed that 'Unless the immediate causes of emigration are counteracted . . . the moral, social and physical life of our native population will be so affected that any attempts by missions, Government or other agencies to maintain, let alone improve upon, the present low standards of health and happiness, will be abortive' (1936 Report). It was concluded that the pace of decline in rural conditions and the volume of unemployment would be considerably reduced by controlled migration. Prior to 1931 labour recruitment was the most important way by which workers were obtained and the Northern Rhodesia Government wanted to return to this system, because if labour were recruited at source instant medical examination would eliminate many needless journeys and only those for whom there were jobs in the industrial centres would leave their villages. As a consequence it was anticipated that the horde of unemployed in the Labour Camps would be drastically reduced.

Beginning in 1936 and continuing into 1937, Government exerted considerable pressure on the copper-mining companies to recruit labour at its birthplace once more rather than await its arrival on the Copperbelt. The companies successfully resisted on the grounds that casual labour was to the advantage of the workers as well as their shareholders. Why should an employee not be permitted to select his own mine and employer, and at the same time benefit by avoiding the cost of recruitment which would otherwise be a charge against his wage? For their part, the mining companies believed that voluntary, casual workers were more content and efficient (1936 Chairman NILAB: 9). This reasoning did not satisfy the Pim Commission when it enquired into the affairs of the country and observed that Wenela found it feasible and profitable to select and medically examine prospective recruits in the villages (1938 Colonial 145: 49). To avoid offending the Government, the mining companies finally expressed their grudging willingness to co-operate in a scheme of labour recruitment if all other employers also agreed to do the same (Saffery 1943: 32). On this the proposal to counteract the Casual Labour System foundered during the Second World War. Nor did anything ensue, at the peak of the copper boom in 1955, when the mining companies were once more urged by the Government to recruit labour directly in the peasant areas (Bromwich).

LABOUR EXCHANGES AS AN ALTERNATIVE TO RECRUITMENT

When Government failed to pressure industry into restoring a Recruited Labour System, labour exchanges were conceived as a second-best arrangement. Though they were in place of rural recruitment by private industry in a strategical sense, they were not equivalent in effect to rural recruitment. This was because for a long while it was only in the urban areas that labour exchanges could hope to equalise the supply and demand for labour; the staff limitations of Government made this inevitable.

To replace the advice about employment opportunities obtainable from District Officers from 1926 onwards, Government in 1940 established a Labour Department to concentrate on this and related tasks. The Provincial Administration had used a variety of devices to prevent the establishment of a special unit of Government concerned both with labour and certain features of life in urban areas. The Provincial Administration, the élite cadre of the colonial service, was wholly rural-oriented, and held the opinion that a Labour Department struck at the very root of its prime task, which was to be the intermediary between its African wards and Government. Whereas the Provincial Administration regarded Africans in urban areas as 'tribesmen' the Labour Department thought of them as 'townsmen' and 'industrial men'. In 1935 the Native Industrial Labour Advisory Board opposed the establishment of a special department of labour but recommended that a greater number of permanent Provincial Administration staff should be stationed near to the Labour Camps (1936 Chairman NILAB). This was in response to the criticism of the report on the rioting of 1935 which complained that along the line of rail the Provincial Administration was preoccupied with matters arising from the presence of Europeans and in consequence had lost touch with urban Africans, whose riotous behaviour was in part due to this lack of contact. But it required the Orde Browne report on African labour in 1938, following on the heels of the widely known recommendation for a specialist labour corps in Tanganyika (1938 Tanganyika Territory: 36), to win the cause for a Labour Department which would be capitalist and urban oriented unlike the Provincial Administration. As a result, in 1942 labour exchanges were opened in the larger towns. These agencies could not create vacancies and seem to have been superfluous throughout the next twenty years. Though they were effective in assisting the resettlement of discharged soldiers after the war on the whole they were patronised by the unemployable and bad employers (1947 ILR 55: 380).

African workers were able to do without labour exchanges because they were well aware that if conditions at one place were unsatisfactory they would have no difficulty in finding work elsewhere during the post-war boom (Gardiner-Browne 1950: 140). The labour shortage became so acute in 1948 that it was thought by the Labour Advisory Board, composed of employers and officials, that new secondary industries should not be established in Zambia until existing employers had filled all their vacant posts; that the Ten-Year Development Plan might have to be deferred for want of labour to implement it; and that a plan for rationing labour supplies was desperately required (November 1948 SEC/LAB/34). A seller's market then prevailed until 1957 when it was replaced by a buyer's market, which lasted almost until the demise of the Federation of Rhodesia and Nyasaland. For this reason the labour exchanges located in urban areas of high unemployment were then permitted to recruit workers for Rhodesian farmers.

When the first rural labour exchange was established at Fort Rosebery and provision made for five others in 1961, consideration and resources were at last seriously devoted to the use of labour exchanges as a mechanism to equalise the supply and demand for labour between the peasant and urban areas. Voluntary employment exchanges were then located in twelve rural centres along the line of rail, and in addition employment information services were first supplied in three towns in 1962 (1962 CCTA: 43).

This rural labour exchange system was preceded by the establishment of a Youth Employment Service in 1959. Its initial purpose was to help European school leavers find paid employment in order to deflect the European criticism of Government, particularly acute during 1959 and 1960, concerning the alleged injustice of the fact that African schoolboys at Munali, the only state secondary school for African boys, were given a better education and obtained superior examination results than European children at what were then known as the Rennie High Schools in Lusaka and on the Copperbelt. This onslaught worried the Government, which feared a large exodus of European parents and their skills around this time. As they slowly agreed to the demolition of the industrial colour bar and its supposed protection of their interests, European parents were concerned that their children should still be given every conceivable advantage. A Youth Employment Service figured in this, alongside apprenticeship training and a psychologist in the European Department of Education, who had responsibility for vocational guidance. Many of the European parents involved had brought their infants with them from the United Kingdom after the Second World War and now for the first time they were confronted with the problem of finding work for these children who were beginning to leave school. No one wanted the Europeans to remove their skills, even from a static economy. As the implications of the march towards independence and the removal of the industrial colour bar swiftly dawned, in the following year the Youth Employment Service was extended to Africans.

INTERNATIONAL MIGRATION OF LABOUR

Though politically separate, Zambia tends to form part of a single labour reservoir, which has traditionally been the area of metropolitan mobility for that one third of all Zambian males employed outside their own country. The achievement of sovereignty by the former territories and the *de facto* independence of Rhodesia have circumscribed this metropolitan area in which migrants in search of work can traverse easily. For this reason it is increasingly inappropriate to conceptualise the supply of and demand for labour in the whole of Southern Africa as operating within a unitary economic system as hitherto. The complementary nature of the economies of Malawi, Rhodesia, Botswana, Lesotho, Tanzania, the Congo, Portuguese Africa and Zambia has been eroded during the past decade. But when the British Government either controlled or enjoyed good relations with the local governments of these countries their overall economic interests were very much its concern.

The salient trends in the international migration of labour point to the relative influence of political and economic boundaries and recognised the particular impact of the latter. Between 1931 and 1962 the number of alien Africans employed in Zambia increased from 10,000 to 44,000 while the Zambians employed in alien countries increased threefold from 31,000 to

94,000. This represents a net loss to the economy of Zambia of 21,000 workers in 1931 and 50,000 workers in 1962.

As the copper-mining companies were major employers in an economy which extolled the virtues of capitalism the local Government was attentive to their requirements. The mining companies wanted a Casual Labour System, the fittest labourers, and the first pick of whatever labour was available inside Zambia. Their desire to select what domestic labour they pleased did not necessarily correspond with the views of Westminster on this matter, and on this Westminster and its local Government were not entirely in accord. This is the root of economic nationalism in Zambia. The competition of foreign employers with the mining companies for such a large proportion of the domestic labour supply was a source of friction.

Even before the domestic money economy had pulled out of the depths of the recession in 1935 the copper-mining industry complained about the unfitness of much labour due to the propensity of so many able-bodied men to emigrate. It was observed that the kind of workers the Rand mines wanted to recruit were precisely those categories which were in short supply in Zambia. Already there were 15,000 Zambians who were second-class labourers on the Lupa Goldfields of Tanzania; between January and August 1934 some 30,000 men emigrated to the south; and there were as many Africans from Zambia as from Rhodesia at work in Rhodesia (1936 Chairman NILAB: 10). The Casual Labour System included the freedom not to work in the domestic economy. This led the mining companies to demand a ban on the emigration of labour and take a keen interest in the free import of workmen.

Not surprisingly in 1936 the Native Industrial Labour Advisory Board, which was representative of all interested parties, on the basis of the evidence which it reviewed, decided that there must be a reduction in the number of emigrants from Zambia. The mining companies were delighted at the prospect of a greater pool of unemployed from which to pick their workforce, and Government was cheered at the idea of fewer men leaving their villages. This led logically to the adoption of a further principle: namely, that Zambians ought to be given preference over others for work in the domestic economy. This led in turn to the practice of discouraging the immigration of Africans, to the great satisfaction of Rhodesia and South Africa. But it was agreed that a small number of 'sophisticated' Africans, e.g. educated Africans from Malawi, who could be expected to improve the general performance of Zambians, should be allowed to work in the domestic economy (1936 Chairman NILAB: 10). This policy in regard to 'sophisticated' alien Africans was implemented, and was long-lasting and in 1960, for instance, sixty well-qualified Africans from South Africa were employed in the domestic economy by special permission of the local Government (1962 CCTA: 88-9).

Even if local employers were not interested in recruitment, the Rand mines were keen to recruit within the country. Under an agreement of September 1936 the Rand mines began full-scale recruiting in Barotseland in 1940, but had to suspend this operation in 1943, owing to the shortage of local labour caused by the war. Wenela was the only agency empowered to recruit labour for export. During the 1950s it was permitted to recruit up to 5,000 men each year from

Barotseland and 500 each year from the Balovale District in the North West Province. As Wenela undertook to return these men to their villages on the completion of their contracts the local Government assented to this franchise.

While not unimpressed by the Malawi report of 1935 about the legions lost from their villages of origin (*muchona*), Westminster was anxious that the development of Rhodesia should not be impeded by a labour shortage. The opinion which prevailed in the 1920s that the expansion of the domestic labour market through the activity of the copper mines would put an ever-increasing check on emigration was proved wrong by, among other things, the continuing interest of Westminster in the economic welfare of Rhodesia. This factor helped to bring together for discussion in Salisbury representatives of Rhodesia, Malawi and Zambia and led to the August 1936 Tripartite Migrant Labour Agreement.

One aspect of this was to promise Rhodesia a fair measure of the labour available to the north and yet implement the recommendations of the Native Industrial Labour Advisory Board, to which reference has been made. This was done in Paragraph 3 of the Agreement: 'Government . . . will implement . . . the principle that the labour requirements of the three Territories shall have the first call upon their available supplies of labour . . .' (1938 Colonial 145: 354). The social aspect of the Agreement was intended to protect the welfare of migrants and their families. The Agreement was revised in May 1942, substantially in conformity with the provision of the text concluded in 1936. However, greater emphasis on the necessity of retaining workers in their native money economies and on the necessity of encouraging them to return to their villages regularly is apparent in this revision (1942 ILR 46: 598). Another revision took place in 1947 and was implemented in 1949. Once more the important part of this Agreement was the reiteration of the 1936 resolve that each Government should ensure that sufficient able-bodied males remained in its territory to meet the needs of the peasant and capitalist economies (1951 Cmnd. 8235: 59).

What were the effects of the Tripartite Migrant Labour Agreement on the flow of labour to the domestic capitalist economy? The effect on the import of labour was soon felt. 'Government has influenced to a great extent the alien curve, for restrictions have been initiated to discourage the alien from entering the territory, and unless the applicant possesses outstanding qualifications he cannot be employed.' The compound manager of the Roan Antelope copper mine – who combined the functions of industrial relations and personnel and staff housing manager – continued this observation by rationalising the change in terms of efficiency: 'It would not be fair to assume that Government restrictions only have made it necessary for us to employ the indigenous native; there has been a remarkable improvement in the efficiency of these peoples, and they are becoming good workers as a result of their close association with trained aliens' (Spearpoint 1937: 52). This compound manager for the oldest copper mine was correct in his belief that the increase in the number of aliens was slight just after the implementation of the Agreement, but this is a misleading impression for the whole history of the Casual Labour System. The number of alien Africans employed in the country quadrupled throughout this phase while the number of Zambians at work for wages only trebled; between 1946 and 1951, for example, the number of aliens employed in the country doubled.* In respect of aliens, the 1936 Agreement seems to have been effective only briefly until the desperate shortage of labour of all kinds led to a failure to implement the Agreement stringently. On this ground it is doubtful if the Agreement was a real barrier to the immigration of alien workers.

The obstacles imposed by the Agreements to the inter-territorial migration of labour, such as they were, were lifted during the era of the Federation of Rhodesia and Nyasaland in so far as they applied to the three territories of Central Africa. Nevertheless the number of alien Africans in Zambia remained static until 1956 when it began to rise, reaching a figure increase of one-fifth by 1962. Thus alien immigration seems to have been due to factors other than the problems of crossing political frontiers.

One way to gauge the effect of the Agreements on the emigration of workers is to examine the principal instrument of control. This was a revision of a system of registration which was first operated in 1931, flowing from the *Native Registration Ordinance* of 1929, ostensibly to protect employers from the desertion of their workmen and their workmen from abuses by their employers. This regulation was conceived within the same cultural framework as operated in Rhodesia, and the meaning that came to be attached to this was identical in both countries. This 'was basically a system of rural registration' whose effect was 'to perpetuate the official outlook that the African has no real home in the towns' according to a witness before the Plewman Commission in Rhodesia, the major official investigation into the state of urban administration. He noted that 'every indigenous African has a rural registration. He is registered and taxed in his rural area. The urban area is nothing but a place of temporary employment . . . You have got to change that fact if he is to be a stable industrial worker.' The Plewman Commission recorded that 'We think there is substance in the statement' (1958 Report: 115). In the sister country north of the Zambesi the situation was no different, and registration was used to attach a man to his peasant system.

But the multi-purpose character of registration was its weakness as a means of control. An African in possession of an identity certificate colloquially known in Zambia as a *citupa* (lit. 'thumb' – due to use of holder's thumb-print) could bring the evidence entered on it about his current work contract to a Government officer if he was in dispute with his employer about the discharge of this contract. In recompense, employers were protected from desertion by the requirements that they must sign the registration certificate when a labour contract was terminated and that a labourer must not be engaged if his *citupa* lacked the necessary endorsement. The Provincial Administration once thought that Africans would not be allowed to leave their villages without *citupas* suitably stamped to indicate that permission to travel had been given (1936 PCs: 35-6), and that the unemployable would thus remain shut up in the society of their kin. This did not materialise. Government adapted the certificate as a device to ensure that wage earners regularly paid their poll tax by requiring that tax receipts should be attached to the identity papers. These devices were revised in 1936 (1936 Chairman NILAB: 17; 1938 Colonial 145: 354) and 1949 (1949

---

* The full impact of this on dissatisfaction and protest along the line of rail is intriguing and has eluded analysis.

Minutes: 9-11). But this form of registration was never really a success (1938 Colonial 150: 59) because a worker had only to 'lose' his *citupa* and adopt another name, which was common for several reasons (Doob 1961: 195), in order effectively to destroy his record of tax payment and his past which was not recorded elsewhere. An African did not fear to do this because in due course a new blank certificate would be issued. Viewed from the imperative of Government to return the adult male to his village this had its compensation: a new *citupa* could not be issued until its claimant had returned to his village of origin and re-established his identity. This accorded with a policy recommendation to defer postponement of urban registration for as long as possible (1949 Report: 34).

The second paragraph of the Tripartite Migrant Labour Agreement of August 1936 determined a further use for the certificate as a testimony that its legitimate bearer was a worker whose emigration had been approved in accordance with the Agreement. In March 1937 the Agreement began to be implemented in regard to what had become passports and from that date all workers proceeding to Rhodesia were required to be in possession of these documents which had been endorsed for work (1940 Northern Rhodesia 1938: 23). A labour shortage immediately followed in Southern Rhodesia whose government attributed this to the failure of the Northern Rhodesia Government to fulfil its bargain (1939 PCs: 19). But the local Government had carried out its obligation faithfully. The inadequate flow of workmen to Rhodesia was due in part to the desire of many tax defaulters to avoid detection by avoiding any examination of their documents. This difficulty was overcome when two papers emerged: a single identity certificate with a work record and a passport restricted to enabling a man to emigrate to an approved job. In addition, the newly introduced registration system for international migrants was not as widely understood as it might have been, and many workers who were ignorant of its existence were stopped at the frontier. To make matters worse there were delays in securing these passports.

There were two other weighty reasons for the slower emigration and the acute labour shortage in Rhodesia immediately prior to the Second World War. Many Africans were reported to be reluctant to leave the country while the discussions and decisions of the Bledisloe Royal Commission, 1938-9, on the future political development of Central Africa, were unknown. There was also an increased demand for labour within the domestic capitalist economy as the sale of minerals in the world market picked up.

Two great weaknesses to the international regulation of migrant labour can be identified. One was that the frontiers of the country could not all be patrolled, and it was easy to paddle across the Zambesi into Rhodesia. There still remained a risk of detection in Rhodesia which would be followed by deportation, but this risk did not seem to materialise for workers who found employment in South Africa. Without the co-operation of the South African Government, little could be done to make the Tripartite Migrant Labour Agreements fully effective. In as much as South Africa was prepared to ignore the presence of immigrants from Central Africa in excess of the number specified in quotas, an early failing (Robinson 1933: 156), a serious leak in the arrangements and stability of the Central African economies prevailed to the point where, in the words of the

Labour Adviser to the Colonial Secretary, it became 'an industrial bleeding artery draining away the vitally necessary manhood of the country' (1938 Colonial 150: 45). Upon the payment of a small fee the Government of South Africa permitted illegal immigrants to remain in the country for limited periods (Burden 1951: 57) at least.

The protection given to the domestic capitalist economy by the Agreements disappeared somewhat with the advent of the Federation of Rhodesia and Nyasaland, which aimed to create a common labour market within which hindrances to the free flow of labour were abolished. The political progression of the country and the regression of Rhodesia and South Africa attracted alien Africans into the domestic economy until the slump of 1957. Then the Federal Government Inter-Territorial Consultative Committee on Labour agreed to restrict the entry into Zambia of aliens from outside the Federation. There were no measures to prevent Zambians from entering Malawi or Rhodesia and then slipping out of Central Africa.

The Second World War drained the labour reserves of Zambia. Recruitment for the Rand mines had to be suspended in 1943, and though the remnants of tribal forced labour had been abolished, by the progression of the 1929 policy of indirect rule, food shortages compelled the local Government to reintroduce some limited compulsion in 1942. Compulsory labour recruitment for European farmers, with a maximum of 600 labourers, was introduced for a period of two months in that year (1942 ILR 45: 746). It became necessary to reissue similar regulations in 1944, with the difference that these did not specify the period during which labour recruited by compulsion would be employed on farm work. The shortage of labourers became even more acute and by 1946 desertions from farms were still very numerous and deserters were believed to destroy their *citupas* and apply for new ones (1946 District Circular 5). Apart from compulsory recruitment for farm work, Government in 1942 introduced emergency powers to form an African Labour Corps (1942 ILR 46: 746). This was used for civilian purposes in 'maintaining supplies and services essential to the life of the community', but only 115 of the 500 men recruited for the Corps in 1943 were enlisted by compulsion (1943 ILR 48: 232). Thus the war effort absorbed more Zambians and denied them to other countries. However, war did not affect labour emigration as much as the trade cycle. Consider the facts that 42,000 Zambians were employed abroad in 1929 and that this number halved to 21,000 in 1933, and recovered to 51,000 in 1936; and compare these data with the fact that during the Second World War the number of Zambians employed abroad only dropped to 44,000.

The Tripartite Migrant Labour Agreements were primarily concerned with the effects of the emigration of adult males on the domestic capitalist economy and peasant systems. During the 1940s at least, the expansion of this economy and the construction of Towns for Africans were retarded by the shortage of domestic labour this caused. It is possible that those economies of Southern Africa which employed Zambians expanded at about the same rate as industry in Zambia, and so the increasing depopulation of the peasant areas, until the position represented in Table 6 was attained, must be attributed to these changes as much as the growth of the domestic capitalist economy. The pace at which Zambians emigrated kept up with the expansion of domestic employment.

Hence the Tripartite Labour Agreements did not significantly reduce emigration. However, these Agreements seem to have done something for the personal welfare of international migrants if not for their villages.

CONCLUSIONS

The government of the Casual Labour System was much less effective than that exercised in relation to the Recruited Labour System. Measures to protect the welfare of migrants appreciably improved their lot but it cannot be claimed that the Tripartite Migrant Labour Agreements did much to slow down emigration, in contrast to the earlier success of Government in curtailing the flow to the Katangan mines. More success resulted from the endeavour to restrict the number of alien Africans employed in Zambia and as a result a tendency developed of not employing unskilled aliens.

The most important direct consequence of the Casual Labour System was that it required more migrants for each job opportunity than did the Recruited Labour System. When the supply of workers does not immediately adjoin a workplace more than one worker must be in circulation, but not in employment, to ensure that one man is continuously employed, and it was a feature of the Casual Labour System that it required if not a whole additional man a larger fraction of a spare man in the pipeline to a job than was necessary under a Recruited Labour System. If recruitment had been universal and compulsory for all workers, this would have entailed the direction of manpower and only those for whom there were known jobs would have left their villages. Competition for jobs would in consequence have occurred at the sources of labour supply in the peasant systems, and unemployment in the urban areas would have been unknown. The Casual Labour System involved competition for work in the urban areas, and as a result far more peasants than there were jobs were encouraged to roam between their villages and through the Labour Camps in search of work. This was a distinct development towards mass migration which was described at the beginning of this chapter as a linked yet indirect consequence of the Casual Labour System. Whereas the Recruited Labour System suited many permanent target workers who were determined to return to their villages regularly, the Casual Labour System was better suited to temporary target workers who wanted to move their homes to the Labour Camps. When they left their villages they had less concern about returning and wanted the freedom to remain in the urban system as long as they pleased.

This is a quite different view from that presented by Prothero, who observed: 'Where labourers are seeking work for long periods, there is usually a greater measure of organisation for migrant labourers' (1968: 253-4). Were this true the following propositions must hold: (*a*) that long length of service in industry is a feature of the Recruited Labour System alone; (*b*) that the circulation of labour, inherent in the Recruited Labour System, is associated with long stretches of industrial employment. But in this and the preceding chapters it has been explained that the contrary was the case in Zambia. Not only did the Casual Labour System displace the Recruited Labour System when it was revealed that the turnover of recruited labour was *higher* than that of casual labour, but the Casual Labour System was closely allied to a growing trend for temporary target workers to drift to towns, stay there as long as possible, and drop out of the circulation of labour at its half way point. Prothero has not detected this one-way drift and the presence of mass migration in his survey of the Sub-Saharan region. These contradictions between Prothero's survey of the African literature and sources and the present study point to our limited knowledge of migration in Africa and the relevance of this study of its governance.

CHAPTER V
WOMEN FOR URBANISATION

LOCATION OF FAMILY UNITS

From country to country women respond differently to the dynamics of industrialisation and urbanisation. One of the Laws of Migration propounded in 1889 was that 'females are more migratory than males' (Ravenstein 1889). With the notable exception of the Andean Indians, this law applies to the inmigrants to the towns of Latin America (Elizaga 1965) and in the older towns and cities of North and West Africa where females sometimes tend to equal the number of males of corresponding age who entered the urban zones (UNECA 1969: 144). But inmigrants to Bombay in particular (Zacharia 1966) and perhaps the towns in the subcontinent of India in general include more men than women. Hitherto males have predominated also in the migrant streams to the faster-growing towns in Eastern and Southern Africa (1969 UNECA: 144) and on the overall experience in these zones it cannot be concluded that there is support for the Law of Migration which postulates that women move more readily than men.

But this requires careful qualification: in the industrial towns of South Africa during 1911-21 the increase in the African population was 'largely accounted from the increase in the native females' (Jones 1967: 164); and in the case of Zambia it is quite likely that by 1960 there were more girls than boys in the young teenage category of inmigrants to the towns, and that during the 1960s the inmigration of all females exceeded that of all males (1970 Census: A10). If, as is sometimes believed, the excess of women over men in an inmigrant stream to an urban area is a sign of an advanced industrial society then it would seem that Zambia has entered this category and now differs from the remainder of Southern and Eastern Africa.

The disproportion among the sexes in these migrant streams affected the ability of the populations at the points of departure and destination to reproduce themselves. In a population where there are fewer women than men the number of family units which can be formed to reproduce the population is dictated by the number of women; similarly in a population where women outnumbered men the maximum number of family units which can be formed to reproduce the population depends on the number of women. It follows that in a society such as Zambia, with a pronounced tendency towards monogamy (1970 Census: A11), the different propensities of men and women to take part in internal migration means that the actual number of family units are fewer than their potential number. This is because it is not axiomatic that surplus women in peasant systems will be absorbed into polygamous households, and in the urban system the scarce women determine the maximum number of family units because of the excess of males and absence of simultaneous polyandrous relationships. At such time as adult women equal the number of adult men in the urban system the necessary condition for enabling the actual and potential number of family and reproductive units to be created to be identical in number will have occurred. From the point of view of the future of the urban system as an autonomous system this demographic state of a balance between the sexes will weaken the present links with the peasant systems. A more dualistic and less heterogeneous form of society in Zambia may emerge from a balancing of the urban sex ratios. For an understanding of the changing social structure and social problems it is therefore of considerable concern to understand the pressures which influence the migration of women in Zambia.

As Government wanted to locate as many family units as possible in peasant systems, the exodus of women from them was looked on askance. While Government wanted every male peasant to become a proletarian for a brief moment to assist industrialisation, it was hoped that the character of the industrial man that he was to assume was no more than a veneer which concealed the identity of a peasant ever longing to return to nature. It was also realised that if women accompanied peasant men to work in factories this would preclude any urge on the part of these men to return to women in peasant systems. Permanent Target-Workers were worthy people and Temporary Target-Workers who had no wish to return to peasant systems were deviants according to this point of view before the 1950s. The issue of where to stabilise family units was reconsidered during the 1940s when it was decided that 'balanced stabilisation' was an appropriate policy. This meant that though some family units should legitimately live in the urban system the bulk should be prevented from doing so and thereby retained in the peasant systems. In consequence, from the early 1950s onwards Government ceased to impede the influx of women into urban systems in order to allow family units in these systems to be formed. In so far as Government regulation of the autonomous processes which brought women to the urban system had been effective before the 1950s this control had contributed to the unbalanced sex ratios of both peasant and urban systems. Looking back over the past seven decades it appears that there has been a tendency for women to follow men to the urban system, but that the government of migration once hindered this and thereby strengthened the pressures to redress the balances between the sexes which have occurred since 'balanced stabilisation' was decided upon.

It is easier to understand the evolution of public policy than current explanations of the migration of women. In two volumes of readings which manifest an awakening of sociological interest in migration, Jansen suggests that a version of push and pull theory is the most fruitful way of interpreting the outmigration from peasant systems of men and women (Jansen 1969: 63-64; 1970: 14-16). Prominence is given to the work of Bogue (1961) who has reasoned that where there is a strong push factor, depressing the conditions of potential outmigrants, differentiation between them by sex diminishes; conversely, there will be appreciable selectivity by sex when the pull stimulus to migration is the greater. When peasants primarily move because they are pushed out of their villages we would therefore expect about equal numbers of men and women to leave. Yet it is likely that if the motivation to migrate is due to the lure of the capitalist-urban centres this will not appeal to men and women to the same extent, and so one sex will have a greater propensity to migrate than the other. As Jansen is uncritical of these notions (1969: 63-4; 1970: 14-16) should we also infer that they are satisfactory as the most general explanation of sex selectivity among migrants? As the outmigration of women lags behind that of men, the push factor as an explanation of migration must be discounted in the case of Zambia if Bogue's reasoning is correct. In order to justify Bogue's hypothesis, which has implicitly received the assent of Jansen, it is necessary to demonstrate empirically that the reason why the migration of women in Zambia has historically lagged behind that of men is that the pull factor has been the paramount motivation and this has favoured the men who have been called to work for capitalism. It follows that the women who have remained behind in the peasant systems have been neither pulled nor pushed to the same degree.

With the help of Tables 6 and 6:1, Bogue's hypothesis will be tested. In Table 6, columns 1 to 3 which concern peasant outmigration are the more relevant. Columns 4 to 6 are of less interest because Zambia is not a closed society and hence many outmigrants never make the urban system of this country their destination. Columns 1 and 2 gauge the propensity of men and women to migrate. It will be recalled that the sex ratio of young people is pretty even so that imbalances between the adult sexes arise from adult behaviour. No variation in the death rate between the Peasant Provinces is known so this is discounted. Hence the relative differencs between the Peasant Provinces in respect of the proportion of adults in their populations were due to migration. It follows that the province with the greatest proportion of adults has experienced the least migration. On average 42 per cent of all the males and 45 per cent of all females in these Peasant Provinces were adults.

It is possible to rank the Peasant Provinces according to the extent of their adult migration. Table 6:1 shows the result of this ranking: on the whole the Western Hinterland is the least migratory and the Eastern Hinterland is the most migratory. In order to ascertain the predictive ability of the 1963 data represented in this table they are compared with the gross population changes in the Peasant Provinces recorded by the 1969 census. The conclusion is that from the 1963 data of outmigration it was possible to predict that the Eastern Hinterland would show the least growth in population in the years which immediately followed. Indeed, an absolute decline in population, perhaps for the first time this century, is recorded for two of the three Peasant Provinces in the Eastern Hinterland.

The fact that compared to men so many women were absent from the Peasant Provinces in 1963 comes as a surprise. There is no hint of this possibility in the study of the Luvale in the North-Western Province. Little economic strain is placed upon women by the outmigration of men from this system where 'women have their own independent incomes from agriculture' (White 1959: 53). In the Southern Province we know that in the late 1940s the outmigration of women was almost nonexistent, and as many as 98 per cent of the married men lived in the villages with their wives among the Plateau Tonga, though we are told of a few nearby Gwembe Tonga women who labour for wages in other peasant systems (Colson 1958: 64-70; Colson 1960: 50-3, 111). A curiosity of the major study of the Luapula is the information that 'women are as accustomed to long-distance travel as men are' (Cunnison 1959: 26), but that this is not important enough to merit consideration with respect to social organisation as is the case with absentee men. Furthermore, as has been noted in Chapter II, apart from Wilson's observation about Lenje migration the ethnographic description of these systems has overlooked the correlation between high outmigration and fairly balanced sex ratios in some peasant systems.

From all this data it is possible to controvert any simple explanation of the allure of lush towns for peasant women in terms of economic self-interest, which seems to be central to Bogue's hypothesis, which mistakenly attributes the outmigration of women mainly to pull factors. No differences exist between the Peasant Provinces with respect to the economic attractions of the towns. This was because employers did not discriminate between potential employees on the basis of their provincial origins and there was scarcely any paid employment for women in the capitalist-urban system. So in order to understand the provincial differences between outmigrants we must turn to the push factor and expect to discover that the most migratory peasant provinces are the poorest. From Table 5 we learn that the most prosperous peasant provinces are those along the line of rail and the Eastern Province, and hence we expect them to be the least migratory. But these same peasant systems exhibit median outmigration and their women leave them at a rate in excess of that of women from the poorer Western Hinterland. Indeed the Western Hinterland is not only the least prosperous but is also the least migratory zone,. Does this conjunction of a demographically viable yet poor peasant zone, with more women awaiting the return of men than elsewhere, refute Bogue? Only the Northern Province conforms to his hypothesis of the combination of the greatest poverty and economic push with the most outward migration by both sexes.

It is the task of the remainder of this chapter to provide a fuller account of female migration than is to be derived from the oversimplified economic hypothesis of Bogue. Thinking within the push and pull framework an attempt will be made to enlarge these concepts from measures of economic conditions towards inclusion of geographical and social influences. Before the factors which facilitate movement are considered a push from the towns which inhibited female migration will be described.

URBAN EMPLOYMENT

When women arrived in the towns of Zambia their hopes of providing for themselves were negligible. Growth in the employment of townswomen has been slow: whereas they comprised 2.1 per cent of the African labour force in Zambia in 1956 they did not exceed 2.8 per cent of the same population in 1961. Of these percentages, the proportion of African women born outside Zambia increased from one seventh (1956) to just under one sixth (1961) (Census of Employees 1965(b): 8). In so far as these figures depict the incomes available to independent women in the towns they are a statement of a weak economic inducement for women to come to towns. Women may migrate as readily as men, given a modern society, if there are equal job opportunities with men (ECA 1968; Southall 1961: 58; Zachariah 1966; Eames and Schwab 1964), but in Zambia there were few jobs for townswomen before Independence.

One reason concerns the nature of employment. Mining and construction industries, the major sectors of employment, by their nature offered few openings for the employment of women (Mitchell 1961(*a*): 212). Not until there was an expansion of secondary industries, a rise in the general level of female education, and clerical employment following the dismantling of the Federation of Rhodesia and Nyasaland in December 1963, which had constrained the money economy to remain devoted to primary production, were jobs suitable for women increasingly available. The lack of growth in the Zambian labour force largely due to the economic effects of Federation occurred at the same time as the number of males entering the towns became a major social problem and there was extreme reluctance to give women jobs which could be performed by men.

To keep women and children in the villages, and so deprive them of legally attainable subsistence in the towns, Government devised the Employment of Women, Young Persons and Childrens Ordinance, 1933. But sex prejudice and the industrial colour bar were of equal effect. The almost exclusive employment of African males in domestic employment will illustrate the local prejudice against the employment of women. Not only will men 'be found undertaking practically every duty in the house; they are occasionally expected to do work which in Europe would be carefully restricted to female servants. For this, no doubt, old-established custom is mainly responsible, together with the fact that at present the African man is more reliable and intelligent than the woman' (Orde-Browne 1938: 27). The Recruited Labour System was exclusively concerned to move men to jobs which were usually located in places where insufficient local labour was available. Initially the labour available for domestic employment was therefore male, in contrast to the situations in other African economies where the employers of domestic labour were closer to a village supply and were thus in a better position to engage women. The shortage of African wives in the early Labour Camps in Zambia also meant a shortage of women for domestic service. African men were also able to overcome the language barrier, due to their longer experience of migration, and were on this count to be preferred as servants. As for the industrial colour bar, this restricted the employment of Africans until the 1960s to unskilled and semi-skilled work. This applies not only to African men but to their wives and sisters. But the really effective barrier to the employment of women was their illiteracy in a country which could only boast of 105 indigenous graduates, of whom but a handful were women, in 1964, its year of Independence.

Why did townswomen in Zambia not become petty traders to the extent found in West Africa? Again the answer seems to lie in differences in the nature of urbanisation in the two areas. In West Africa urban growth tended to take place in African towns often established before colonisation; whereas in Zambia entirely new 'European' towns were built in which women were scarce, where no official housing was provided for single African women, and where illegal housing was under the threat of demolition from the 1940s onwards. About the only occupation available to a single African woman in the towns was prostitution, but even 'paid prostitution is uncommon' (Orde-Browne 1938: 24). Although this occurred, it was prohibitively expensive; for in 1940, one man discovered that a night's 'casual intercourse' would cost him one or two whole days' wages (Wilson 1942: 66). Even so, some men were reluctant to live with women who did not have jobs because the level of male wages was determined with a view to the needs of bachelors and not heads of family units (McCulloch (1956(a): 217).

PEASANT SYSTEMS

In part the conduct of a woman is a product of her socialisation and interpretation of the immediate situation in which she is placed. It also arises from social facts which are pressing and external to her. A peasant system is composed of such external facts which embody the ends and means of social existence. With regard to Zambia, the government of migration, divorce, marital residence, authority and kinship ties were the major social facts of the peasant systems which influenced the migration of their women until nationalism intervened.

Government of Migration

Ethnic and cultural restraints have been cited as reasons why women and men do not migrate in the same proportions (Sjoberg 1966: 242; Caldwell 1968: 21), but the nature of these controls have been made clear less often. It would seem, according to a general line of explanation, that while modern societies do not interfere with the migration of women, traditional societies keep them 'locked up'. In practice, however, the matter is more complex. For instance, the Plateau Tonga (Southern Province) disapproved of married men leaving their wives and while only the unmarried men went to work in the towns (McCulloch 1956(b): 16) family life in the villages was not disrupted. With some seventy-three tribal and linguistic groupings in Zambia it is clearly impossible to comment on their unique features which hindered the migration of their women, but it is possible to single out a few variables which affected more or less all these societies.

First to be described among these are manifest regulations and controls on migration which can be said to have contributed towards induced social stability in these societies. It was a premise of District Officers and Native Authorities that social stability was best ensured when there were balanced sex ratios over time in the rural societies; second best, a measure of social stability was preserved if adult women in their prime were kept in the rural societies even if their husbands were absent. Social stability was absent when men and women in their prime made haste towards the towns. Thus the government of migration was motivated by beliefs which failed to understand that a high rate of migration by women as well as men may be consonant with social stability.

Regulations concerning the movement of single women, the registration of marriages, and schemes to augment peasant incomes were the major devices whereby Government sought to sustain peasant systems by means of family planning. Following the introduction of indirect rule in 1929, the Native Authorities were encouraged to prohibit the movement of women and children to the towns, and this they were glad to do on three grounds. First, it was realised that if they left the peasant systems the men would not return or make further remittances (Moffat Thomson 1933: 79). So by regulations the women were bound to the villages as hostages for the return of the absent men. The second ground concerns the complaint that African men were losing control over their womenfolk. A senior official thought that 'women have a harder time than men who live in the villages, in the towns they do not have the same amount of labour to perform' (Moffat Thomson 1933: 78). When asked why they were going to the Copperbelt in 1958, three elderly women said: 'We want to rest; there is no hard work in the towns, but plenty in the village' (Taylor and Lehmann 1961: 72). To escape from hardship was a real incentive to migrate but this was restrained on a third ground: that the sole occupation of a single woman in a town was immoral. A study of Ghana reveals an 'extraordinary concentration on a single theme in the opposition to female migration. It is not the destitution, crime or loss of family ties which are feared; it is the temptation of prostitution' (Caldwell 1969: 107). In Zambia a similar moral conservatism was displayed which caused the Great East Road from Malawi to Lusaka to be nicknamed the 'conveyor of prostitutes' (Marwick 1965: 48).

Many Native Authorities made Orders to prevent the movement of unmarried women. In 1924 the High Court quashed the conviction of a woman who had been found guilty of disobeying an Order issued under Proclamation 8 of 1916 that no unmarried woman or married woman unaccompanied by her husband should leave the Mumbwa District (Central Province) without the permission of the Native Commissioner. This Order was declared to be restrictive of movement amongst individuals. It was also criticised for the hypothesis that the accused was guilty until the contrary was proven. In the case of girls and young unmarried females, any Order by an Authority would of course be valid if it prohibited the taking of an unmarried girl under the age of sixteen years out of the custody and protection of the person having the lawful care or charge of her and against their will. The movement of a girl in the face of such prohibition would be an offence against morality under the Penal Code. District Officers, under the system of indirect rule, were therefore instructed to restrain the Native Authorities and not support Orders which were merely to the effect that unmarried women or married women unaccompanied by their husbands should not proceed to the towns (District Circular 9 1931).

But it seems that Native Authorities sometimes ignored the cautions of District Officers. Three instances of this must suffice. In the case of the Mambwe (Northern Province), 'single women are prevented by law from going to the Copperbelt to find work by themselves. Apart from the legal restrictions, Mambwe ideas of decorum forbid women to attempt to seek work on their own. A woman showing such a degree of independence would be considered immoral' (Watson 1958: 44). Among the Ngoni (Eastern Province) women were forbidden to leave the tribal area except in the company of their husbands, 'or with a pass of leave from the Native Authority. ... These laws are quite energetically enforced, principally by the placing of Native Authority police at strategic points along the lorry routes. These police inspect the passes of all passengers on the lorries, and bring offenders before the nearest Native Court' (Barnes 1959: 246). Likewise, the Cewa (Eastern Province) insist that women passengers on lorries 'unaccompanied by their husbands have to produce marriage certificates before passing westward out of the Province' (Marwick 1965: 48).

By means of the regulation of marriage registration the peasant systems exercised some control over the movement of women until 1953. The peasant systems in this case were the Native Authorities. These were never established in the towns and were organised as the formal, grass roots, local governments. There were two issues: should the registration of marriages be made compulsory? and who should register marriages? In 1934 a number of Native Authorities brought into force a scheme for the voluntary registration of marriages by peasants resident in their areas. These rules of registration did not alter the forms of marriage, which in order to be legally valid must still be in accordance with peasant law and custom. In some peasant systems today it is an offence not to register a marriage and in others registration is optional. After Government had considered whether to assume direct responsibility for the registration of marriages and provide for civil registration it decided that registration should remain a discretionary responsibility of Native Authorities, that Government officers should have no hand in the registration of marriages, and that the question of marriages among urban Africans be considered only when special Urban Native Authorities were appointed for them (1935 PCs Conference: 12; 1936 PCs Conference: 32).

Popular demand, new means of urban housing management, and the bureaucratic ineptitude of the peasant Native Authorities led to the urban registration of urban marriages. The decision of the mid-1930s that the Native Authorities were the sole agencies for registration was challenged in 1939 by a request to the Government from the newly created Urban Native Courts. This asked that, in order to meet popular demand, Urban Native Courts should be permitted to register the marriages of those urban dwellers who could give evidence that their kin in the peasant systems approved of their marriages (1939 District Circular 39). This antagonised the Provincial Administration, which was less concerned over the fact that the concepts embodied in peasant marriages would be preserved in the proposed rearrangement than by the by-passing of the peasant Native Authorities upon whom the evolution of African society depended, according to official theory. It was therefore reaffirmed that only Native Authorities should be allowed to register, but that there was no objection to Urban Native Courts forwarding applications in writing, with their own comments, for registration by the Native Authorities concerned (July 1943 Circular Minute NAT/K2).

Hardly had this slight rearrangement come into practice when a revision in the method of housing management in the towns set up pressures to permit the urban registration of marriages. In 1945 the mining companies began to insist on the production of a valid marriage certificate prior to the allocation of married quarters in the townships. This was of critical importance in a situation where other employers followed leads given by the mining companies and where the vast majority of housing in the towns was controlled by the local authorities on behalf of employers, allocated only to employed men, and was usually not suited to the needs of families. Without a marriage certificate a couple whose union was not registered might be denied married quarters. The problem was that the sanction of a peasant system to a marriage must be obtained before a certificate of registration would be issued and this meant that urban 'pick-up' marriages would not be recognised by the peasant authorities and hence quarters would not be available to partners in such marriages. Either a marriage must be contracted in a peasant system with the assent of all concerned; or it must take place between a man and woman who came from the same peasant system and who received the approval of an Urban Native Court who passed on their application to their Native Authority. What was at stake was the power of the peasant Native Authorities to control the lives of those who had left them even while they lived in the urban system. Apart from the question of creating an entitlement to married accommodation, a certificate of marriage equally served as an entitlement to a marriage allowance from those employers who paid these. In a situation where the 'legal status of most urban marriages is doubtful, registration by providing for a marriage certificate facilitates proof of marriage when there is a dispute' (Native Courts Advisor 1961: 9).

Had the peasant Native Authorities been less dilatory and inefficient they would not have provided the necessary cause for urban registration of marriages. From early 1944, the Native Authorities often failed to reply to applications for the registration of urban marriages or simply rejected them. An attempt to speed up the legal marriage process was made but still the Native Authorities had to decide each issue. A good reason why they failed at first to cope was that situated outside the urban system they were not in possession of the facts pertinent to each application. So the Urban Native Courts gladly assented to the instruction to investigate marriage proposals carefully and reject "irregular unions", marriages between persons from different peasant systems, and other cohabitations which the Native Authorities would not approve (1945 District Circular 6). Even so the Native Authorities could not cope with the "screened" applications which they received. The educational standards of Native Authority clerks were too low to enable them to deal with registration.

Their failure to meet the urban demand had two further causes. They were suspicious of the parallel urban system and its institutions, which seemed to be making demands upon them, and no doubt were inclined to derive some satisfaction from slowing down the processes of this dangerous competitor. Another related reason is that the Native Authorities could not understand why they should sanction the marriages of their women to men they did not know, had not seen, and would never see in their own peasant systems.

The matter was resolved without legislation. Government recognized not only the inconvenience of the system of peasant registration of urban marriages but also the need to create urban institutions appropriate to the Towns for Africans it created in the 1950s. Hence an administrative circular of 16 April 1953 instituted a reform and permitted Urban Native Courts to issue marriage certificates. Marriage certificates could thenceforth be issued when the Urban Courts were satisfied that the partners had 'severed normal connections with the rural areas' provided that a state of marriage existed, or when the Native Authorities had failed to issue their own certificates.

Undoubtedly this facilitated the migration of women to towns where they could marry whom they pleased. The general implication of the pre-1953 policy is clear: the Native Authorities wished to ensure by this that their absentee men returned to their villages. As marriage between persons from separate peasant systems made it unlikely that they could batten down on the parties involved, such 'inter-tribal' marriages were not registered. It is of interest that even the Urban Native Courts approved of this and were opposed to 'irregular unions' (Epstein 1953: 61). They, the Native Authorities, and the Government believed that the rightful place of men was in the villages. As long as they returned, the pressure on women to leave for the towns was diminished.

The probability that a man would return from town as long as he sent money and presents to his village was high. Several arrangements, not particularly successful, require mention. In 1911 R. W. Yule instituted the system of deferred wages (Colonial 145 1938: 30) which were once of territorial-wide importance and linked expatriates and their families. Some £52,000 was paid as deferred wages in Zambia in 1928, but this dropped to £5,200 in 1934 and £8 in the depths of the recession in 1935 (Orde-Browne 1938: 55) – no doubt partly because of the emergence of the Casual Labour System. There was hardly a recovery, and merely £227 deferred wages were paid in the territory in 1939, probably as a result of the implementation of the Migrant Labour Agreement. Paragraph 10 of this Agreement stipulated that the Government of Southern Rhodesia would experiment for two years with the organisation of a voluntary remittance scheme and would employ seven itinerant officials for this purpose. But this was unsuccessful and the 1947 revision of the Agreement did not alter the voluntary nature of the scheme, despite strong feelings that it ought to on the part of the Zambian Labour Department. In as much as workers were recruited, they enjoyed vague contracts and tended to avoid the scheme as a result. The deferred wage system, designed to encourage thrift and 'form a real incentive to a speedy arrival home' (Orde-Browne 1938: 49), was thus ineffective.

In November 1938 the Native Industrial Labour Advisory Board considered whether the deferred pay scheme, already in operation for Africans who were recruited for service *outside* Zambia, should be introduced for Africans within the country. The mining companies and Government agreed in January of the following year to introduce a similar scheme for indigenous Africans employed in the domestic money economy. This scheme would be voluntary and interest at 3 per cent would be paid on deposits. Between the inception of this savings scheme in 1939 and June 1942 £132,760 was deposited and £68,956 withdrawn, leaving a balance of £63,804. But whether this scheme had the desired effect, namely to ensure a steady flow of wealth to the rural families, is difficult to gauge, but the impression of the compound managers and others was that 'the money saved is spent in the urban areas, and that the benefit, if any, to the villages is in the form of goods and clothes and not in cash' (Saffery 1943: 24). Unlike the deferred wage system for men recruited for work outside Zambia, the domestic Voluntary Deferred Pay (Savings) Scheme, the 'Mine Bank' which lasted until 1965, while providing for regular deductions from the wages of miners once they joined the scheme also permitted them to make regular withdrawals. Another point of difference between the foreign and domestic schemes was that in the latter withdrawals could be made in the towns. In combination these factors meant that 'a real incentive to a speedy arrival home' was absent from the local scheme.

In 1949 Government considered for the last time introducing a system of family remittances by Africans working in the towns to their rural families. But it was decided not to adopt such a scheme because of the difficulties of administration and because 'it was not a suitable way in which to educate the African to realise his responsibilities to his relatives' (1949 Administrative

Conference: 22). The relative failures of these schemes gave more reason to deserted wives to join their husbands in the towns.

Controlled recruiting seemed a more promising way of alleviating hardship and persuading married women to remain in their villages. An instance of the humane and realistic aspirations of Government officers in respect of recruiting is provided by Kalabo. This was the most backward district in Barotseland but possessed a strong tradition of recruitment by the Witswatersrand Native Labour Association. The Government minimum wage in this district in 1959 was £3 a month, and the average miner recruited by Wenela returned with eight months' wages at the local rate, i.e. £25 (Armor 1962: 28). Without this the district economy would have collapsed and an urgent incentive to rural exodus would have operated: tax collected in the district in 1959 was £7,500 and the Native Authority budgeted to spend £24,000. How was this deficit to be overcome?

CONTRIBUTION TO KALABO ARISING FROM WENELA OPERATIONS, 1959

	£	£
Wenela payment to Native Authority	1,200	
Remittances of deferred pay to Kalabo repatriates:	39,000	
Local payments by Wenela for labour, rations and materials consumed by recruiting posts:	9,200	
Total:		49,000
Expenditure in Kalabo by Angolans being repatriated by Wenela:	5,000	
Grand Total		54,400

Wenela as a South African organisation was forbidden to operate in Zambia after 1965, but in that year it paid to Zambians and in Zambia £117,537 in the form of remittances and deferred pay. These remittances were crucial to peasant families because they were often the sole link between a wife in a village and a husband at work in a mine. In some cases they may have been the remaining reason why women stayed in the villages and thus it is interesting that the individual remittances paid in Zambia were about one-third of the total deferred earnings paid to Zambians (1967 ARDL: 78), or 833 years' wages at the rate of £3 a month. One can only conclude that though all these efforts failed in the long term they were probably once important in stemming the rural exodus of women.

In spite of all these arrangements a government officer complained bitterly that the 'real damage to village life in Northern Rhodesia has been done not by the temporary absence of men on the Copperbelt (or by the permanent settlement there of families), but by the much longer absence of migrant labourers in Southern Rhodesia, and, unless they have been properly recruited, in South Africa' (Bradley 1952: 25-6). By 1956 some 19,737 Zambians had been employed continuously in Rhodesia since 1949 and in 1961 it was recorded that 44,840 Zambians were employed in Rhodesia (1965 Census of Employees: 32). All that the Northern Rhodesia Government could do was to acknowledge the power of autonomous social processes and by Clause 24 (2) of the Inter-Territorial Agreement on Migrant Labour, negotiated between the three territories in Central Africa for the duration of the Federation of Rhodesia and Nyasaland, it was agreed that Zambians who had been continuously resident in Rhodesia for ten years should be permitted, with their families, to remain there indefinitely (Cmnd. 1149 1960: 333).

Divorce

Phenomenal and epiphenomenal explanations of divorce have been evolved and as they are both fashionable and have contrasting implications for the connection between divorce and migration, they will be examined in turn. In the phenomenal explanation of divorce a distinction is made between migration during the initial phase of capitalism, when primary production is all-important, and in the second phase when more resources are devoted to secondary and tertiary production. Zambia is now moving into the second phase of capitalism in these terms and this analysis concerns the first phase.

Bogue has noted that during the beginnings of capitalism most inmigrants to towns are young and mature adults who are single, divorced or widowed. With respect to Africa, Gugler affirms that marital instability 'be it traditional or a product of new forces ... pushes women into the city' (1969: 139), and Colson has observed a connection between marriage break-up and migration (1958: 67). Southall observed the product of this: the 'women living singly, or without legal husbands, and in economic independence', which constituted 'one of the most striking characteristics of Africans in towns in contrast to rural areas' (1961: 51). Behind this phenomenal explanation a three-part theory may be detected: that urbanisation creates inmigration of the men who are pulled to new jobs; this imposes a strain on the wives they have left behind and divorce follows; and as a wife is dependent upon her husband their divorce leaves her destitute and to escape from her predicament in a peasant system where marriages are arranged and every woman wanted has been spoken for, she flees to a town and its surplus of men in search of relief. Thus the exodus of women from peasant systems is in part attributed to their rates of marital instability.

Superficial support for some such hypothesis is available. Table 11 reveals that marital instability is endemic in the peasant systems of Zambia. For these reasons Southall has observed that in Zambia it 'appears that there is little difference in the stability of urban and rural marriages' (1961: 63-4). His further comment is crucial: 'This may be because the traditional marriage of most of the tribes concerned is of the low stability type and consequently allows for the new urban pressures.' Peasant systems which are prone to marital infidelity and instability are seen to be characteristic of Zambia and in consequence to facilitate the pathological upheaval of their systems by creating the pressures which can most easily be alleviated by the outmigration of women. As this tends to be much more of a one-way affair than it is with men, it may be contended that certain social spaces in peasant systems are permanently vacated by this outmigration. Because of divorce, the bonds which knit together peasant systems are untied.

The epiphenomenal explanation asks whether it is true that divorce has these multiple and devastating repercussions on the fabrics of peasant systems. Bohannan is of the opinion that a high incidence of divorce is not necessarily pathological ((1963: 114) and Mitchell considers that 'one social system may be able to tolerate a high degree of marital instability which would be dysfunctional in another' (1961(*c*)). Thus women, even if single, may in certain circumstances remain an integral part of a social system and remain subject to its pressures to keep them incorporated following divorce. A study of the Luvale discovered that only 7 per cent of the divorce cases arose from the absence of a labour migrant husband, and that the 'small number of divorces arising from labour migration is consistent with the fact that many labour migrants are young bachelors, few stay away over four years, and women have their own independent incomes from agriculture' (White 1959: 53). On the other hand sterility may drive a peasant woman into a migrant stream. In the early history of migration to the urban system, it is suspected that many barren women participate. Sterility may have rendered them incapable of remaining a useful part of a peasant system where the begetting of children cements relationships and creates valuable property rights. The epiphenomenal explanation will be preferred here but it may not be consistent with the circumstances of other societies. Though divorce rates in Zambia are high they make little impact upon outmigration from the peasant systems typical of Zambia, though it is suspected that the contrary may pertain in some other societies.

The factual observation that 'divorce is rare and difficult in those (African systems) organised on a system of marked father-right, and frequent and easy to obtain in other types' (Gluckman 1950: 190) prompted the current explanation of differential marital instability among peasant systems. This rests on a distinction between rights in a mother, particularly with regard to the control of her child, and rights to her domestic and sexual services; that is, genetrical and uxorial rights respectively. Hence 'our argument . . . has been that the main stabilising influence in marriage is the legal transfer of genetrical rights to the husband' (Mitchell 1961(*b*): 328). Marriage obtains new recruits to patrilineages by securing rights over the reproductive powers of women from exogamous groups. Rights over reproductive powers are permanently transferred to the husband's group 'so that the marriage cannot easily be dissolved' (Mitchell 1961(*b*): 318); nor can a mother transfer her children to her original group in the event of a divorce in a patrilineal society.

By contrast, marriage in a bilateral or matrilineal society mainly involves the securing of uxorial rights by a husband (Mitchell 1961(*b*): 318, 323) and so does not automatically separate a woman and her matrikin from the guardianship of her children. Hence the network of most important relationships in which a woman is involved in nonpatrilineal systems need not be disjointed by divorce. It is as if the husband in matrilineal systems is but an instrument through which various ends of the group to whom he is married may be pursued. Personality differences are reflected by divorce under these circumstances and not the structural ties which bind a woman to her kin. For this reason divorce in matrilineal systems is an epiphenomenon which does not necessarily make women available for outmigration.

If it is asked whether or not the payment of a large bridewealth constrains and supports a marriage and reduces the likelihood of the outmigration of a woman, it must be answered that this is not necessarily the case. Underlying such a question is the notion that the bridewealth must be returned if a marriage fails, and that this gives the extended kin who receive the bridewealth a vested interest in the success of the marriage. But 'It seems clear to me that the size of the bridewealth and the ways in which it is contributed are determining factors but by no means the only ones' (Richards 1950: 250) in influencing the perpetuation of a marriage. The Azande and Ganda are patrilineal peoples who make low marriage payments 'but nevertheless had stable marriages', and there are records of matrilineal peoples with high divorce rates who make high marriage payments (Gluckman 1950: 205). Indeed it is claimed that it is 'rare divorce which allows high marriage payments, rather than high marriage payments which prevent divorce' (Gluckman 1950: 192).

Under changing conditions, in the urban system especially, there has been a tendency to raise marriage payments for uxorial rights (Lehmann 1961: 30; Mitchell 1961(b): 32) as a 'sort of insurance policy against the possible dissolution of a marriage' (Mitchell 1957: 25). This may help to stabilise the increasing number of 'inter-tribal' marriages where uxorial rights are chiefly in question (Mitchell 1961(c)). But this refers to the evolving forms of marriage where the emphasis is on diffuse rather than extended kinship and does little to influence the availability of peasant women for outmigration.

This epiphenomenological explanation of divorce and marriage payments pertains to matrilineal and bilateral peasant systems. The likelihood that a divorcee will migrate is probably greater in a patrilineal than in a nonpatrilineal system. Empirical and comparative verification for this is still required, yet in one of the rare patrilineal systems of Zambia 'some women will go to extraordinary lengths to get to the towns' (Watson 1958: 45-6). Most peasant systems in Zambia are matrilineal and bilateral, and divorce is to them an epiphenomenon which makes little contribution to the outmigration of their women.

Perhaps too much importance may be attached to the autonomous forces which make matrilineal and bilateral divorces an epiphenomenon. Among the Luvale the percentage of divorces arising from labour migration may have been greater than seven had it not been for the attitude of peasant authorities. If divorce does not free a woman to migrate, it may reduce the urge of men to return to a peasant system. Through the sexual imbalance which this indirectly creates, the propensity to bring this back to normal by enabling a woman to have a man of her own in a town is increased. Continuous pressures are often exerted to ensure that absent husbands had a peasant home, and so the pressures on a deserted woman to continue to behave as if she were married may be strong in her village. Desertion for under two years or so does not seem to be a general ground for divorce, and among the Lozi of Barotseland a woman can only apply for a divorce on the ground of desertion, and succeed in her petition, after three years (Gluckman 1950: 182), because the court will hold that a 'woman marries a man and not a blanket.' So the husband must periodically return, care for and sleep with his wife. In the 1950s a divorce was only available to a woman who had been 'five years without help' in a part of the Northern Province (Taylor and Lehmann 1961: 83). But in the Southern Province 'a Tonga woman married for a husband and not a remittance' (Colson 1958: 68), and after a short interval approved by custom could apply for a divorce. Among the Ngoni of the Eastern Province a woman not content to be alone will be told by a court to write to her absent husband and ask him for the fare to join him in the town (Barnes 1951: 85). A common test of the perseverance of a marriage and the obligation of a woman to remain in a village was whether an absentee husband treated her with consideration. This involved giving her clothes, but only rarely took the form of providing her with food (Barnes 1951: 88; Richardson 1959: 20). If these attitudes are associated with the information contained in Table 6:1 it will be observed that, with the exception of the Plateau Tonga, these attitudes were manifested in Peasant Provinces in which the propensity of men to migrate was considerably greater than that of women. The Tonga women who expected to marry men and not remittances are understandably prone to follow their husbands to the urban system.

Residence, Marriage and Migration

Customs which decide the residences of marriage partners will affect the availability of wives to migrate with or to join their husbands. A useful distinction may be made between those kinds of marriage with immediate rights of bride removal and those with deferred rights of bride removal (Richards 1950: 209). The latter is the practice over much of Zambia and ties a man as well as his wife to his in-laws' homestead until such time as he has qualified to act independently.

But this practice is fast disappearing, for instance among the Ndembu in the North-Western Province (Turner 1957: 23). In the Southern Province, the Ila-Tonga (Richards 1950: 236) and the Gwembe Tonga (Colson 1960: 96) remove their wives immediately after marriage, and this may also happen among the Lenje and Sala peoples of the Central Province (Richards 1950: 237). It is a norm among the Plateau Tonga that they should live where they please (Colson 1958: 25). With a right to remove his wife immediately after marriage, a man is in a better position to take her with him to town than when he must defer this movement. Today many men become impatient of the demands made upon them by an uxorial marriage and they are tempted to terminate residence with their in-laws before the time set for the removal of their wives from her kin's homestead. Uxorial marriage is the custom among the Luapula peasants with a tendency to move out of the wife's village after the husband has been 'accustomed'. But increasing mobility appears to be the keynote of modern marriage conditions here: 'a wider choice of spouses and the opportunity of marrying further afield' because the 'density of village settlements, the constant mixing of peoples around schools and missions, in fishing camps and on motorboats, the commercial beerdrinks, hotels and tearooms have all helped to increase the movements of individuals, men and women' (Cunnison 1950: 19, 21). Thus in the more prosperous provinces the migration of married men and women is facilitated by the erosion of marriage customs and the present of Ila-type virilocal marriage.

There may be another factor at work which affects the practice of some women following their husbands to towns. If, for instance, Ila-type and Luapula marriages are compared with Ndembu marriages the fact that there is less emphasis on companionship in the latter will be remarked. Undoubtedly a variable reflected in Table 6:1 is that on the whole those provinces which experience more companionate marriages watch their men and women leave them in roughly equal numbers.

Status to Contract

There is reason to suppose that women migrate more readily from peasant provinces where social relationships tend to be governed by contractual considerations than from those where status is paramount. The provinces from which women migrate in numbers just a little less than men, with the exception of the Northern Province, attach increasing importance to contractual inter-action so that there 'is a feeling that Luapula life is not rural backwood life' (Cunnison 1959: 25) and, to explain a basic Tonga formulation, 'those who help one another in a particular fashion are relatives, and those who do not so help one another are to be considered unrelated' (Colson 1958: 20).

On this depends the ease with which migrants are reabsorbed on returning to their villages, the importance laid upon material advancement, and the tendency for nuclear marital partnerships. Take the case of the re-absorption of absentees and it will be seen that not only are they made welcome but they are likely to have gained from their absence. For instance, in the Serenje District of the Central Province differences 'in wealth, education and style of life are often expressed in terms of a dichotomy between town and country' (Long 1968: 165), and the greatest prestige is attached to those who once lived in the urban system. To the south the Gwembe Tonga see labour migration as advancing their prosperity in their peasant setting (Colson 1960: 51), and in the Luapula it is believed that men 'who have sought work abroad need not fear to return home, for opportunity exists there to make money and enjoy the attractions of the Copperbelt in their native surroundings' (Cunnison 1959: 29). This is partly achieved through the communication links between absentees and villagers, for migration 'need not involve any great separation from family and kinsmen' (Colson 1958: 68) when periodical trips home, remittances, letters of advice and information keep the outmigrants involved in peasant life. Return to the villages is much more likely if there is social space for the prodigals and if the villages offer attractive livelihoods not unduly constrained by the demands of kinship and status. It is not surprising that there should be what the Tonga call 'farmers for profit' (Jones 1966) when it was 'recognised that a man could improve his lot above that of his fellows' (Colson 1967: 94). Cash cropping and commercial fishing in these provinces are achievements of individuals rather than traditional groupings. This in turn affected the nature of marriage which is moving towards economic partnerships, so that it is reported that Plateau Tonga couples 'work together as a team for the welfare of their own households' (Colson 1958: 64) and this seems to be the trend among the Lala in the Serenje District (Long 1968: 20-25). In those peasant systems where the individual more and more arranges for his or her own welfare there is decreasing opposition to outmigration.

Nationalism

Political agitation by women in the African struggle against the European dominated Federation of Rhodesia and Nyasaland (1953-63) earned them citizenship under the 1962 constitution. Peasant systems reeled under the national political turmoil during the 1950s, and after victory was achieved there was no return to the *status quo ante* as recorded by anthropologists for the Cewa, Ngoni, Bemba, Plateau Tonga and Mambwe peoples. Native Authorities, chiefs, and village headmen were often attacked as the symbols of European authority. When their power weakened, the Northern Rhodesia Government had no choice but to reintroduce an element of direct rule (Heisler 1965: 188). Assaults on the authority of Headmen, whose 'position is the key to understanding the relation of kinship and political bonds' (Gluckman 1963: 151), struck at the core of the organisation of peasant systems and thus at the pressures which kept women in their clutches. African national political organisation began to emerge as alternatives to indigenous and colonial power at the grass roots (Mulford 1967). As individuals and through membership of the women's brigade, women played a part, sometimes violent, in undermining the continuity of peasant systems. This took place more or less everywhere except in Barotseland where this process did not come into being until late 1961. Political emancipation of women strained all other aspects of the webs of relationships which once secured them to peasant systems; if women showed disrespect to a Native Court or headman who sought to enforce regulations about contour ridging or smallpox regulations by the non-payment of fines and refusal to proffer customary salutation, why should they heed Native Authority orders which would bottle them in their villages? If the Luapula, Southern and Central Provinces had flexible societies in the 1940s which enabled them to use for their own ends migration and development, their developmental difference from the remaining provinces began to be cancelled in the 1950s by the political changes which opened the towns to all women. To the individualisation of married life in these three provinces in the 1940s must be added the impact of nationalism on the other provinces in accounting for the outmigration of women.

OPPORTUNITY

When two women with similar motivations who are members of separate social systems exhibit dissimilar behaviour this cannot be attributed to these systems. The similar motivations of the dissimilarly located women would indeed point to a close resemblance between these social systems and so the sources of dissimilar behaviour by these women must be sought in other circumstances. These may be referred to conveniently as opportunities which are regularly distributed so that all women in similar situations are aware of them. Communications are opportunities which were not equally available to every Peasant Province and which as a result did much to facilitate only the movement of women close to the urban system in spatial and familial senses.

Once more the advantages of the Luapula, Southern and Central Provinces is striking. 'Living in the bush is a Bemba custom' (Cunnison 1959: 25), and as it is better to be in touch with the outside world the Luapula peasants live near the main highways. From these 'some eight or ten buses link the valley every week with the Copperbelt, and the Luapula steamer, motor-boats and a number of lorries link it every day with Elizabethville' (Cunnison 1959: 26). In Lusaka in the Central Province it was found that the neighbouring Lenje and Soli tribes provided more women than men to the population (Bettison 1959: 66), similar to the case of the Lenje at Kabwe (Broken Hill) 90 miles to the north. As a result these three provinces supplied an important element of the female population available for 'intertribal' marriages. In the 1940s about half the women who entered the towns were not already married to men in the towns, and it is probable that neighbouring peasant systems supplied a greater proportion of these than distant systems whose women went to the towns mostly if they were already married to absentees. If distance was a barrier to migration, fewer women from distant systems than from nearby ones should be found in the towns. Column (7) of Table 6 supports this conclusion: the sex ratios in the urban system of those who came from the adjacent provinces was about 105-6 and more evenly balanced than the sex ratios of peasants from more distant systems. Thus transport, the cost of movement and the initial urban facilities for migrants will be considered as the major opportunities for the migration of women.

Transport and Costs

Improvements in road maintenance, transport and cost made journeys easier (Ridley 1955; Niddrie 1954; Scott 1954) and until this happened few women went to the towns until the Second World War. Until motor transport – first lorries and later motor buses – became generally available, migrants walked. With babies and bundles (*katundu*) this taxed the strength of women more than of men. But in the 1930s the majority of men could not avail themselves of the scarce transport available because they could not afford the road and rail fares (1935 Emigrant Labour: 24-5). Not surprisingly, they found it even more difficult to pay for the travelling costs of women at a time when the Bemba on the Copperbelt paid 35s. for a lorry fare to their rural areas (Northern Province) at a time when their unskilled wages were 12s. a month (Richards 1963: 45); and in the late 1940s the lorry fare for an Ngoni was 20s. from Fort Jameson (Eastern Province) to Lusaka (Barnes 1959: 245) when the median wage in 1947 was 44s. a month. As the Pim Commission put it in 1938, 'the costs at present are prohibitive for a family . . . Men travelling alone have difficulty in doing the long journey of 400 or 500 miles on foot, and for families it is practically impossible' (1938 Colonial 145: 48). Rises in the cost of transport were checked in the 1940s (Cost of Living 1950: 267), but it is likely that only the wives of the better paid workers could afford to use transport facilities. Probably of greater importance to women than transport before the 1960s were the labour routes established by the Government, which were described in Chapter IV. The general result of this early transport difficulty was that in the main women from tribes adjacent to the line of rail were to be found in the towns in greater numbers than women from elsewhere.

In the 1960s it became increasingly normal for all women to complete part of a long journey by bus or lorry. Based on a twenty-one-year concession dating from 1955, the Central African Road Services Ltd. now operates transport over all the main routes. The quality, schedules and fares of these services are subject to review by Government. C.A.R.S. provides the necessary complement to the single line of rail and has made the whole of Zambia the migration hinterland of the lone public railway – the Zambezi sawmills line from Livingstone towards Barotseland is privately owned though it takes some passengers. Underpinning this, at public expense, the Zambezi River Transport Services provide a road and river service between Livingstone (Victoria Falls, Southern Province) and Mongu (Barotseland). These services were developed as part of the development planning implemented from 1948 onwards. Road improvements must also be noted: for instance, £5,000,000 was spent to improve and lengthen roadways between 1954 and 1960. All this provided speedier journeys, reduced wear and tear on transport and thereby lowered costs and fares, and made possible the cheaper migration of women to towns.

Town Relatives and Housing

Relatives established in towns induce women to leave the villages and join them (Caldwell 1968: 272-4; Taylor and Lehmann 1961: 71). Help and encouragement is given by urban relatives and migrants usually join them or a person from the same village until such time as they can fend for themselves. In a study of Lusaka in 1957 it was found that 41 per cent of the primary family-type households contained 'additional persons'. Broadly speaking, these were new arrivals to the town. Less than one per cent of these households contained unrelated males, all households being related to 'additional' females. Two times as many of the 'additional persons' were related to the husband as to the wife, and females tended to find accommodation with a male relative, 'but to a lesser extent than did males . . .' 'The evidence points to the conclusion that settled urban families act largely as temporary hosts to relatives seeking either to settle in the urban area or merely to visit the town for some special reason or other' (Bettison 1959: xiv-xv). The facilities provided by these staging-post urban family households created ties with the villages of origin which, once established, gave momentum to the peasant exodus.

Temporary accommodation is a scarce facility in Zambian towns where housing has been tightly controlled and where local authorities made difficulties for persons without approved residences, until the very early 1960s. A reason why male relatives are joined by single women must be that they make a legal claim for housing if they are employed but no provision is made for accommodating women not in employment. Even when housing was available its standard might be so low as to deter women from coming to a town (Kay 1960: 21; Taylor and Lehmann 1961: 72).

Broken Hill

The greater the distance from town the more absolute became the break between village and town kin. To the extent that villagers were aware of this, the motivation to migrate must have been more intense in distant than in near villages. Quite apart from knowledge of the hardships of migration and the restraint on movement because of the shortage of cash, women about to migrate from distant villages must have been much more aware of being about to take an irreversible step than women in villages near to towns.

This is brought out in the first classic study of urbanisation in Zambia. 'The greater the distance the fewer the people who migrate' is a general fact brought out in Table 4. 'Distant' here means in excess of 200 miles from Broken Hill on the line of rail. Migration to Broken Hill brought more married men than single men and youths. There were fewer married men from distant tribes than from nearby ones. Proportionately fewer men from distant tribes left their wives in the villages. It may be that before beginning their journeys they were more determined than nearby men to make a firm break with their kin. The other reason is that to bring their wives to Broken Hill minimised strain. No doubt the nearby men could visit wives in the nearby villages more regularly so they were not impelled by this consideration to the same degree. But there is the additional possibility that men from afar visualised their migration more as a break with village organisation than did nearby men, and if the wife was valued it would be easier to make this break if she also lived in Broken Hill.

Evidence on this point is provided from data on the transfer of wealth in the same study. Miners from villages near to Broken Hill transferred 20.3 per cent of their income to their villages, but miners from afar managed to transfer only 13.7 per cent of their income; married men whose wives were with them transferred the least, and married men whose wives lived in the villages transferred about one-third of their income to them. These figures refer to the oldest industrial town in Zambia which may be atypical yet indicative of a trend.

DEPRIVATION

Deprivation is commonly described as an emotional state induced by the way a woman interprets her situation, and the lessening of deprivation is often explained as the motive for many kinds of action. For our purpose of explaining migration as an outcome of deprivation it is necessary to distinguish between two kinds of deprivation. One is known as relative or social deprivation and involves *ego* comparing herself with *alter* and deciding either to imitate or avoid imitation of *alter* in some respect. Approval from others is sought by this kind of behaviour. Hence European goods such as bicycles, clothes and food are now highly valued by Africans as being the means by which a 'civilised life' may be lived and the esteem of peers acquired.

Material deprivation is of no less importance (Jones 1962: 40) because 'in the beginning there is the body' (Wrong 1961: 191) which requires access to the utility of material goods. Near Kasama, Richards 'watched from a distance a woman running down a hillside and up the slope opposite to her village, wailing in short staccato cries as she ran. It was like the lamentation at a funeral ceremony, and people stood aside to watch her as she passed. They explained as an apology for such an unusual display of emotion: "That is a single woman . . . She is alone. The pigs came to her garden last week, and then the other night, and now today. And so her heart has become heavy. She has no more food . . ." it gives some idea of the depth of despair to which widows or deserted women are sometimes brought at the present time for want of male help in economic tasks' (1939: 298). The line of causation in this episode seems to be economic deprivation, leading to physical deprivation, leading to socio-cultural deprivation, leading to behavioural disorder (Roach 1967: 309).

Relative and material deprivation was the lot of most rural women because of a shortage either of cash or of male labour for certain essential tasks in husbandry. To the materially deprived, migration is an alternative to begging, behavioural disorders and the lack of material possessions which will gain the pity of more fortunate neighbours. Relative deprivation is bound up with the proximity of urbanisation. Seemingly in support of the law that females are more migratory than males, it has been postulated that the pace and length of urbanisation experiences are important variables which affect this. Hence it would be suggested that because Latin America is more urbanised, fewer men migrate than in Africa and Asia (Sjoberg 1966: 242-3). This assumes that traditional men are more exposed than their women to urbanisation and comply with its opportunities without irrevocable commitment to its way of life. By contrast their womenfolk, given the opportunity, will make an irrevocable commitment to urban life. The urbanisation experience in Zambia first made an impact on rural men, and much later on their women, who were more firmly insulated and embedded in the peasant systems. The more closely peasant women witness the attractions of capitalism and urbanisation, the more they will be motivated by relative rather than material deprivation. A comparative view sees this as the probable circumstance of women in the Luapula, Southern and Central Provinces which possessed the most viable peasant economies in Zambia and people with a disposition to migrate in search of capital (Cunnison 1959: 29; Colson 1960: 51-2) or adventure (Colson 1958: 67), rather than subsistence. To the women in these provinces the needs of the body were less pressing than they were to the women in the Bembaland of the Northern Province.

CONCLUSIONS

A monocausal explanation of the migration of women was considered at the beginning of this chapter and as it did not fit the facts it was abandoned. It was decided that there was no direct economic pull exerted on women to bring them to the urban system and that in consequence much of their movement had to be accounted for by the nature of the pushes they received, although their propensity *vis-à-vis* men to outmigrate conforms to the erroneous explanation of Bogue which ascribes this to urban pulls.

Next the influence of peasant systems on the outmigration of their women was considered. It was found that until 1953 the inability to register marriages in the urban system impeded the outmigration of women, as did the activities of peasant authorities which discouraged women from leaving their jurisdiction. The bolstering of peasant economies with the aid of remittances from absentee men once helped to keep peasant life attractive to women. Divorce played a minor part in the migration of women, but the trend to allow husbands to remove their wives from their kin soon after marriage seems to make a more positive contribution to the migration of women. In those peasant systems which expect individuals to make their own way in the world it is likely that women were free to migrate. Through the nationalist offensive women were involved in the wider world and repudiated restraints by peasant authorities on their freedom of movement.

Nearness to the urban system not only helped a woman to minimise the expense of moving but in addition enabled her to escape the restrictions of peasant authorities. But the growth of real earnings by men in the 1950s, coincidentally with the improvement and cheapening of the real costs of transport, removed this handicap. But distance might be an index of communication isolation and in the case of the Western Hinterland might have helped keep the women penned in the villages. Perhaps of equal importance is the related probability that though these women were often hungry they did not aspire to enjoy the easy life and comforts of women in the urban system.

The migration of women requires three sets of explanations. The first is the determination of why the volume of female outmigration appreciably varied between some Peasant Provinces. If one takes an objective and measurable factor such as the value of output as a clue to the push behind female outmigration, it is discovered that the Western Hinterland is the poorest zone and yet retains more women than other zones. This means either that poverty involves a disinclination to migrate or that the motivation of relative deprivation is hardly known in the Western Hinterland, whereby a powerful incentive to potential migrants is lacking. Instead of an objective variable, the woman's interpretation of her situation has been selected as a more accurate guide to her motivations.

The second task of explanation is to account for the relative parity between the men and women who leave the Central, Southern and Luapula Provinces. Two factors not equally applicable to the other provinces stand out: the transportation proximity of these provinces to an urban system and the contractual nature of relationships in their peasant systems.

The third task is to explain why women migrate and the brief answer is that they do so to join their men. It is possible that in those systems where it was known that men would be absent for some considerable time, or unlikely to return, a positive incentive for women to follow them existed. When such absentees valued their wives they were more likely to summon them to the urban system when quarters and work had been found. But when there was real hope that their men would return while in their prime, women showed greater reluctance to migrate.

CHAPTER VI
LABOUR CAMPS

TYPES OF URBAN SYSTEMS: IN SEQUENCE

In this and the next chapter several of the resources involved in urbanisation in Zambia will be examined. For conceptual purposes this urbanisation, the transformation of urban social systems, will be split into two phases or systems to be known as Labour Camps and Towns for Africans. The latter will be discussed in the following chapter with notes about their replacement by contemporary African Towns.

Developmentally, 1945 to 1950 was the watershed during which Labour Camps began to give place to Towns for Africans. The devaluation of the pound sterling in 1949 and the start of the Korean War seemed to guarantee an economic future for the copper industry which hitherto had always been in some doubt. With this assurance the economic incentive to make Towns for Africans was provided. It was in these years that preparations were made for the establishment of a Department of Local Government and African Housing, intent on demolishing Labour Camps and erecting Towns for Africans. Equally important, it was decided in these years that the way to prime the pump for the development of the whole of Zambia was first to generate increased wealth in the industrial centres and then redistribute it to the peasant systems with the logic that for a time little aid would be supplied to peasants.

Industrial centres — which accommodated the Labour Camps — was a term often employed until the 1950s to denote the areas of industry and dense settlement adjacent to the line of rail, which stretched north from Cape Town in South Africa to Elizabethville in the Katanga Province of the Congo. Free movement of Europeans occurred throughout this line. In the European imagination this and its settlement were areas where European interests must predominate. Accordingly, Africans in the industrial centres were alien visitors and Europeans indigenous hosts. Thus the industrial centres were composed of modern communications, European Towns, and European-dominated Labour Camps in which African labourers lived. The very vocabulary then in use — industrial centres and Labour Camps — denied the legitimacy of the urbanisation of Africans and protested that this was a social system devised to serve the needs of international capitalism and the Europeans who controlled it.

The Labour Camps simply grew until they became large or menacing enough to command White attention. Then a location manager was appointed to safeguard the interests of the Natives in the interests of the Whites. All workers, male and female, domestic and others, who had not been definitely requisitioned in writing to live on the premises of their employers, were domiciled in these camps (Davis 1967: 78). In respect of mining Labour Camps, where conditions were better than elsewhere, each 'is a township in itself, and the responsibility for housing, drainage, sanitation, health, discipline and general welfare of the inhabitants, is vested in the compound manager and his organisation. The natives employed by the Company; their wives and children; all look to the compound manager for almost everything they want done to help them during the time they are dependent on the mine for their livelihood' (Spearpoint 1937: 18).

The Village Management Proclamation of 1913 transferred direct control of these camps from officers of the territorial Government to European Village Management Boards. Until 1963 'unofficial' Europeans continued to control the local authority successors to those Boards, and this dictated a bundle of issues in national life. But not until Towns for Africans took shape did the opposition of political class interests reflected by these issues crystallise (Heisler 1970); without Towns for Africans the challenge to the European stake in national life would have been weaker and for long delayed. The legacies of the Labour Camps were finally scrubbed out and the victory of urban Africans over urban Europeans proclaimed by the termination of Towns for Africans and their replacement by African Towns in 1963. The legal enfranchisement of urban Africans in the government of their towns in that year marked the transition. This was a most important metamorphosis in urbanisation in that it signified not only the durability of the urban areas, so long in doubt, but the fact that Africans who worked in the towns were at last permitted to end their lives in these African Towns whereas in Labour Camps and Towns for Africans they had been obliged to return to their villages to die.

In Table 10 the resources of urban social systems (cf. Roth and Wittich 1968: 1212ff; Mitchell 1966: 48-50) are described. It will be seen that the mixture of resources differed for each kind of social system with which this enquiry is concerned. Thus the particular mixture of resources defined the succession of Labour Camps by Towns for Africans. Urbanism is a way of life which is derived from the resources of urbanisation. Urbanisation imposes limits on many kinds of social interaction which occur within urbanism and as the constitutive resources of urbanisation alter so does the way of life of the people involved. As was explained in Chapter I, for this same reason the types of African towndwellers changed and finally, corresponding to Industrial Man, an Urban Man who was totally committed to African Towns appeared.

A few comments on the resources of urbanisation listed in Table 10 will make them more intelligible. Mobility refers to the growth of urban population from inmigration, in contrast to natural increase: as time passed the capacity of urban areas to sustain their own level of population by means of their own reproduction increased. Labour Camps could not sustain their populations from their own resources; Towns for Africans were increasingly peopled by town-born persons. The average length of service with mining companies is a rough measure of mobility; even if a man did not return to his village immediately on leaving a job, the probability that he would if he were a blue-collar worker was considerable. During the lifetime of the Labour Camps the length of service increased from under six months in the 1920s to eighteen months or so in the 1930s. In 1958, when Towns for Africans were under construction, the average length of service was double that of the 1930s.

The number of Africans who lived in the urban system showed a considerable increase. The main Labour Camps accommodated between 22,000 and 25,000 Africans in 1931, but by the mid 1940s their number had grown fourfold. The population then doubled in five years, and if 1950 is taken to inaugurate the history of the Towns for Africans, it may be recorded that the main towns started with a population of 243,000, which had reached 570,000 by 1963. The 1969 Census of Population recorded some 1,100,000 Africans living in districts which are mainly urban. During colonial times the urban local authorities wielded more and more power; they checked the sprawl of population and the problems of environmental control by means of town planning and expressions of hostility to those who preferred to live outside their boundaries and yet work in the official urban areas. After Independence and the start of African Towns in 1964 the sprawl began once more.

Heterogeneity refers to the cultural and social origins of the urban population: well over 100 peasant systems were represented on the Copperbelt. The shortage of women in the urban areas created a serious demographic disproportion. When estimates of the urban population were prepared in 1944 there were about 23 women for every 50 men in the Labour Camps; but by 1963 there were 26 women for every 30 men in the Towns for Africans.

The capitalist economy in Zambia was overwhelmingly dependent on mineral production, and only slowly did secondary manufacturing and other economic activities grow. For example, in 1931 9 per cent of the Africans in the camps were engaged in manufacturing and commerce but thirty years later this had increased to only 16 per cent.

Urban local government suited to the needs of Africans was not evolved until the permanence of the Labour Camps was assured. For this reason the inhabitants of the camps were not treated as townsmen but as rural visitors. Though beyond direct tribal controls these visitors to the camps did not think and behave as townsmen. In terms of social evolution, the Europeans thought these visitors were intermediate between tribesmen and townsmen. Not surprisingly the inhabitants of these camps were called 'detribalised' and the camps were sometimes known as 'detribalised areas'. What need was there to construct another classification for the inhabitants of these camps if their sojourn was temporary? A soldier on leave away from his unit still remains a soldier, and this way of thinking parallels European orientations towards Africans in Labour Camps. Apart from a military code a soldier on leave is subject to a civil law; apart from customary law a tribesman at work on the mines was subject to mine and camp regulations.

It may be that this has caused some confusion among anthropologists who insist that 'detribalisation' is not an apposite description of the condition of these people. Anthropologists contend that an inmigrant acquires a positive identity as a townsman the moment he steps outside his 'tribe' and over the urban threshold where a completely new array of pressures then constrain him to stop acting as a 'tribesman' and behave as a townsman (Gluckman 1961: 69; Mitchell 1966: 48, 1969: 471-2). There is an element of exaggeration in this, more so with respect to the analysis of Labour Camps than the later Towns for Africans. Mobility in Labour Camps was so rapid that the time for newcomers to learn and identify with camp ways was often too brief to make much impact on their behaviour before they returned to their 'tribes'. There was less mobility in

Towns for Africans and so the anthropological model of situational response and behaviour is more apt for the 1950s.

But there need be no contradiction between the anthropological viewpoint and the position taken here: the anthropologists are concerned about socio-logical concepts which serve purposes different from the meaning of 'detribal-isation' in the social consciousness of élites in Zambia with which this discussion is concerned. What was so important for the political and administrative limitations on urbanisation in Zambia was that 'detribalisation' encouraged European élites to think of wage earners as tribesmen and not townsmen, as visitors and not as residents in the Labour Camps, and as persons with few rights to urban amenities because they had prior claim to those in the peasant systems. It was as if Africans in camps were foreigners living in a European society. All this was evoked in the public mind by the thought of 'detribalisation'. An instance of the interaction of urbanisation and urbanism may be culled from this: when sufficient people were accustomed to an urban way of life they pressed for better amenities, which are part of urbanisation, and urban local government for Africans was among these. African urban government followed when it was conceded that Africans were at last townsmen.

Official opinion adopted a 'wait and see' attitude towards the Labour Camps: if their migrant populations were to continue to swell and show reluctance to return to their villages every year or so, then the status of these camps and provision for them would merit revision. After the traumatic unemployment experience of the 1930s no one doubted that another catastrophe would close down mines and empty settlements once more, and for how long? No, it was thought better not to invest public resources where the yield did not look certain. Hence 'for years the Anglican Mission refused to accept the Mines as an area of evangelistic responsibility, on the grounds that a man's residence in the Copperbelt was so temporary that it was impossible to guarantee sufficient continuity of instruction' (Taylor and Lehmann 1961: 36). Anglicans preferred baptisms to be performed at rural missions rather than on the Copperbelt in 1936; and in 1940, while this had changed and missionaries on the Copperbelt were sure of the desirability of a 'stabilised urban community', others 'as for instance the Bishop of Northern Rhodesia and certain Government officials, foresaw possible difficulties inherent in such a policy' (Taylor and Lehmann 1961: 36-37).

The question whether stabilisation of the population of the camps should be discouraged, and what services should be provided for a stabilised population, were considered by the Native Industrial Labour Advisory Board established after the 1935 disturbances. Representing industry and missions, as well as Government, the Board advised in November 1935 that though there was a tendency towards stabilisation, 'no special steps are necessary or desirable to encourage or discourage this tendency at present.' But then the mines had not long been back in production.

When questioned by the Colonial Secretary as to what was to be done about the growing stabilisation of Africans in the camps, Government was more apprehensive and the Governor replied in October 1941 that he was anxious that stabilisation 'should not be accelerated with the resultant loss to tribal areas' (25.1.1944 SEC/LAB/71). Public revenue was insufficient to provide for a horde of unemployed should another depression hit the economy, with the difference that the men in the camps had lost contact with the villages which would not be able to reabsorb them as in the early 1930s. Labour was the only economic asset of the peasant systems which depended on the wealth from the camps in the form of remittances and money brought back by returning migrants. To be indifferent to the growing stabilisation of the camps entailed abandoning the peasant systems to decay. And what was more desirable than rural life? The Secretary for Native Affairs (his was the third most important post in Government) reflected the concern of most of his colleagues when he complained that 'in the past too much attention has been given to the development of the urban areas to the neglect of the rural districts' (December 1942 SEC/NAT/351).

In the rest of this chapter some of the factors involved in the continuity of Labour Camps are reviewed. If the peasant population could not be stabilised and the flood to the towns were to continue, then camp conditions must be improved. Such aspects of poverty as arose from inadequate accommodation would in this circumstance become a priority for improvement. But there was little chance that the camps would be converted into towns if they remained the accommodation of bachelors. However, the mining companies began to lean towards the view that if their workmen lived with their wives in the camps, productivity would be raised. To encourage the residence of women and children in the camps would enable them to generate their own population in the future and this would give them a durability which they would otherwise lack. As the demographic imbalance began to be redressed, young people without experience of peasant ways and Native Authorities would require social control agencies specifically built for their urban requirements.

PEASANT STABILISATION

The future relationship of the White and Black races in Zambia was the fundamental issue in official thought which affected not only the stabilisation of the peasant population but whether the Labour Camps would one day be replaced by Towns for Africans. As the peasant areas were occupied by the Black race, the public resources devoted to them were determined by the roles assigned to them in Zambian life. Peasant stabilisation was also influenced by the viability of the peasant systems as places where Africans might choose to live in preference to Labour Camps. Thus the stabilisation of the peasant population, arresting the drift to the Labour Camps, was a political as much as a socio-economic issue. Whether Labour Camps became towns very much depended on prior decisions about the peasant areas — whether they should develop into autonomous and self-sufficient racial reserves or be permitted to interact freely with the industrial centres.

The Hilton-Young report on the political state of Eastern and Central Africa in 1929 declared it was desirable that the White and Black races should be geographically separated: 'In the complicated racial conditions which prevail in Eastern and Central Africa local government institutions, provided that native and settled areas are arranged in homogeneous blocks of adequate extent, offer a field in which each race can control and direct its own more immediate affairs and learn to exercise responsibility unhampered by the complicating presence of the other. In this way they can allow free room for the expression of the individuality of communities entirely diverse in their traditions, habits, experiences and requirements' (1929 Report: 180). With the introduction of a system of Indirect Rule for rural Africans in the same year, the local Government had the option of delegating to the new Native Authorities specific duties or granting them originating and discretionary power of government. The latter would involve what was believed to be genuine decentralisation of the power of the Central Government and was the target towards which Indirect Rule was to be developed (15.6.1936 SEC/FIN/23; 2.3.1939 SEC/NAT/277; 1.9.1941 SEC/NAT/343). As the Secretary for Native Affairs put it, 'the fundamental principle must be to encourage the native to develop his own areas and his own form of government by gradually absorbing ideas of civilised government as he can understand them' (February 1940 SEC/NAT/92).

When measures to plan the future of Zambia after the Second World War were taken this belief in parallel development momentarily was assigned an important place by officials who had not caught up with the implications of the shift in policy from the paramountcy of African interests in 1930 to the partnership of Europeans and Africans, often living as neighbours, announced in 1932 and reasserted during the 1940s at Westminster and in the Legislative Council. The plan was first broadly sketched by the Chief Secretary who wrote in 1943 of 'The problem of educating and developing Africans in such a way that they can form a useful complement to a community which is non-African and can at the same time satisfy their own legitimate ambitions' (Stooke 1943: 6). Two years later in the blueprint for the post-war plan the chief planner explained that there 'is no need for any conflict between white and black if a policy of *complementary development* is followed' (Clay 1945: 5). Whereas the chief planner thought of functional complementary development the old guard civil servants and Europeans thought of geographical complementarity. Ingrained in these habits of thought, located almost in the recesses of the official mind, was the presumption that the peasant areas were truly African and the industrial centres European – in its own area each race would be politically dominant. To extend peasant institutions of local government to the industrial centres would trespass on European territory; to allow Africans to become stabilised in the Labour Camps in these centres would doom them to European domination; to stabilise the Africans in the peasant systems would ensure their freedom. On the assumption that the races could not live in the same geographical zone without either European domination or conflict it was tacitly agreed that Towns for Africans were impossible and that the repercussions of trying to build them were best avoided by not making the effort. Racial conflict would be avoided by peasant stabilisation and the accommodation of wage labourers in camps instead of towns.

But if the stabilisation of peasants was to be achieved, social services for Africans, among which the local Government classed agriculture, must create attractive conditions for them to live in. As long as there was hope that this might be achieved, to invest resources in the industrial centres and convert their living quarters from camps into towns would detract from the attractions of peasant life and make imminent open disagreement between the races whose economic interests would conflict in the industrial centres. As long as the local Government felt free to devote its resources to Africans, hope for self-sufficient peasants was sustained. But when resources were concentrated in the industrial centres urban conflict and peasant poverty were joined by the same cause.

Until the mid 1940s at least it was believed that the paths to peasant reform were known and accessible. Although 'in 1929 a development programme of some magnitude was inaugurated' (1932 Report: 4), which necessitated the creation of a Public Debt, the lean years of the recession which followed curtailed any effective advance. Yet it was realised that in itself the recession was not responsible for the growing plight of the villages, denuded of their young men and hemmed in by infertile soil and erosion. The Chief Secretary, C. C. F. Dundas, and one who was not an official, Sir Stewart Gore-Browne, thought of a Native Development Board as a panacea and suggested to the Legislative Council in December 1935 that this would supply the organisational solution to the lack of stability in the peasant population. Through such a Board extraordinary expenditure on development could be introduced and the initiative for this could be removed from the Central Government to the Native Authorities. But the timing was not quite right and it needed an increase in public revenues and the criticism of the Pim Report on the neglected state of the country in 1938 before it was decided to establish a Native Development Board to expand African services as fast as funds permitted (1938 PCs: 3). Though a Board was established in 1938, it only handled small projects which scarcely lowered the scale of rural population destabilisation.

Simultaneously, the greater effort was directed through newly created or expanded departments of Government, which in 1939 presented plans for the following quinquennium, contrary to Gore-Browne's advice over the previous four years that the fault of Government planning had been the lack of integration and co-ordination inherent in departmental activity not centrally controlled. These five-year plans, with realistically modest targets, were mostly achieved within the planned period. This raised confidence in the efficacy of planning and encouraged the belief that all that was necessary would be done immediately after the interlude of the Second World War.

To this end in 1942 a draft plan for further development was agreed. Two features of this were of importance to the future of the Labour Camps. Planning was now to be on an areal instead of a departmental functional basis and was to be directly concerned with the stabilisation of peasant populations by concentrating them around provincial community centres where easy access to public services was possible. Perhaps of most importance, planned development in Zambia was taken to mean the provision of extraordinary aid to Africans in their rural setting and ignoring the conditions of the Labour Camps. For this purpose 'full use should be made of these demobilised soldiers in the prosecution of a campaign of Native Development throughout the Reserves' (Stooke 1943: 1). A subcommittee of the Native Development Board became a major body and prepared blueprints. These were revised by the Joint Development Adviser in the *Memorandum on Post War Development Planning in Northern Rhodesia* which was published in 1945, entirely in sympathy with the 1942 scheme. This plan sought to secure maximum co-ordination by overriding the authority of specialist departments, by focusing on areas rather than specialist services, and devoted most of the available funds to raising the welfare of peasants. By defining these targets the Labour Camps were intended to survive as such. But this only lasted until the early post-war days when new priorities were set.

POVERTY OF THE DETRIBALISED

Poverty in the Labour Camps became public knowledge during the Second World War. Reports to the Government by Saffery (1943) and Eccles (1944 Native Locations) defined the state of welfare among urban Africans as desperate, demanding a political solution, and therefore a social problem. According to these reports, the first step towards a remedy was the adoption of balanced stabilisation as the policy guideline for reform. It was reasoned that once it was accepted that camps were at last permanent features on the social landscape, investment in their welfare would be the only way whereby the official conscience — which was appalled by what it witnessed in them and secretly hopeful that they would vanish and let the bush take over again — would be appeased.

What the Labour Adviser called a 'discreditable situation' in housing in 1938 became worse as the population of the Labour Camps increased by 10 per cent between 1940 and 1943 at a time when scarcely any new permanent housing became available. A conservative estimate is that 94,000 people experienced this pressure on physical facilities in 1944. These people were composed of the following categories: children 27 per cent; women 23 per cent; self-employed men 2 per cent; male wage earners 40 per cent; unemployed men 8 per cent, making a total of all men of 50 per cent. On average in the urban local authority areas 8.1 persons squeezed into each housing unit and 7.3 persons into each room — from which it may be inferred that only 10.3 per cent of the housing units were made up of more than a single room.

To make matters worse, two-thirds of the houses were distinctly sub-standard in construction: half were made of sun-dried brick which could not withstand a climate such as this with much more than the 11 inches of rain a year, which was the maximum this brick could withstand. As a result plaster would not remain attached to walls, rain and ticks entered through the many crevices, and pieces of wall fell away. The other half were the first 'houses' to be built along the line of rail and were made of grass and mud, which gave even less protection than sun-dried brick. No piped water to individual houses was available; except at Fort Jameson, latrines were communal and only at Kitwe was there one lavatory seat for as few as twelve persons. 'Their inadequacy is only too obviously supplemented by the luxuriant crops which grow to within a few feet of the compound' (Orde Browne 1938: 62). Conditions were scarcely better in the accommodation provided for Africans by the Mining Companies.

To withstand this exposure to the elements Africans needed to be well fed, but those in this fortunate condition did not live in either the Mining Company areas or the urban local authority locations. Scurvy, pellagra and local diseases of a nutritional origin such as *chuifa* and *onyalai* were rife, and tuberculosis arising from the bad housing was becoming noticeable. Saffery estimated that an average family required £6 11s 7d a month to have a reasonable standard of living, exclusive of luxuries, in order to keep the family functioning and able to attend school, work and so on. But the income of no occupational group reached this first poverty datum line. The self-employed were comparatively well-off with £4 a month; men who worked in secondary industries earned £2 5s 10d a month; those in domestic service did better at £3 12s 0d a month. Even the miners, who were the best paid of all Africans, received no more than £4 14s 7d.

Their low wages had risen little since they had been fixed during the Recruited Labour System when it seemed obvious to an employer that a wage earner was a single man, unencumbered by a family the cost of whose transportation and feeding would have deterred the very keenest of recruiting agents. Before employers could be persuaded to pay wages appropriate for family men their stabilisation with their families in the Labour Camps was necessary, and in 1944, when the Eccles Commission on urban affairs reported, this still awaited a decision by Government. As for malnutrition, its primary source was the shortfall between the poverty datum line and the wages cited.

But a cultural cause of malnutrition, which can still be observed among middle class Africans in Zambia in the 1970s, arose from the self-imposed restriction on expenditure for food. Until recent years the incomes of most employees were composed of a rent subsidy, wages and rations. At first rations were in kind and Africans believed that they alone were to be the source of their food, leaving their wages to be used for other purposes. When rations were commuted into cash − say, 5 to 10 shillings a week − Africans usually continued to retain their former levels of food consumption and restricted their purchase of food to this commuted sum, even though their families had moved from the villages to the camps to share these rations. While wages rose in recognition of family needs, rations hardly increased, as the trend was towards a composite income; thus the paradox developed of the well-dressed African suffering from malnutrition.

However, as Saffery warned, malnutrition was not the only problem that arose from low wages. The 'danger of serious upheaval' was growing as the Africans observed their poverty and the affluence of their European co-workers, and formed the belief that it was they themselves who did the work while the Europeans contributed little to economic activity.

Provoked by the 1941 Forster Report, and the indignation of the House of Commons, about the strike and violence in July 1940 on the Copperbelt, a serious effort to improve recreational provision began, and more was being planned in 1944 by the newly-appointed social welfare organiser to the Government. But as the Africans who appeared before the Eccles Commission explained, 'it is illogical to provide expensive recreational halls . . . cinemas and the like, for people who are housed in hovels.' In spite of recreational facilities, 'the locations . . . present us with a miserable picture indeed. The usual lay-out is of rows of houses in straight lines, very often too close together, and in many cases open spaces are inadequate or absent. Natural features have seldom been used to advantage and in some cases all indigenous trees have been cut down . . . The African living in these locations, therefore, has no encouragement to develop family life and is deprived of the privacy to which he is entitled' (1944 Native Locations: 11). At the root of the concern of the major employers and government officers was this lack of privacy: privacy would permit the African to escape from customary communal life, and enable him to emerge as a modern man capable of assuming increasing responsibility for his own affairs; privacy among Africans would mark the time when it was appropriate for Europeans to remove their paternal mantle over urban African life. The future of urban African society was thus involved in the amelioration of the poverty of the Labour Camps in 1944.

LABOUR EFFICIENCY

In the belief that this would increase efficiency, the Mining Companies edged towards a policy of stabilising their African workforce. On their behalf, Sir Auckland Geddes pointed out in 1933 that the high labour turnover of the Recruited and early Casual Labour Systems prevented individual workers from benefiting from their experiences and increasing their skills. Geddes, drawing on his Rio Tinto experiences, believed that workers must be induced to remain in employment for long periods. But the world recession made the future bleak and little could be done to induce greater labour stability. With a steadily rising world demand for Zambian minerals to satisfy, the mining companies decided around 1938 to expand output not by new investment of capital but by the better use of labour: the future of the copper industry was still not assured, at prevailing wage rates labour was cheaper than capital, and in the event of a recession labour would be dismissed without cost to shareholders whereas idle capital would hurt their pockets. Social security was not then part of the employers' cost of labour which covered housing, food, wages and recreation.

It was believed that labour inefficiency was due to two factors. The separation of workmen in the Labour Camps from their families in the villages tempted miners to remain seasonal, and not long term migrants and continuous employees, and maintain links with their families by regular trips to the villages. Secondly, a high rate of abstention from work was in part due to sickness which could be prevented by improved nourishment and the ministration of housewives.

Every employer was obliged to provide 'good and sufficient rations' in order to comply with the Employment of Natives Regulations. A committee reported to the Native Development Board on nutrition in Zambia and whether rations were indeed 'good and sufficient' (1938 Meetings of NDB), this report had been prepared in liaison with the mining companies. It was found that the employers who were the worst offenders against these regulations were the Afrikaner poor whites who themselves suffered from malnutrition. In general, too much carbohydrate and too little protein appeared in most rations and the Government decided to provide a more balanced diet for its own employees.

Government scales for the diet of mine employees were revised in a similar direction, and from 1937 onwards the mining companies were permitted to undertake experiments in feeding their employees. An early assessment of this scheme showed only limited success because though the mess feeding of bachelors was producing encouraging results, the diet of the control group of married miners was known to be insufficient (23.6.38 SEC/H/4). At the time the addition of weight was the sole criterion of success, and to encourage this bachelors were allowed to eat as much as they liked; at one sitting in a mess a man ate 12 lb of food. In 1939 the rations to the wives and children of married miners were increased, and as a result the married miner shared less of his own ration and improved his own health. In the first and third month of an engagement the risk of illness was higher than in other periods, pneumonia being a serious risk, but in correlation with the progress of the Rhokana mine nutrition experiments the rate of illness and absenteeism declined. By 1942 it was clear that sickness among married miners was appreciably lower than among bachelors. This was attributed to the care taken of married miners by their wives who, it was observed, supplemented the restricted fresh foods available for sale, gave time to their preparation and generally helped their husbands to relax after work. Moreover, in 1937 'we have found that the married native remains in employment for longer periods than the single native' at the Roan Antelope copper mine (Spearpoint 1937: 53); and in 1942 at Nkana mine it was known that the average period of contract of a married man was 23 months compared with the 12 months of single men (Saffery 1943: 83).

In spite of this information Nkana remained opposed to stabilisation in 1943 though Roan Antelope and Mufilira mines were in favour of building up a stabilised labour force. Nkana noted that a decision to stabilise the labour force would weaken their ties with their villages and asked to whom the unemployed would turn if another depression such as that of 1931 should hit the country. This was the precise question which led Government to refrain from supporting Geddes' initiative in 1933 and made the Provincial Administration cautious about committing itself to stabilisation a decade later.

SOCIAL CONTROL IN TOWNS

While the Christian mission report by Merle Davis and his colleagues on *Modern Industry and the African* (1933) had first brought to public notice the social problems of the Labour Camps that clustered beside the line of rail, as well as the incipient stabilisation of the population of these camps, this made little local impact because of the recession extant at the time of publication. The trudge of thousands of unemployed labourers back to their villages emptied the camps and seemed to dispel their problems. But there was rioting on the Copperbelt in 1935, following the ill-timed disclosure of an impending tax increase, and more rioting in 1940 in association with a disciplined and well organised strike by African miners for higher pay. Both these events were subject to commissions of enquiry, newspaper comment and attention in the British House of Commons. In a manner which could not be achieved by the Pim report on the state of the government and the Orde Browne report on labour, which were published in 1938 and attracted mostly official attention, the riots of 1935 and 1940 publicised the presence of what the local Government was most reluctant to treat as a persistent urban problem.

An analogy between Government and the proverbial ostrich which buries its head in the sand in the hope that what is unwelcome will go away appropriately describes official reaction to the revelation of three unwelcome categories of persons resident in the Labour Camps. In addition to honestly employed men there were many unemployed who were regarded as having no business in these camps. After all, these were Labour Camps and not towns; therefore no one without work had a claim to their facilities and so it was surmised that the persistently unemployed in these camps were vagabonds and thieves. Nor was there space for camp followers in these hives of industry, but the presence of increasing numbers of women and children was revealed. Because, according to the official myth-anthropology of the time, workmen were married to women resident in the villages, and because there was no industrial employment for the women in the camps, they could only live on immoral earnings. As for the young people, it was evident that they were unruly, rarely under what was considered effective parental control, and inclined to steal their food.

An urban authority is perforce compelled to live with and accommodate itself to such categories on the presumption that they are stabilised town-dwellers, but those in control of Labour Camps emphasised the temporary nature of their activities, claimed that unwanted categories of persons remained the responsibility of the peasant systems whence they had come, and sought to expel these categories from their camps. This was the official response to the presence of juveniles, unemployed men and women in the Labour Camps. Until this response changed, a necessary condition for the creation of an urban society with Towns for Africans was not fulfilled. Peasant solutions were sought for the social problems of the industrial centres until a policy of urban stabilisation was adopted.

There were three components within the attitudes which wished to preserve the environs of places of employment as Labour Camps. It must be remembered that not until 1944 was a District Officer assigned full time to the affairs of the industrial centres, hence it is not surprising that rural-minded District Officers influenced public policy. They saw the unemployed as deserters from the villages in their care and worried about the effects of their absence on family and village life. To create institutions to control and care for these categories in the Labour Camps would negate the efforts of the rural based District Officers to administer justice and raise welfare. Bourgeois-minded District Officers and missionaries could not be expected to adopt permissive attitudes to urban prostitutes when part of their mission was to impose a new and better moral tone on morally degenerate and heathen Africans. And it was plain that the temporary civic-industrial structures of Labour Camps, essential for the continuing production of minerals, would be dislocated if further disturbances were not prevented by excluding the trouble makers, along with the women whose presence induced them to remain in the camps.

Deportation

Peasant social control institutions inserted into Labour Camps, the harassment of the unemployed, the repatriation of women and children, and the administrative deportation of men were the devices contemplated to keep the undesirable categories in the camps under the control of peasant agencies. In 1935 the unemployed in the camps were identified as the most immediate social problem in Zambia. Undoubtedly the number of men in Labour Camps had increased much faster than the number of jobs available for them, and this left the unemployed without adequate means of subsistence. But the phenomenon of the inmigrant sponging off relatives and fellow tribesmen with housing and secure jobs until he in turn became settled in a similar manner became important in the later post-stabilisation situation in the Towns for Africans, rather than before the decision to stabilise urban people was taken. Until then the high rate of labour turnover, and the fact that the available accommodation consisted of already cramped bachelor quarters, meant that relatives and friends in employment could offer little help to those unemployed who felt they had some claim on them. As a result there was little help to save the unemployed becoming destitute in the Labour Camps.

The Commission on the 1935 riots considered the presence near the mines of great numbers of unemployed or unemployable Africans, who were not under any effective public control, to be one of the most important predisposing causes of the temper which led to the disturbances (1935 Report: 38). But the situation was seen to be not entirely the fault of the unemployed, according to the Commission: 'To a certain extent, it suits the mines to have unemployed in or near the mines as a labour reserve' (1935 Report: 38).

The Commission believed that many of the unemployed were not physically capable of undertaking arduous labouring work and were parasites who shared the scarce facilities of their employed relatives, who were thus led to complain of the shortage of rations and the cost of living. Indeed the unemployed were parasites of the order of thieves and gamblers (1935 Report: 37-38). It was believed that, but for them, existing conditions would have been more tolerable and the employed would have felt less need to complain about the proposed increase in taxation. The Commission undoubtedly exaggerated the discontent of the employed arising from the need to support the unemployed. The Bemba were the largest grouping on the Copperbelt and recognised limits to the tribal rules of the division of food. In Bemba villages the tribal rules of division of property did not apply to food bought with money and those who obtained food in this manner were entitled to consume the whole of their purchase (Richards 1961): 152-3). As this custom was growing on the fringes of peasant systems it was much more likely to be prevalent in the urban system. The Commission disregarded the absolute poverty of the many unemployed. The District Commissioner of Ndola reckoned that half the Africans who entered his camp in search of work were unsuccessful and roamed the camp (1936 Chairman NILAB). The Governor fully shared the apprehension of the Commission on this matter (1935 Report: 3).

The Native Industrial Labour Advisory Board, which was immediately established to examine some of the suggestions of the 1935 inquiry into the disturbances, considered the matter of deportation at its first meeting. As deportation on the order of a District Officer, without an appeal to the High Court, was repugnant, and the use of judicial enquiry was seen as too slow and unwieldy to deal with an urgent problem the Board did not recommend blanket power for the Provincial Administration. It confined itself to recommending that the following should be deported: those unemployed through physical ill-health, persons living on their wits, agitators, and persons living on immoral earnings (1936 Chairman NILAB: 11-12). The Chief Secretary further argued that criminals should not be repatriated to their peasant areas of origin, thus 'passing the buck', because their behaviour was not a product of peasant systems; instead, criminal behaviour in the camps should be prevented by removing potential criminals, i.e. those unemployed for a long time, before they committed offences. This fascinating explanation of delinquency and its cure 'amounts also to racial discrimination, but I imagine it would not be rejected by the Secretary of State on that score' (1935 Conference of PCs Appx G).

Now that the potential criminal had been identified the Governor ordered an amendment to the Penal Code enabling administrative deportation to take place with the possibility of appeal to the Provincial Commissioner and then the Governor (1935 Conference of PCs: 19). But it was decided not to proceed with this until the proposed Commission on Native Labour reported. In the meantime the provisions of section 18 of Ordinance 41 of 1933 were employed. As the *Vagrancy Ordinance* of 1929, which stipulated that a man must return to his village or country if he could not find work within a prescribed time, did not apparently discriminate against Africans it also seemed useful (1936 Conference of PCs: 34).

While the report on *Labour Conditions in Northern Rhodesia* in 1938 found some of the unemployed undesirable it avoided comment on administrative deportation and was of the opinion that 'there is no ostensible reason why the urbanised community should inevitably become a nuisance' (Orde Browne 1938: 60). However the increased demand for labour around this time lowered the volume of unemployment.

The problem was not properly considered again until 1945 when once again a distinction was drawn between the parasitic population and the stabilised, employed industrial population. The notable difference on this occasion however was that the gainfully self-employed traders, charcoal-burners and the like, were lumped with thieves and prostitutes among the undesirable. It was observed that the mining companies favoured a nearby pool of unemployed and, though they initiated prosecutions of Africans who were without cause within the areas under their own control, they did not actively discourage the presence of unemployed adjacent to these areas (23.7.1945 SEC/LAB/27/62). As a result the Government came out strongly in favour of stricter control and administrative deportation (5.9.1945 SEC/LAB/27/79).

But despite considerable discussion little guidance was given to District Officers as to how to behave towards the unemployed. Little indeed is known about their practice, and the information that the District Commissioner in Luanshya in 1955 sifted the African population to force those without legitimate employment to return to the rural areas (Munger 1955: 361) raises the suspicion that this was the exercise of discretionary pressure rather than legal authority and may have been widespread. But in 1958 it was recorded 'that there is no great number of genuine loafers in towns, but recently an unemployment problem has arisen, and many Africans would support some sort of control of influx into the towns' (1958 Urban Problems: 224). The expanding demand for labour in the money economies of Southern Africa, and the gradual implementation of the policy of stabilising urban populations, effectively checked pressures to introduce administrative deportation.

Women

Following the enquiry into the 1935 rioting the regulation of the movement of women was reviewed. It was recalled that in 1931 it had been laid down that Native Authorities were not empowered to prevent the movement of women to the labour camps. In view of this could they be repatriated from these camps back to their villages of origin? Only under the authority of the penal code would this be countenanced and so a bill was drafted for the *Repatriation of*

Natives from Urban Areas, but it was deferred for implementation until the Commission on Native Labour reported (1936 PCs Conference: 34). As this report in 1938 anticipated a stabilised African population in the camps it neither recommended the repatriation of women nor, for that matter, men. This was inconvenient to the local Government and so this part of the report was ignored.

It was decided that Native Authorities should be assisted in enforcing the rules for preventing this departure of women from their areas, unless accompanied by husbands or other authorised persons, and enabled to collect women who were unaccompanied by their husbands or guardians from the labour centres and so return them to their villages (1938 PCs Conference: 8-9). Nothing was then done during the war, but this resolution of 1939 was reaffirmed in 1945 with the additional proviso that Government should provide free transport to assist repatriation (1945 PCs Conference: 7-9). Deep concern about the prostitution of young women and children, in addition to the wish to bolster a flagging rural society, led the *Report of the Financial Relationship Committee* to recommend repatriation in 1949 (1949 Report: 65). In 1952 this became policy when repatriation in pursuance of an Order of a Juvenile Court, Urban Native Court or rural Native Authority was legalised (2.8.1952 Circular Minute N/0082/1). At last the practice of rounding up Barotse women in Livingstone, for instance, and returning them under the escort of a member of their Native Authority back to Barotseland (McCulloch 1956: 19), was legal. In so far as these regulations were enforced in the 1950s in the Towns for Africans they were animated by morality rather than hostility to women living with men near their places of industry.

Children

The Report on *Labour Conditions in Northern Rhodesia* in 1938 drew attention to the presence of delinquent children in Labour Camps (Orde Browne 1938: 67-69) and produced hastier official action than did the presence of women. The Department of African Education undertook a survey of the child population on the Copperbelt and its educational needs (1939 District Circular 3) and it was decided that £1,000 should be spent on repatriating children who were not under parental control nor attending school from the camps (1938 PCs Conference: 23). This policy was reiterated in 1939 (1939 PCs Conference: 10) and the authority for moving the children was found in the *Juvenile Offenders Ordinance*. The Mining Companies opposed the more extreme proposal that all African children be sent to the villages irrespective of the wishes of such of their parents who lived with and cared for them in the camps (Bromwich). By May 1942 a mere 300 children had been returned to their villages (1943 PCs Conference: 5). But then the possibility of introducing compulsory education for children in the camps came to be seen as a more positive attack on juvenile delinquency. The Mining Companies had instituted classes for children and adults in 1930, but the unpublished 1938 survey of the problem by the Department of African Education showed this to be woefully inadequate. However, by 1942 the 1938 five-year development plan was almost completed and the problem was at last thought to be soluble.

It was then realised that there must be delay before another plan was formulated and implemented. So between 1942 and 1944 a further 220 children were repatriated and the rural Native Authorities were once more encouraged to restrict the exodus of children from their areas (September 1944 SEC/LAB/34). By 1947 the effort had almost fizzled out and only £85 was spent on the repatriation of children from the camps (1948 Financial Report: 42). Except in so far as this brought public authorities into contact with the growing and changing needs of Africans, this seemed a waste of effort for 'those orders are ... very freely ignored or evaded, and even after periodical round-ups and repatriation many of those repatriated drift back to the towns' (1949 Report: 65). This was even more true of unaccompanied women.

Peasant Controls in Labour Camps

Until it was decided to stabilise the African population of the Labour Camps in the mid-1940s, it was policy to attempt to control them by the adaptation of peasant institutions to their conditions. As the first mine on the Copperbelt came into production in 1929, it is not surprising that this policy was of relatively recent origin. The issues were clarified by the reports of the riots of 1935 which complained that there was an absence of measures to control the African population of the camps because the Provincial Administration was preoccupied with the affairs of Europeans. These camps were considered to be but temporary affairs and not in need of new and permanent regulative institutions. The model of local administration being evolved for the Europeans was considered inappropriate for labourers. In the industrial centres it was decided that Europeans and Africans should be administered by institutions which resembled those extant in their societies of origin. It was decided in 1936 that rural government must be applied to the camps, and the urban labourers should be governed by District Officers through paid (village) headmen and peasant Native Authorities. It was further decided that 'the establishment of native courts and location elders give District Officers means of control over native affairs (in the camps) that is lacking at present. The courts will provide knowledge and means of control of the domestic affairs of the community; and elders, even though they may be directly under the control of Compound Managers, will provide opportunities for consulting opinions that are lacking where neither elders nor courts exist' (1936 Chairman NILAB: 1).

Urban Native Authorities were thought of but were never introduced and the elder system persisted until 1950. The meaning of the arrangement for influencing African labourers through elders cum 'Tribal Representatives', which was partly intended to prevent the formation of trade unions grounded in a capitalist-urban society, was radically transformed in 1945 when it was decided that the elders should not feel themselves beholden to either the District Commissioners or the Mine Managements. At long last, they were to be representatives of the people in the camps. Urban Native Courts were established in 1939 and in 1948 it was clear that 'urban court members were not representatives of the chiefs' in the rural areas. It would seem that the policy of stabilising the population of the camps coincided with fundamental changes in the ways in which camp populations were led and represented.

Pass Laws

To ensure that Africans in camps were aware that they had no business, apart from work, in European areas the Township Regulations of 1929 required them to be in possession of passes, valid for one night only, if they wished to be outside their camps or employers' locations between 9 p.m. and 5 a.m. This regularised the position at Livingstone where, in accordance with Government Notice No. 14 of 1914, no African had been permitted to live outside the Labour Camp since the town became the capital of Northern Rhodesia. In 1933 the Ndola Council introduced quarterly passes for 'civilised' Africans of well-known and good character. The system worked so well that in 1936 it was recommended that this arrangement for the 'civilised' should become universal (1936 Local Government: 22). It was observed in 1940 that the pass laws were 'not strictly enforced' (Hailey 1941: 9), partly because the European local authorities were too poor to enforce them. But as urban conditions came under scrutiny during the Second World War, the finances of these authorities improved, and their private police became more active.

The evidence that the Provincial Administration, the urban local authorities and their staff, and the Northern Rhodesia Police harassed Africans in Labour Camps to drive out the unemployed is conclusive. They were able to harass Africans who were not properly equipped with passes. These were of two kinds. According to the Native Registration Ordinance an African must possess a *citupa*, issued in his peasant system, which included particulars of his work history and to which was attached a receipt for any poll tax he had paid. The second form of pass required in a Labour Camp was a visitor's permit which authorised an African seeking employment to be in a particular camp; it was issued by the local authority responsible for the camp. Local authority police would raid living quarters, frequently at midnight, and inspect visitors' permits. Under the African Exemption Ordinance certain Africans were exempt from carrying any of these passes.

Between 1947 and 1956 there were 94,858 convictions for violations of these pass laws: around 90 per cent of the violations of the Townships and Urban African Housing Ordinance were for residing in a camp without a visitor's permit; and 95 per cent of the violations against the Native Registration Ordinance were for failure to obtain or carry a proper identification certificate. About a quarter of the offences were contraventions of the Native Registration Ordinance of 1929, thus three-quarters involved the European local authorities and their police (Commissioner of Police: Lusaka: August 1957).

At one time or another the great majority of Africans must have been stopped and questioned about their passes, and the Eccles Commission recorded that 'the location police are strongly disliked by the Africans and with good reason' (1944: 18). Their abolition was proposed by this Commission in 1944 but not carried out till 1960. Despite the number of prosecutions under pass laws, the situation in 1958 was that the 'control on these various passes is largely ineffective because of the size of the town and because there are no physical barriers to entry at any point' (1958 Urban Problems: 224).

The 'pass system in Southern and Central Africa was designed not only to control the flow of cheap labour, but to keep the African attached to his happy tribal home, which our Victorian forefathers thought was not only his rightful place but the best one for him' (John-Wood 1960: 40). This conclusion of a talented District Officer, with previous experience of a different social system in West Africa, as to the underlying meaning of the pass laws informs us why the squalor of temporary Labour Camps proved to be so much more desirable to many of the ruling class than modern Towns for Africans. That the overwhelming majority of Africans who lived in peasant systems deserved help rather than the men in the camps was the point of view of many District Officers. And the antipathy towards industrialisation which they had brought with them from England did much to reinforce this fact.

CONCLUSIONS

The future of the Labour Camps precipitated the major crisis in imperial policy regarding Zambia. Rural peasantries had become idealised in all British imperial policy which contended that the imperial mission was to improve their welfare. With the scarce funds and men available it was impossible to better the conditions of peasant systems and the Labour Camps simultaneously. But the issue was political as well as socioeconomic, because what was at risk was the wish that through the improvement of peasant systems competent peasant elites would emerge who in time would assume the mantle of the imperialists and take charge. The growth of the Labour Camps sapped the life of peasant systems, in part by alienating their elites from peasant life and attaching them to the urban system. Not surprising, this alarmed the imperialists who profoundly mistrusted urbanisation and certainly did not wish an urban-led society to evolve in Zambia.

Three factors challenged the peasant-oriented imperial policy. Peasant planning and development had started too late, was on too small a scale geared to the needs of specialist departments instead of peasant systems, and not grafted on to a vigorous Native Authority System. In consequence the peasant flood to the towns was not arrested. Secondly, though the local imperialists comforted themselves that the squalor of the Labour Camps was for the good of the peasant systems, Westminister did not see things this way, especially when it became clear that the urban miners and railwaymen would make the more important contribution to the war effort. Westminster exerted pressure to improve the camps. Thirdly, the large employers of urban men became aware that the productivity of their African labour was needlessly low. It could be raised by encouraging their male employees to bring their families to live with them in the urban system.

Government became conscious that it could not quickly resolve the crisis of the future of Zambia by making peasant systems attractive. But at the urban end of the migration path it tried to repel the peasant boarders. Until the 1950s its efforts created considerable irritation among the peasant inmigrants who refused to be deterred by the repatriation of families and the harassment of municipal police. The slumlike quality of housing deterred women and children from becoming inmigrants more effectively than did the police and regulations; the economic boom, by absorbing many inmigrant men, was similarly effective in keeping unemployment in the urban system low. The failure of mutual self-help among urban Africans and the termination of aid to the unemployed beyond a certain point also persuaded them to return to the peasant systems.

CHAPTER VII
TOWNS FOR AFRICANS AND AFRICAN TOWNS

Urban poverty that could not be hidden, the desire of Europeans to make the line of rail as modern as any other social system, the aspiration of capitalists to raise the productivity of their workforce without investment in more capital equipment, and the insistence of Westminster, which was entering the terminal phase of colonialism and becoming more sympathetic to radical and modern elements in African societies, brought about the metamorphosis of Labour Camps into Towns for Africans. The first task of this chapter is to describe how this was rationalised. Next, we shall consider the impact of Towns for Africans and African Towns on social action. This had two aspects: the increase in commitment to the urban system and the replacement of short term migration by urban residence during the working life of males.

BALANCED STABILISATION

Government and the Copper Mining Companies separately announced their intention to assist the stabilisation of the African inhabitants of the Labour Camps in the mid 1940s. They proposed to do this by constructing Towns for Africans. As the Governor explained to the Secretary of State for the Colonies in 1945, 'endeavours should be made to provide a balanced stabilisation in rural as well as urban areas . . . I suggest that the declared policy in this matter should be the recognition and provision for that degree of urban stabilisation which exists from time to time and the progressive development of the rural areas to keep pace as far as possible with progress in the urban areas' (2.1.1945 SEC/LAB/27).

There was an outstanding qualification to this which eventually distinguished urbanisation in Zambia from that of Eastern and Western Africa. The Governor concluded this same despatch to the Secretary of State by pointing to the 'special provision being made to encourage the retirement of urban workers to village life with the object of achieving a balanced stabilisation in both urban and rural areas'. If it was beyond the power of Government to induce men to live in peasant systems during important periods of their most active working lives, then an attempt must be made to force the tired and worn-out urban workers in middle age to leave the towns and take up peasant life once more. Over a lifetime a worker would achieve 'balanced stabilisation': during his childhood he would live in the peasant areas, then he would spend the most productive period of his life in the towns, and finally he would retire to a village which had become bankrupt because there had been no one to take care of it while he was away.

That this became typical and remains so today was largely due to several factors, some of which were beyond the control of the local Government, which was obliged to reflect the compromises reached in Westminster. The important factors were land and social security arrangements for Africans, and the inability — and unwillingness — of Africans to own urban property during the colonial regime; these substantially account for the habit of people leaving towns and retiring to the peasant systems.

This policy was identical with that adopted by the Mining Companies and pithily described by one of its leaders as 'stabilisation without urbanisation' (Prain 1956: 307). About 1941 and 1942 such a policy was first contemplated by the Mining Companies (Bromwich). Yet it was not until 1946 that the Companies 'formulated the policy that detribalisation and urbanisation should not be encouraged in any manner' but that 'stabilisation of African labour on the mines should be encouraged' (Prain 1956: 307). Thus, in terms of policy, stabilisation had come to refer to lengthening periods of employment until they filled a worker's economically active life; this contrasted with urbanisation which the public mind reserved to denote 'severance from rural ties combined with a tendency to settle down forever as a towndweller' (Prain 1956: 306); urbanisation was in this way used to convey the same meaning as 'detribalisation' (Prain 1956: 305); balanced stabilisation meant a rural childhood, long service in an industrial occupation and early retirement in middle age to peasant life. Without a circulation of population this policy must fail. For this reason some of the policies first associated with Labour Camps, designed to squeeze unemployable Africans out of the towns, continued well into the 1950s. But history is never neat, and there were opponents of this who hesitantly laid some of the foundations for African Towns during the colonial regime. Nevertheless, this does not detract from the accuracy of the characterisation of thought which is presented here as typical until 1964.

There is little evidence for a clear perspective and the difficulty of interpretation involves cognisance of adminstrative practices and the paucity of official statements on this issue during the 1950s. But it is likely that 'stabilisation without urbanisation' remained policy until Britain abdicated her sovereignty over Zambia in 1964. Afterwards the African government continued to give the same lip-service that the colonial government had given to peasant development. But by allowing periurban areas to grow, and be given community services, the probability that many people would continue to seek a peasant retirement was diminished. In future an old or unemployed man would shift from accommodation provided by an employer within the official limits of a town to a periurban area outside it instead of returning to a peasant system as was once customary.

It is tempting to make this one source of a distinction between Towns for Africans and African Towns. Towns for Africans were loaned to workers for as long as they were employed; African Towns now belong to their inhabitants throughout their lifetimes. The shift in the political control of towns which occurred with Independence reinforces the usefulness of distinguishing between towns supplied to Africans to use for only parts of their lives and towns owned and run by Africans throughout their lives.

Behind balanced stabilisation lay a remarkable agreement in the philosophies of many senior civil servants and mining executives. Fundamentally it was agreed by the civil servants that the peasant areas ought to be the true homes of Africans and that the areas must be made to provide suitable incomes (1948 PCs and Heads: 5). Sir Ronald Prain, long the outstanding captain of the Roan Selection Trust group of mining companies, spoke for the Colonial Service as well as his lieutenants when he declared that a 'balance-sheet' of Zambia would show 'an undue concentration in the urban areas both in terms of wealth and people to the detriment of the rural areas' (Prain 1964: 153). Plainly

'I am not blind to the consequences . . . which may result from the creation of large-scale mining industry. Foremost among these . . . is the possibility of upsetting the normal balance between town and country. Mines, by their nature, are apt to pay higher wages than other industries, and as a result you will find people who flock to the mining towns and perhaps upset the balance in the rural areas. Mines, furthermore, can bring social problems, problems of disparities of wealth, and problems of the type that follow those of large urban communities with only one interest, unlike the diversified economy of towns in the more developed countries of Europe and America. Mines too, by their nature, may have a short life . . . The impetus which a mine thus gives to a country may slow down and eventually cease altogether, and leave in its place a gap . . . a realisation of this point places upon managers of a mining industry and on government some responsibility for seeking not only to correct any imbalance that may arise between town and country, but to create something that will continue after the life of the mines. Such responsibility cannot be better discharged than by ensuring that some of the short term benefits of mining are put at the disposal of the long term interests of other industries such as agriculture' (Prain 1964: 33).

Urbanisation was thus the major social problem thrown up by industrialisation in Zambia, and it was planned to minimise it by stabilising workers in Towns for Africans which would kick them out when they could no longer serve industry, but when with their savings and failing strength they might still prop up peasant life. With taxes, such as the £38,000,000 levied on the mining companies in 1968, peasant development could be financed directly; with a gift of £500,000 the Roan Selection Trust financed experiments to grow food by irrigation at the Kafue Polder; with an interest-free loan of £2,000,000 from the Roan Selection Trust, earmarked by the Mines to assist the birthplaces of their workforce, the Government embarked on an intensive development drive in the Northern Province, of which programme the Mungwi agricultural settlement and training scheme was the most important part. Who could devise better ways to create and inject new blood into the peasant systems where life awaited the improvements of twentieth century technology? As Government and the mining companies often contended, 'it was essential to marry industry and agriculture . . . so as to promote the welfare of the whole territory' (Guillebaud 1953: 8).

Urban social problems, industrial strategy for expanding output, and economic self-sufficiency were the major facts which brought about the creation of Towns for Africans and the neglect of the peasants. It is likely that following the discovery of every kind of urban problem in 1935 the Labour Camps grew by ten per cent each year to a population of around 100,000 Africans by the time that Government settled upon a policy of balanced stabilisation. This very growth illuminated the ineffectiveness of the peasant stabilisation policies agreed upon by Government in 1936: the fostering of economic progress and the reduction of tax rates in peasant areas, a strengthened system of passes, and cheap transport for those wishing to leave the Labour Camps and return to the villages (1936 PCs: 27).

New and more radical forces emerged to negate this tinkering to support stagnant peasant arrangements. War rather than industry paid for the subsistence of the 15,000 Zambians who served in the East African Command between 1939 and 1945. Many of them chose not to return to their dreary villages when they were demobilised. Accompanying the revelations of the Eccles Commission on housing and the Saffery Report on the levels of living of people in the Labour Camps was a new appreciation of the purpose of government, civilisation, and progress symbolised by the Atlantic Charter and the Colonial Development and Welfare Act of 1940. If it is reflected that the latter was in large part an outcome of disturbances in the slums of the West Indies in the 1930s, and the wish to remove the conditions which were supposed to breed riots everywhere, one can understand another motive for urban improvement. Welfare replaced law and order as the imperative of imperialism around this time, and in 1940, following the strike and riots by African miners, the House of Commons, the Christian Churches, and the Aborigines Protection Society in Britain had identified the poverty of the Labour Camps as the most pressing social problem in Zambia. Moreover the people in these camps directly contributed to the war effort and were needed to supply strategic minerals to aid Britain's post-war recovery, hence their contentment became a matter of more than merely humanitarian concern.

According to the mining companies, the productivity of labour depended on housing, stabilisation, and urbanisation. The quality of labour on the mines was lower than it might have been had there been more family units for experienced miners. In addition it was believed that many better miners took employment in Katanga rather than in the Copperbelt of Zambia because they were uncertain of obtaining married quarters in Zambia (Jones 1951: 23). In the late 1940s all kinds of material developments by industry and government were arrested by the shortage of labour. Indeed, an investigation commissioned for the Mining Industry around 1950 showed 'that the male labour available for work is in fact at work, and no further supplies are available' (Jones 1951: 21). This investigation reckoned that 15 per cent of the employed labour force in Central Africa could be released for newly created posts if labour were used more efficiently. But this depended on the stabilisation of the workforce which in turn required family quarters. 'The stabilisation of labour results in a better use of African labour, and more continuous work leads to more intelligent work and the development of skills . . . There is, through urbanisation, less waste generally through the lesser turnover of labour' (Jones 1953: 40).

As the policy of stabilising their workforce was implemented, the mining companies became aware for the first time that labour was no longer plentiful and must be employed more intelligently in order to raise production per unit of labour and thus meet the rising world demand for Zambian minerals. The alternative was to undertake large-scale investment in labour-saving machinery. Apart from the cost, this needed time, and would leave demand unsatisfied, with the possibility of world consumers switching from copper, zinc and lead to the use of other minerals not produced in Zambia. If the stabilisation policy of 1946 was formulated unhurriedly after 1941 as part of a rational plan for an unknown future, its implementation assumed an air of desperation as world copper prices and demand soared towards the end of the decade at the time when the reserves of labour in the peasant systems were at last exhausted.

Economic self-sufficiency became the target of the Ten-Year Development Plan when it was revised in June 1948. Its objectives in order of importance were the increased production of food for sale to urban people, more housing for Europeans and Africans in the urban areas, and better roads in the urban areas and along the line of rail which linked them (1948 Plan). When it was discovered that Britain would contribute little finance for the development of Zambia, it was decided to displace the priority accorded to the peasant areas in development plans in favour of urban progress. The Europeans led by Roy Welensky reasoned that the peasants were Britain's responsibility but that their own self-interest lay in the urban areas, and the commercial farms close by them, and so these should receive priority in Government spending. As 'development' was assumed to depend on the settlement and goodwill of Europeans, they were allowed to call this tune.

This complete displacement in emphasis in development was the most profound event in the imperial experience of Zambia. It was made necessary because the British Treasury received from Zambia more than the Zambian Treasury received from the British (Heisler 1971). This detracted from the ability of Westminster at the time to dictate the course of Zambian development. The scale of Zambia's need can be illustrated from her income from Colonial Development and Welfare Funds and local expenditure on recurrent and capital accounts. Between 1947 and 1954, the central years of the post-war plan, the expenditure of the local Government amounted to £134,200,000 and to offset this a derisory £2,400,000 of aid was received from Colonial Development and Welfare Funds. If British public funds were insufficient to finance the development of Zambia, and the repayment on public loan issues remained costly, Zambia must finance as much of her own growth as possible.

Without all-weather roads to connect the commercial farms, fortuitously adjacent to the line of rail, with the townspeople, prices would be high and all other forms of distribution costly. However, the tarred road did not extend north of Broken Hill to the Copperbelt when this plan was revised, and most other roads were corrugated and impassable during the rains. With the building of these roads an urban enclave knit with the nearby commercial farms was formed quite distinct from the peasant systems. Improved roads were as essential for the infrastructure of towns as were houses. Domestic food production for the towns must be stimulated to improve the balance of payments because 'it is one of the outstanding characteristics of the Northern Rhodesian economy during the period 1939-47 that in no important consumer goods was the Territory self-sufficient' (1950 Report: 63). African farmers then produced about half of the maize sold but otherwise contributed little to the urban economy. Development resources were therefore concentrated for the benefit of the urban system. Those who looked beyond their immediate interests in urban growth could save and the savings could one day be injected into the sick peasant systems.

PEASANT-URBAN DIVORCE

Nevertheless, after the Second World War the peasant and urban systems drifted apart. This was due to the vast improvements in all kinds of capitalist-urban facilities and the comparative lack of change in those of the peasant systems. Whereas for half a century the possibility of combining subsistence and money incomes was the condition under which the majority of peasants were persuaded to sell their labour services, because money earnings in themselves were insufficient incomes, with the advent of Towns for Africans the real income and standard of living of urban residents improved to the extent that they no longer felt the need to 'keep in' with their peasant kin nor to maximise their welfare through a combination of peasant and urban incomes. Henceforth, they were tempted to believe that the capitalist-urban system would provide for all their needs, and town-dwellers became autonomous of the peasant systems. In Government development plans, wage, education and housing policies produced this divergence of systems, and the trend towards dualism in societal organisation which became manifest in the 1960s.

The Enclave Society

Behind the line of rail lies a hinterland of backward technology, ignorance, poverty and hopelessness which is absent from the Enclave Society united by this rail. This Enclave Society is composed of two elements: urban areas and commercial farming areas rarely more than 15 miles distant from the railway. It is likely that in the terminal phase of the Labour Camps, in the mid 1940s, this Enclave accommodated a mere one-eleventh of the population of Zambia. But by the time that Towns for Africans were replaced by African Towns one in four of the residents of Zambia lived in the Enclave, and by 1970 two-fifths of them lived there. The dynamics of this Enclave have attracted men and women away from the hinterland and, since the time Towns for Africans have been built, have prevented increasing numbers from returning to it. Investment in industry and all sorts of services account for this dynamism which has created the Enclave Society within the National Society of Zambia. At first the flow of resources from the Enclave to the hinterland was appreciable, but with the demise of the Labour Camps it almost dried up. From then on the manpower resources of the hinterland were drained by the Enclave without reciprocal exchange and the two zones have drifted apart. Public spending has accelerated this divorce.

The Pim Report of 1938 reliably summarised previous favourable treatment for the Enclave as follows. 'Under the administration of the British South Africa Company attention was concentrated on the development of the European areas and the mineral assets of the country, and the first essential step was taken towards economic advance by the construction of the railway. Except for law and order practically nothing was done for the outlying areas covering by far the greater part of the Territory.' Following this, 'in the earlier years of administration by the Imperial Government there was little progress in the outlying areas' where 'little had been achieved towards improving conditions when the slump hit the Territory in 1932 ... The retrenchments and general reductions in expenditure of 1932 and 1933 were disastrous and this was particularly serious for the outlying areas as plans for development were only beginning to be thought out' (1938 Colonial 145: 333, 337).

The neglect of the hinterland continued with new investment activity after the interlude of the Second World War. As a consequence of the Ten Year Development Plan, between 1947 and 1953 only one quarter of the monies spent on economic services were allocated to the peasant systems. In 1952 around £9,600,000, out of a total expenditure of £12,500,000, was used by Government on the development of the Enclave Society. When but one quarter of the total in this year found its way to the development of the peasant hinterland this cannot be accounted a fair exchange for the health and vitality supplied to the Enclave by the labourers from the hinterland.

During the life of the European-dominated Federation of Rhodesia and Nyasaland between 1953 and 1962, when 'European' development was the special responsibility of the Federal Government, the Enclave Society received even more favourable treatment. Looking back in 1962 planners reflected that the 'Government had been hard pressed to keep pace with the needs of the urban areas for the corresponding expansion of normal Government services . . . Meanwhile, the rural areas have not seen any similar expansion of economic activity . . . Consequently, there is now a very widespread disparity between the economies' of the peasant hinterland and Enclave (1962 Draft Plan: 1). The reason for this is clear: 'In the Federation, the evidence indicates that the major aim of European policy has been to effect the most rapid rate of economic growth possible in the European-controlled section of the economy' (Taylor 1963: 244).

To redress this imbalance it was proposed that during the years 1961 to 1965 Government should invest about the same amount of capital in the economic development of the hinterland as in the Enclave Society. But when the First National Development Plan of 1966-70 was announced it became clear that this parity of treatment was not to continue and the major colonial trend was to be reintroduced by the African regime. It was decided that 70 per cent of the capital investment in the plan should be in the three provinces in which the Enclave Society was situated (1966 National Plan: 81).

Economists have disagreed as to whether the scarce resources available to induce higher agricultural output should be spread thinly over all the subsistence cultivators or concentrated on the relatively few cultivators who have taken a keen interest in commercial farming. There has been doubt whether weak injections of agricultural resources to the mass of cultivators will effect any lasting improvement in production; there has been much more certainty that strong injections of agricultural resources to the few most enterprising and modern-minded African farmers will prove successful. These improved peasant farmers will not only enter the twentieth-century money economy but, in addition, through their optimum use of the help they are given, will 'demonstrate' to backward villagers the virtues of their new rural enterprise. They will light the path from age-old and anachronistic custom to the scientific technology of the present for ignorant villagers to follow. As the ignorant masses were located in the hinterland and the improved peasant farmers in the Enclave Society the outcome of this dispute among agriculturalists affected resource allocation to one or other of these zones.

The issue was publicly raised for the first time in the Ten-Year Development Plan of 1947, and later in the investigation of agriculture which set the guidelines until the imperial power abdicated (1961 RED Report: 34). In both instances support for African commercial agriculture in the Enclave Society was agreed upon. Despite the protestations that the 'majority of subsistence farmers who remain practically untouched by any of the advanced productive techniques' must be the focus for agricultural development, in the First National Development Plan it is noteworthy that it was proposed that 50.1 per cent of the capital investment in agriculture during 1966-70 should be in the three provinces which contained the Enclave Society and, with the exception of the Eastern Province, the bulk of the improved farmers (1966 National Plan: 81).

Apart from a decision that known techniques of induced change do not allow us to materially uplift the 'majority of subsistence farmers', the trend to favour agriculture in the Enclave Society has been occasioned by the needs of urban peoples. For instance, maize imports were negligible in 1936-7. But with the growth of Labour Camps they exceeded 9,000 tons in 1939 and 29,000 tons in 1943-4. However, in the 1960s the country has become self sufficient in maize production and this has reduced pressure to extend maize cultivation in the Enclave Society. But as long as there are food imports the handful of cultivators in the Enclave Society will receive disproportionate support from Government. However, it seems that the problem is soluble for whereas in 1964 food imports amounted to 11 per cent of the total this figure had dropped to 7 per cent in 1967. With this move towards self sufficiency the justification for shifting resources for economic development to the peasant hinterland should become irresistible.

When Rhodesia unilaterally declared its independence from Britain on 11 November 1965 the third greatest boost to the expansion of the Enclave Society followed. Copper exploration and the establishment of the Labour Camps in the 1920s was the first, the decision to build Towns for Africans in the 1940s the second. Zambians interpreted UDI as meaning that not only would a White group run Rhodesian affairs exclusively on their own behalf to the detriment of the interests of Rhodesian Africans, but that they would take advantage of Black Africans everywhere. Without delay Rhodesia put the economy of the Enclave Society in jeopardy. At least 35 per cent of Zambian imports came from Rhodesia at the time of UDI, but this is a figure which conceals the difficulty experienced by Zambia in switching from Rhodesian supplies to others. Power, railways and airways were owned jointly with Rhodesia and the communications and energy required to keep the Enclave alive could be sabotaged by Rhodesian action. Rhodesia did not hesitate to effect a huge rise in the price of coke and coal to Zambia which was totally dependent on the Wankie industry in Rhodesia for all this fuel; all the petroleum came from Rhodesia; Rhodesia controlled the operations room of the Kariba Dam which provided light for the Enclave. Between Zambia and her international customers for minerals lay the Rhodesian railway system. Without exports Zambia would starve, without energy and communications the Enclave would grind to a halt.

The strenuous efforts to make Zambia free of Rhodesia will have two results, one immediate and the other in the near future. The first is that the Enclave has grown in self-sufficiency by undertaking activities formerly accomplished by

Rhodesia. Secondly, by means of a road and rail link with Tanzania and the Indian Ocean, to circumvent Rhodesia and Portuguese Angola, a ribbon of development has now been laid through the hinterland. This parallels in socio-economic importance the building of the trans-continental railways in the U.S.A. in the 1860s and will provide a source of growth and urbanisation alternative to the present Enclave. The railway link is scheduled for completion in 1973 and the hinterland of the long depressed Northern Province will finally be dragged into the twentieth century.

Wage-Earners

Differences between the urban and rural earnings of Africans hastened the trend for urban life to seem more attractive than peasant life. The effect of a rise in urban income compared with that earned from subsistence production was to increase a migrant's opportunity cost of not engaging in urban work, and this was the major incentive to seek and retain employment in the towns. Economic theory suggests that the substitution effect associated with a rise in wages increases the time spent by the typical migrant in employment' (Baldwin 1966: 118).

It is hazardous to compare the values of urban and rural incomes and so the following figures must be treated with caution and understood merely as an attempt to ascertain gross differences between them. *Per capita* incomes of Africans in 1946 were £16 in the Labour Camps and £4 in the peasant areas; in 1954 they were £24 in the Towns for Africans and £9 in the peasant areas; in 1964 they were £43 in the Towns for Africans and £12 in the peasant areas. In proportionate terms the attractions of the peasant systems remained fairly constant and the *per capita* incomes of people engaged in indigenous enterprises were one quarter to one third of those in the urban areas in 1945-63. Given differences in the cost of living, the urban level of living during this time was probably a little more than twice that of the peasant systems. But it must not be forgotten that peasants not only admired the clothes of men who had finished a spell of work in the towns but were impressed by their tales about the deplorable conditions they had lived in. The Commission of Inquiry into the Cost of Living in 1947 considered that 'the present predicament' of the people in the camps was 'sufficiently grave' for Government to continue to subsidise the price of the staple food in the Labour Camps and in addition to prohibit the sale of maize at more than 15 shillings per bag (1947 Interim Report: 6).

During the last decade, urban conditions improved dramatically and between 1964 and 1969 the income gap between the peasant and urban zones yawned. While the value of peasant incomes remained stationary at around £13 *per capita*, incomes in the African Towns had shot up to £90 by 1969. In this year peasant incomes were a mere one-seventh of urban incomes and even allowing for the soaring cost of living in the towns, which raised the consumer prices of the working-class townsmen by 43 per cent between 1960 and 1968, this rise in town incomes helped to pull more people out of the peasant systems.

The differences between the incomes of urban Africans and those still tied largely to subsistence production reflected the changing organisation of Zambia. The fact that wages were initially set for single and not married men has already been cited as an instance of this. When a government officer giving evidence to the Commission investigating the riots of 1935 made the point that an African wage-earner did not need wages that did more than keep him alive while employed, pay his poll tax, and during a number of labouring stints allow him to acquire one or two essential durables such as a bicycle and a sewing machine, he did so in the hope that wages would continue to be fixed by the peasant status of the recipient. Not only were the needs of a peasant supposed to be low but they must be kept low to keep him in his station and prevent him from trying to reach above himself like the odd and well-dressed African townsman. Otherwise the peasant wage-earner would be deterred from re-entering a peasant system.

Though infrequently spelt out, this was a point of view which impressed the European élites and provides the context for the historic judgement which concerned African wage-earners in general as well as African mineworkers. Because they were paid peasant as well as bachelor wages, African miners once reasoned that much was omitted from their wages 'that was needed to make even a tolerable existence' (Guillebaud 1953: 7). In 1953, fresh from Britain, the arbitrator who uttered this judgement dealt with a major dispute between the mining companies and the African trade union. The mining companies told him that they were perfectly capable of paying the miners what they asked for but stressed that the arbitrator should consider the effect of this on the growing divorce between the peasant and urban areas. If he awarded a sizeable increase to the wages of mine-workers this divorce would be accentuated because the disorganisation of the peasant systems would be hastened. But, 'vitally important though such considerations undoubtedly are for the future well-being of the territory, I cannot regard them as constituting in themselves a bar to the claim by the Union for a substantial increase in wages ... Urbanisation and industrialisation have come to stay, so long at least as the copper ores continue to be worked. With this development arises the opportunity of giving the African a higher standard of living than any he has known in the past' (Guillebaud 1953: 14). This pointed the way to providing levels of living appropriate to townsmen just as surely as the trend to pay family wages in order to avoid urban poverty. The latter was concerned with the minimum welfare of Africans in towns; the Guillebaud judgement of 1953 was determined that they should receive a fairer share for their contribution to capitalism.

If the acceptance of Africans in urban areas as persons participating in an urban civilisation was a major change in social organisation, no less important was the removal of the industrial colour bar between the European and African urban estates during the 1960s. To illustrate, in Divisions I and II of the civil service in 1963 only one-third of the officers were African, but by 1968 two-thirds were African. Whereas in the 'field of expatriate employment' 8.4 per cent of the jobs on the mines were filled by Africans in 1964, this rose to 55 per cent in 1970. A dual wage structure stood in front of the industrial colour bar, and in 1960, for example, European salaries were twelve times as great as those of Africans. With the removal of the industrial colour bar Africans began not only to occupy 'European' jobs but to receive 'European'-level incomes. To improve matters for white-collar Africans a *de facto* policy of Zambianisation has meant that black Zambians have increasingly been given preference for all jobs and have displaced whites irrespective of their nationality. Now an industrial colour bar in reverse operates and Europeans can compete on even terms with Africans only for short-term contract jobs which require specialised experiences or training.

Three major effects for the pattern of migration ensued from raising the incomes of urban Africans. Undoubtedly these rises aroused the envy of townsfolk felt by villagers who wished to imitate their style of life by moving into the urban areas. Not only consumption patterns were involved. Africans who earned more than £10 a month showed 'evidence of appreciable savings' (1965 Urban Budget: 5) which would eventually be translated into consumer durables such as tea rooms, sewing machines and taxis. As this was within reach of the majority of wage-earners, they all experienced a disincentive to become peasants once more. The second effect was to reduce the outmigration to the villages of blue-collar workers and their families. In 1960 it was found that there was a significant difference in the sizes of the families of the poorest 20 per cent and the richest 20 per cent of the urban African population – there were 3.8 persons in the former and 5.4 persons in the latter. It would be strange if the poorest were to employ birth control and breed the fewest children. The explanation for these figures was that the poorest families could not afford to feed all their children, nor their wives sometimes, in the towns, so sent them back to the villages (1965 Urban Budget: 7, 12). The increasing wealth of the 1960s and 1970s has probably made this no longer necessary.

In passing, a comment on mutual aid is apposite. Of the average poorest family of 3.8 persons 0.1 person was not a parent or a child, in contrast to 0.5 person in the richest quintile, and so it would seem that mutual aid to 'friends' was not provided by the poorest. Even the 0.5 person who lived with the average rich family does not represent the horde of spongers that the myths of African hospitality and custom have spread. An unemployed blue-collar family did not last long in the towns under these conditions, and the keen resentment felt by white-collar Africans about any obligation to render hospitality indicates that as their incomes increased they were unlikely to encourage the visits of peasant 'friends'.

The third important consequence of rising urban incomes concerns white-collar workers. More than blue-collar workers, they were prone to wander from town to town rather than town to village when they became unemployed. Increasing incomes and European styles of living widened the social distances between these men and their village relations. White-collar workers in Africa increasingly experience secondary poverty which is incomprehensible to peasant relatives. In future times of trouble it is unlikely that they will turn again to the peasant systems for help.

How these changes in incomes directly affected migration is unknown. An examination of the migratory pattern of wage-earners at distant points in time is possible, but does not reveal much information about urban stabilisation. For what it is worth, a comparison of the Labour Camp at Nkana in 1941 and the Towns for Africans run by the mining companies on the Copperbelt between 1957 and 1959 reveals no change. Some 36 per cent of the workmen who joined Nkana came from other Labour Camps and the remainder derived directly from peasant systems (Saffery 1943: 82). Similarly, between 1957 and 1959, 34 per cent of the men engaged by the copper mining companies came from other Towns for Africans (1957, 1958, 1959 Yearbooks). One-quarter of those who joined the copper mines came directly from villages where there was no previous experience of mine employment. When between 1957 and 1959 men left the copper mines, 37 per cent declared their intentions of returning directly to their villages. If those who came directly from the peasant systems were the same men who returned to them directly on discharge from the copper mines, it would seem that just under a half chose to remain in the urban areas a while longer after leaving the copper mines. From this body, as well as the old timers on the mines, the stabilised urban population grew. The available data does not permit comparison on this point with the earlier Nkana experience.

Social Security

Forms of social security provision appropriate to each phase of urban organisation were evolved. Basic social security for the people in the Labour Camps was their right to utilise land in their place of origin. Some 94 per cent of the land in Zambia was reserved for Africans in 1947 and chiefs and headmen safeguarded the interests of migrants in land pending their return. To make this more of a reality the overall distribution of population is still low, at around twelve persons to the square mile, and though there is overcrowding in some areas by the standards of Eastern and Western Africa, there is ample land for the African people of Zambia. But peasant production entailed more than making a garden, burning bush, and harvesting once a year. It involved more labour than a nuclear family could provide and exposure to the demands of social and political custom which, if not respected, would make peasant life intolerable. Thus the right of re-entry into a society as well as the peasant economy had to be preserved during absence in town. By retaining reciprocal obligations with rural kin this re-entry into peasant life was arranged. The African in a Labour Camp paid his social security contribution by remitting goods and money to the villages.

Marking the transition from Labour Camps to Towns for Africans was a large fall in remittances for social security. Cash-flows from miners and urban areas in general to the peasant areas in 1931 were around 20 per cent of earnings (Robinson 1967: 179, 184); they were 18 per cent at Broken Hill in 1941 (Wilson 1941: 43); and 7 per cent from the urban to the peasant areas in 1964 (1964 UN/ECA/FAO: 53). This is an outstanding symptom of the replacement of Labour Camps by Towns for Africans filled by people with little interest in returning to the villages before they retire.

In this connection the differences in the remittances of single men and married families resident in towns is of interest. Young unmarried men tend to visit their villages more frequently than married men. This throws light on the budget survey of 1960 which revealed higher remittances by single men than by married men. Single men in the median income quintile remitted 3 to 4 per cent of their income to their relatives, but married men remitted only half of this (1965 Urban Budget: 37, 40). These remittances to relatives were to those in urban as well as rural areas, but it is possible that with the money personally handed over by savers, the figure of 7 per cent for 1964 which has been cited is a fair reckoning.

Arising from the wish of Government and the Mining Companies for Africans to seek retirement in the peasant systems, during the 1950s pensions were introduced which would deliberately be insufficient for pensioners to subsist on in towns (Baldwin 1966: 138-9). Thus in 1955 the Mining Companies introduced a pension scheme which allowed past service to count immediately and in full for pension. Of the first fifty-five pensioners under this scheme fifty-one immediately returned to their home districts (Prain 1956: 307). When in 1958 the question of pensions for urban Africans was raised in the Legislature one of the arguments used to resist this and leave matters where they stood was that this would ensure that 'retirement will be on the easier conditions of the rural areas' (Fosbrooke 1958*a*; Fosbrooke 1958*b*).

With the inauguration of African Towns Government became concerned with the needs of urban Africans in general and not just long-service employees. Labourers and semi-skilled workers will be the prime beneficiaries of this. For the unestablished, low-grade wage-earner a National Provident Fund was established in 1966. Employers and employees are compelled to contribute and benefits are paid from the age of fifty-five onwards. Active consideration as to how to widen the basis of the scheme to forms of dependency other than old age has been undertaken (Rockett 1966). As important for the future demographic composition of urban society as cutting ties with peasant systems has been the conferral of 'European'-type pensions on the many Africans who through fair competition and Zambianisation have succeeded in obtaining 'European' posts.

Before there were African Towns most Africans were in a similar plight in old age. But now there will be a distinctly better-off class of retired men. The ease with which they can buy their own accommodation in African Towns will enable them to remain there until their death. It is possible to infer from several observations that while there were Towns for Africans, middle-class Africans were most noticeable among those who returned to villages (e.g. Richards 1958: 312; Long 1968). Traditionally the ambition of every African was to acquire status by commanding the services of others and by engaging in rural enterprise on 'retirement' from the urban areas; the prodigals certainly won considerable esteem. Within the next decade this way of evaluation may well continue and many middle-class Africans may prefer the esteem, and relative discomfort, of village life to being ignored by bustling younger townsfolk while enjoying the comforts of urban life. But there will be others who have been absent from the villages for so long that they will not know how to arrange a re-entry, so they will cling to the towns when they have stopped work. It is not certain whether the social security provision for former blue-collar workers will enable them to do likewise. They may have no choice but to return to the villages. Status may be the prime motivation concerning place of residence after retirement in the case of middle-class Africans, but material needs may dictate a peasant old age for labourers.

Houses and Wives

The provision of suitable housing in the Towns for African couples detached them somewhat more from the peasant systems. According to the Employment of Natives Ordinance of 1929 an employer was responsible for the rent of his employee. In this lies the origin of Towns for Africans which are basically housing units provided for Africans, paid for by employers, and closed to the unemployed. However, by 1946 the failure of some employers to pay the rents of employees was identified as a problem (February 1946 SEC/DEV/21) and in 1949 it was realised that the most important sections of the African Housing Ordinance of the previous year, relating to employers' obligations to provide family accommodation and the local authorities to build and lease this, could not be enforced because of a shortage of accommodation due to the financial inability of local authorities to shoulder their new task and the scarcity of men and materials to build houses.

The pattern of accommodation which structured Towns for Africans had been decided upon when there were only Labour Camps. On the one hand Europeans feared the disease and contamination to which uncontrolled building by Africans would expose them (cf. Davis 1967: 82; Orde-Browne 1938: 61); on the other hand there was the problem of controlling a dispersed African population (1936 Chairman NILAB: 6). The solution was to house Africans in blocks segregated from European housing. Thus Africans lived in areas reserved for them and nowhere else, and apart from the unemployed and self-employed, the majority tended to live in accommodation paid for by their employers and leased to them by a European local authority. This latter practice conformed to a policy agreed in 1935 (1935 PCs Conference: 11).

The Central Government decided to provide the finance required by local authorities to accommodate the 24,350 adult males who in 1946 were found to require housing (13.2.1946 SEC/LG/1). To this end, in December 1947 a Department of Local Government and African Housing began business and generous provision for housing was made in the Ten-Year Development Plan when it was revised in 1948. This might be described as a family housing programme. During the lifetime of Labour Camps the emphasis had been placed on providing accommodation for bachelors, now the accommodation of workers with their families became the objective.

Three reasons for this may be noted. Following the rioting on the Copperbelt in 1940, public opinion in Britain as well as in Zambia decided that the trusteeship obligation of the imperial power had not been adequately discharged in respect of the welfare of urban Africans. Secondly, the return to industrial productivity from the stabilisation of the urban African population became desired. 'We are convinced', explained the Eccles Commission, 'that the extra cost of good houses would be offset by a higher level of performance and that considerable economy would be effected, as reduction in the number of employees, which must follow improvement in health conditions' arising from better housing, 'would naturally result in a reduction in the number of houses needed' (1944 Native Locations: 6). Thirdly, it was believed that through better housing a more contented urban population would emerge. For instance, in 1953 the Executive Council was advised that housing shortages in Kenya had contributed to the rise of Mau Mau and the same must not happen in Zambia. Furthermore, the European-controlled Federation was imminent and there was need to give local African opinion encouragement, a psychological fillip, to reassure it that African interests were still of some account (8.10.1953 102/4). Thus between 1948 and 1964 the mining companies and various public bodies built some 100,000 houses for Africans in urban areas at a cost of not less than £32,000,000. As a result, it was reported in 1961 that only 7 per cent of the housing under the control of urban local authorities consisted of semi-permanent and temporary structures (Mitchell 1963: 16). This wellnigh satisfactory achievement in constructing permanent dwellings was obtained by allocating to housing one-fifth of all the investment in the capitalist economy during the 1950s.

In consequence the local authorities felt justified in demolishing the unauthorised huts which had sprung up in the Labour Camps and which were 'most of them unhygienic and squalid in the extreme and their presence so near to the townships constitutes a hazard to the public health' (1944 Native Locations: 1). Which is to say that, in general, until the 1940s Africans in the Labour Camps erected their own huts on sites allocated to them whereas in Towns for Africans they lived in accommodation built for them by employers and local authorities. Towns for Africans were built most rapidly on the Copperbelt.

Lusaka is a place where unauthorised housing remained a more or less intractable problem. People in these illegal housing areas could not be driven from the Enclave because 'there is no doubt that the vendors of herbs and dried caterpillars, the indigent carpenters and shoe-makers, the wise women and snuff-grinders all have an established position in the Urban African Society, and that at present they operate almost exclusively in the Unauthorised Locations' (Armor 1958: 3-4). In 1957 these inhabitants of the unauthorised settlements constituted 45 per cent of the total African population of Lusaka and lived in 6,699 condemned structures (Armor 1957: 4). In spite of prodigious efforts to contain the problems accentuated by a boom in the urban population – some 6,000 additional souls seem to have become illegal squatters in Lusaka between 1956 and 1957 – by the end of 1964 there were still 2,032 unauthorised structures standing with a population of not more than 12,000. This is creditable compared with the later growth of the peri-urban area in Lusaka where there were 90,000 inhabitants in this area in 1969.

But the satisfactory quality of housing achieved in the Towns for Africans soon fell as a new housing boom failed to keep pace with the influx of inmigrants to African Towns. Two instances of changes in housing between 1963 and 1969 will suffice to illustrate this point: in 1963 there were 1.9 persons to a room and in 1969 there were 2.7 to a room; in 1963 3.7 per cent of the walls of dwellings were pole and *dagga* or grass whereas in 1969 these inferior construction materials occurred in 9.4 per cent of the dwellings. The true changes in these years are understated because of the nature of the urban units available for comparison. This increase in pole and *dagga* housing units is a symptom of the spread of peri-urban areas in African Towns.

During the terminal years of Towns for Africans the housing requirements for African Towns became understood and accepted by public bodies. The Coleman Commission which reviewed the Financing of Services and Amenities of Africans in 1961 and the Economic Survey Mission on the Economic Development of Zambia in 1964 believed it was psychologically wrong for urban Africans not to own or rent their own accommodation. Therefore, with the establishment of African Towns, the attack on unauthorised locations and their health problems was modified. The following characteristic lament to an African newspaper had not passed unheard.

I am a self-employed carpenter and could not get a municipal house as there are none empty and even so the rents are too high for my pocket, having five children. So I built our house with burnt brick and thatch all myself at Kalingalinga where were not supposed to stay but are allowed because there is nowhere else for us. We have no water, no lights, no schools and no lavatories but the Municipals say that they will build us a big beer-hall. If we drink beer to give profits then one day there will be water supplied to us in taps. How much beer must I drink before my children can drink water? (Hall 1964: 135).

In African Towns the answer was to provide site and service plots with either individual or grouped services. Between 1966 and 1970 Government provided help to 63,410 housing units of this kind. The switch in emphasis will be better appreciated if this figure is contrasted with the 15,993 houses built on behalf of Government during the same period (1970 Yearbook: 162). An outstanding instance of this growth of unauthorised peri-urban areas where a public body supplied some help of this kind to would-be house-owners was the sudden emergence of Zambia City, near Luanshya on the Copperbelt, in the mid 1960s.

People in Towns for Africans reciprocated by regarding themselves as stabilised for the duration of their working lives but not urbanised. Security during their working lives became a novel objective. Increasing numbers of employees preferred to pay their own rents and discontinue living in 'tied cottages'. Artisans who were intermittently out of work liked to do this in Livingstone (McCulloch 1956: 5) and in 1958 a rent increase seemingly levied on employers produced a riot in Ndola. It was found here that 41.7 per cent of the people in the zone paid all or part of the rent and its increases (Hancock 1958). By contrast there was clear reluctance on the part of Africans to own their own houses, despite encouragement. From 1950 onwards the local authorities offered assistance to this end and from 1958 the Mining Companies also offered help. But in 1964 there were no Africans in the Mining Industry who owned their urban homes and only seventy-eight permanent owner-occupied houses in the controlled local authority high-density areas in Zambia (1966 Copper Companies: 15). Africans who planned a rural retirement had no need to own their own urban homes and preferred employers to make some contribution to their rent. With the growth of African Towns this reluctance to be committed to urban life through ownership of an urban home began to disappear. By 1969 28 per cent of urban people owned their own homes.

As urban people, Africans had no voice in the arrangements for the administration of Labour Camps which were completely dominated by European interests. To erase the impression that Africans lived in European towns, while at the same time preserving such *de facto* segregation as occurs in any advanced industrial country between a working-class and middle-class population, quasi-autonomous Departments of African Affairs were formed within the European-run urban areas around 1950. As the Member for Local Government explained to location superintendents, soon to become Directors of African Affairs in this reorganisation, the new African housing areas were to be self-contained units for the African community. To be successful they must have not only housing and recreation groups but shops, schools, clinics – in fact all the normal facilities of the town (February to March 1950 SEC/LG/49). In these towns to assist the officers of the Central Government 'in keeping in touch with African views and opinion African Urban Advisory Councils were established in

1947' (1960 Cmnd. 1149: 102). In time African members of these Urban Advisory Councils were enabled to comment constitutionally on the affairs of the Departments of African Affairs within the European-controlled local authorities: they could advise the Europeans through their membership of the African Affairs Committee of each municipality which included persons who were also members of the Urban Advisory Councils. Nevertheless, their influence was restricted to advice because Europeans composed half the membership of African Affairs Committees, plus one (Mitchell 1963: 4, 15-19). Unlike the Labour Camps, Towns for Africans were to be operated in consultation with Africans, although executive power still resided with European elected councils in urban local authorities.

Turning to the impact of housing on behaviour we may begin with Wilson's classic study of Broken Hill. In this, the oldest industrial centre in Zambia, attempts to encourage family life had taken place well before the Second World War. Family housing had been used to encourage this on a larger scale than elsewhere. In 1940 Wilson found that an average married man whose wife lived with him had spent nine years and eight months in a camp; a man whose wife was in a village had spent four years and one month; and the typical single man or youth had spent three years and ten months. This was the first glimpse of the pattern which would be set when Towns for Africans replaced Labour Camps everywhere. Wilson's portrayal of behaviour which was ancillary to the stabilisation of married men accompanied by their wives will serve as a handsome description of Towns for Africans.

> The circulation of population between town and country has changed its character; it now consists more in movement of general population, less in movement of young men. Young unmarried men still go home fairly frequently, but married men whose wives are with them do not; they normally stay where they are in towns, while their wives go home on visits, and their parents, parents-in-law and mothers' brothers come from the country to visit them. Elderly men and women from the country who have four or five junior relatives living in one town very often find it more profitable to visit that town themselves than to wait for visits from it (Wilson 1941: 48-49).

The major difference between this pattern and African Towns is that in the latter young men marry women of their own choice within the town and neither feel the need to visit the country. In fact the large number of Africans who nowadays find the countryside strange is amazing to a European.

Family housing units did not merely bring women and children to towns to join husbands. Once there they helped commit a worker to town life, perhaps because he could discharge his family responsibilities more effectively in this milieu with its ample facilities. Following in the tradition established by Wilson of careful sociographic study of urban life, Mitchell (1969) has constructed a measure of urban ties among which marriage and housing are considered. This involves measuring the extent to which one indicator is correlated with other indicators. How far marriage and living with a wife in town, for instance, interconnects with other indicators reflects the influence of family life in keeping a man in town. Weights measure the degree of interconnectedness of a particular indicator and the combined weights of all indicators of urban commitments total 100. A weight of 11.5 was calculated to be the contribution that living with a woman made to the involvement of a man in a Town for Africans in the early 1950s.

Thus the ability of family housing to influence commitment to urban residence was considerable. From 1931 onwards, when the Casual Labour System had undermined the Recruited Labour System, the Mining Companies did not deter their employees from bringing their wives to the camps at the expense of the Companies. But not all Mining Companies supplied family quarters and in the main married mineworkers had to make do with bachelor quarters. This reduced the number of mineworkers whose families lived with them. Table 3 shows that in the 1950s about one third of all urban men actually lived with their wives.

At Broken Hill in 1940 45.8 per cent of the mineworkers had their wives with them, but in 1948 in the Labour Camps of the Mining Companies on the Copperbelt less than 40 per cent of the workers lived in family units. Yet by 1951, as the family housing programme got under way, this figure had increased to 60 per cent (Jones 1951: 8). By 1954 this figure for the Copperbelt had risen to 78 per cent. The trend spread to all the main towns, where 87 per cent of mineworkers lived in family units by 1960 (1961 Demographic Surveys: 6). From the demographic repercussion of the drive for family housing to stabilise the employed population came a generation of youngsters who resisted any move to transport them away from their places of birth to the decrepit villages. In this way Towns for Africans laid part of the demographic foundation for African Towns.

Education and Children

During the age of Labour Camps it was not unusual for parents to send their children to the peasant systems. Overcrowding in the camps was intolerable and could be relieved if children were sent to relatives in the villages, but, in the case of girls, probably of greater importance was the wish that they be taught peasant customs and thereby prepared for a peasant life.

But, as an official working party reviewing educational changes since the demise of the Labour Camps has remarked recently, 'To the outsider, development on the line of rail has been spectacular. In the hinterland, however, in much of what we have seen, time has frequently stood still. We are fully mindful of the efforts that have been, and are being, made to make the rural areas more attractive, to introduce more education and to provide better housing. But it is still correct to observe that in many areas an air of resignation and hopelessness prevails. An attitude which many hold is that improvement cannot be expected, and will not be seen, in their time' (1968 Teaching Service: 30). For a people who were largely indifferent to education and its opportunities during the inter-war years, but who now clamour for education, this means that their children's life chances will be handicapped if they remain in the peasant systems. 'It is a simple belief of many rural people that if they can only get their children to the urban areas, then places in schools will be guaranteed, often an all-important consideration' (1968 Teaching Service: 30). Beginning with the growth of Towns for Africans (Mitchell 1954: 6) there has been a tendency for children whose parents live in the villages to be sent to live with relatives in towns.

The reasons for this are clear. First, Africans have long recognised that the best teachers are to be found in the Enclave. For instance, the pioneering and only state-run educational institutions — Hodgson Technical College, Munali Secondary School, and Chalimbana Teacher Training College — which provided the models for local education authority schools, were located within the Enclave Society; so too was Chipembi Girls Secondary School which led female education. In the 1950s no distinction was made between pupils on tribal criteria: Bemba, Barotse, Tonga and Luvale might occupy the front row of a classroom together, thereby creating an important condition for a united nation. As English was the compulsory tongue of the dormitory as well as the classroom tribal differences were eroded. But the sovereign African government at first made a faint effort to disperse secondary schools away from the line of rail (1965 Transitional Development Plan: 27), partly to demote Munali from its seminal position and to ensure that children received secondary education close to their birthplaces, partly to decelerate rural-urban mobility. However, it was soon realised that this would lead to parochialism and hinder the mixing of people with diverse backgrounds which is necessary for national unity. The colonial pattern was restored and students encouraged to undertake secondary education in areas away from their homes (1966 Development Plan: 56). But as interchange between peasant areas is extremely difficult and often takes several weeks it is probable that peasant children will find it easier to attend urban schools in pursuance of this policy.

Undoubtedly the best teachers and the intelligentsia cling to the Enclave Society and will change their jobs if this is the only way they can continue an urban way of life. It requires saints and not teachers of ability to endure the housing provided for rural teachers. In some peasant areas 75 per cent of the teachers live in 'semi-permanent houses' or pole and *dagga* huts (1968 Teaching Service: 20). As long as teachers are paid less than their educational equivalents in other occupations, or believe this to be the case, and there is a shortage of teachers, as seems likely for another decade, the trend to keep the best teachers in African Towns will continue. This situation has become so serious that in 1968 the Ministry of Education was compelled to consider a recommendation that all teachers in the national teaching service must serve two years in a designated peasant area before they could be promoted.

The second reason why educational resources are concentrated in African Towns and enhance their attractiveness is that it has been believed that education is a greater necessity for urban children than it is for rural children. It will be recalled that it was planned that the juvenile delinquency rife in Labour Camps should be stopped by providing schools for potential delinquents and making attendance compulsory. Thus in the late 1940s 'compulsory education areas' were designated in the new Towns for Africans, but nowhere else. The building programme this involved even included the replacement of 'condemned buildings, particularly in the Copperbelt' (1950 Reports: 4) — an unheard-of luxury in peasant areas where there were few schools to replace and where the need was for schools in areas where none existed. Undoubtedly the aim of providing schools for all urban children in the 1950s contrasted in the minds of parents with the slow growth of educational facilities in the peasant system.

The post-Independence educational arrangements have reinforced this view of the availability of education in urban areas and the lack of educational opportunities in the hinterland. On arrival at State House in 1964 the President discovered that there were only 105 African graduates available to Zambia. For many jobs which required no more than a secondary education the country was dependent on expatriate labour. Manpower independence then became a priority for security reasons, buttressed by the realisation that the expansion of the economy would be delayed until all the manpower demands of the booming economy were satisfied. With the resources available the most economical way of accelerating the output of secondary education was to concentrate educational expansion in the African Towns (1965 Transitional Development: 21-9). This became a longer term objective in the 1966-70 Development Plans which allocated 58.5 per cent of the capital to be invested in education to the three provinces in which the line of rail and the major African Towns were situated. At the least, the gap in educational provision between the Enclave and hinterland was preserved in this plan. To emphasise the importance of education in African Towns this same plan aimed at providing an upper primary education for *all* children in the towns but for only 75 per cent of peasant children (1966 Development Plan: 55).

Thirdly, the African middle class now has access to the former European schools with their superb facilities, located in the urban areas. European and African Education were administratively merged after Independence but in order to continue the supply of education to children of much needed expatriates the former European schools were designated as fee-paying, with the proviso that they would be open to Africans who could afford their charges as well as to non-Africans (1964 UN/ECA/FAO: 114). Unlike the non-fee-paying schools, English is the medium of instruction in fee-paying schools from the age of five onwards. Instruction is often given by expatriates who are relatively well-educated and to whom English is the mother-tongue. The advantage of this has not been lost on Africans. They do everything possible to enrol their children in the fee-paying schools and thus entrench their middle-class position. The same has occurred in the health services. The 'brain drain' will depress peasant activity even further and deepen what the educational working party described as the 'danger of creating one Zambia, two Nations – the line of rail on the one hand, and the rural areas on the other' (1968 Teaching Service: 19).

CONCLUSIONS

When it was reluctantly agreed that it was impossible in the short run to imprison peasants within their own social systems, 'balanced stabilisation' became policy. To the cynical this was a formula which combined recognition of the realities of the flood to the urban system with the hope that there would be an ebb of worn-out people to the peasant systems. One positive feature of 'balanced stabilisation' was the intention to generate so much wealth in the Enclave Society that appreciable portions of the resultant savings could be ploughed back into the peasant systems to give them new vitality. The other positive feature was that the levels of living of the urban population were raised.

A balance between the sexes in the urban population was sought through measures to increase the attractions of the urban system. Urban schooling became immeasurably superior to that available in peasant systems, and induced parents living in these systems to arrange for their children to be raised in the urban system. The outmigration of children from the Labour Camps was therefore reversed in Towns for Africans. To check juvenile delinquency compulsory education for urban children was introduced. Though this was soon abandoned, in the early 1950s its repercussions were great: peasants believed that education was sure to be available in the urban system and did not note the end of the scheme. Then in the African Towns, to make good quickly the manpower shortfalls projected in the National Plan, preferential treatment was given to urban education. This has crippled peasant education because able, successful, and ambitious teachers are determined to avoid the hardships and limited advancement opportunities which await them in peasant systems. The best teachers and facilities have gravitated to the urban system.

Provision for old age while the Labour Camps lasted was by maintaining and creating individual rights in land and engineering a social atmosphere in a village that would make re-entry into peasant life congenial and tolerable. Trips back to the villages every two or three years at the most were an important means of providing for this kind of retirement. But these trips became less frequent when men lived with their wives in the Towns for Africans, and some urban men may have sold their parcels of land in consequence. What little pension provision was made by employers was designed to be inadequate for an urban retirement and to compel the retired worker to return to a peasant system. For the duration of Towns for Africans, arrangements for retirement to peasant systems tended to be neglected and greater difficulty was experienced at the point of re-entry into peasant life. This is still the case for perhaps the majority of urban people, but is less of a problem now that it is policy to extend pension coverage to all urban employees and to try to pitch the incomes from this at a level more adequate for old age in the urban system.

Since before the break-up of the few and uncharacteristic stockaded settlements at the turn of this century, peasants have lived in small dispersed villages and homesteads which have proved difficult to govern. A norm of adequate space for living has emerged as a result. Thus, when confronted with a choice between sharing cramped urban bachelor quarters with a husband or remaining in a homestead many a wife preferred her homestead. This was the situation of the Labour Camps. The alacrity with which new married quarters were filled in Towns for Africans reveals that this must have been a major consideration in the migration of women. If wives were eager to become townswomen, given the right sort of encouragement, it is less certain that their husbands felt indefinitely committed to the Towns for Africans. Although many tried to obtain security for themselves while they lived in the urban system by paying their own rents, in place of employers as was the official norm, they refused the chance of becoming urban houseowners. One day they would return to the peasant systems, and as a market for African urban houses did not exist they could not conceive of making any kind of profit from owning their own urban homes. The establishment of African Towns is beginning to change this and the number of property owning urban dwellers is increasing. Buying a home means more than acquiring a piece of property and involves liking its setting. For

many urban people this was not right until African controlled towns emerged
and it is in conjunction with this political change that urban home ownership
and urban commitment must be considered.

With better housing, social security, and education, levels of living improved
immensely as a result of 'balanced stabilisation'. Whereas the government of
migration to dam the flood to the towns on the whole failed, the policies to
create a balanced and self-perpetuating urban population have succeeded
admirably because they accorded with the desires of the people involved.

CHAPTER VIII
MIGRATION AND ZAMBIA

Social mobility or social mobilisation (G. and M. Wilson 1945; Deutsch 1966) are terms which describe the kind of migration which has been the subject of this enquiry. One or more of three features were present whenever such social mobility occurred. Sometimes this meant a change in the nature of a migration pattern. An example of this was the replacement of the short term circular migration, typical of the Recruited Labour System and Labour Camps, by the longer absences from peasant systems by temporary target workers involved in the Casual Labour System and Towns for Africans.

A qualitative distinction between metropolitan and local movements indicates a second feature of migration. Metropolitan moves involved contact with alien social systems. The relocation of villages necessitated by the periodic soil exhaustion inherent in the *citimene* modes of cultivation or hunting parties were once characteristic local moves. Slave caravans and perhaps raiding parties were more metropolitan movements away from the centres of small-scale African systems. In their place outmigration to wage labour and urban life have become the characteristic metropolitan moves. There is a vital difference between the metropolitan moves of the past and present. Apart from a few elderly women, it is likely that at present all African adults have experience of metropolitan moves whereas in the past this was the experience of a minority.

Nation-building provides the context of a third feature of migration in Zambia. Migration takes place in social systems or societies within which a migrant can move freely. In the nineteenth century, a clan or tribal system encapsulated the widest possible movement of a normal African. Today the national society of Zambia, incorporating the peasant successors to seventy-three tribal systems plus the capitalist and urban systems, represents the widest area within which free movement by a Zambian is possible. Though the constitution assumes a homogeneous society, Zambia is in fact a heterogeneous society. A Zambian is not free to migrate and live in each of the heterogeneous parts of Zambia. This is especially true of mobility among the peasant systems. But compared with the tribe to which a man was restricted in pre-contact times, the extent of metropolitan migration has expanded enormously within the supra-system of Zambia. For instance, in 1969 almost 33 per cent of the population of Zambia lived in districts other than those in which they had been born. The Director of Census regards this movement as a blessed 'bond uniting the people of Zambia into one nation. This is a very happy situation in the context of the national motto "One Zambia, One Nation".' Thus by establishing new positions peasant, capitalist and urban systems were created; by supplying the appropriate personnel for these positions migration met a necessary condition for the formation of Zambia.

The novel entity of Zambia was the culmination of a chain of reactions initiated when tribesmen were induced to fill positions created by the imperial Government and capitalism. Whereas capitalism in the concentration known in Zambia is rare, imperialism has been a force in much of the Third World. Capitalism therefore distinguished the country from so many others. In response to its rewards, tribesmen committed social suicide and acquired new social personalities.

The three steps in this process involved characteristic personalities. Step one involved the worker in a strictly limited contract with mammon. While he worked for this god he was unhappy because he remained devoted to his tribe and village. So a man would work a tolerably short stint and save most of the wealth he received. When a predetermined target was achieved, his contract with the god was at an end and he set off quickly to his village with his booty. The village served him as a base from which he would set out on several occasions in his lifetime to raid the capitalist system instead of a neighbouring and prosperous tribe. The Permanent Target-Worker describes this conduct.

Step two was reached when the rewards of mammon were wanted more than the combination of wages and subsistence production enjoyed by the Permanent Target-Worker. The worker now wanted to earn money not in order to accumulate savings to be transferred to his village, but rather to earn his subsistence as well as consumer durables from capitalism. Unemployment, ill-health and old age prevented a man from permanently exchanging his labour for money, but until misfortune struck he would not return to a village. This was the Temporary Target-Worker, the man who set out to work only a short while for capitalism but then was persuaded to work for as long as possible.

Step three concerns the Industrial Man who has no choice but to work for capitalism. Unlike the preceding social personality, an Industrial Man is dependent on capitalism for his livelihood, even in old age. A minority now behave as Permanent Target-Workers and Industrial Men; the majority are Temporary Target-Workers.

This study of migration has examined capitalism in the aspects of the labour markets which match the supply and demand for wage labour. Three aspects of the labour market became important to the labourer. Initially he knew nothing about capitalism and its products and did not desire those things that could be obtained through wage labour. To overcome this inertia of ignorance and indifference, capitalism and Goverment compelled men to migrate to centres of employment. Recruitment of labour in the villages was the instrument whereby this was achieved. No matter how high the rewards offered by capitalism, they had no meaning for a villager to whom they were unknown and who did not want the products they could purchase. The labour recruiter, however, provided a villager with an opportunity to earn enough to pay his poll tax. Once a man had experience of wage labour, he readily appreciated the utility of some of the goods he could buy with his cash. At first the greater utility of manufactured goods for clothing, utensils and other necessary equipment became impressed upon the labourer, who recognised their superiority over those he could make for himself. Only later did he aspire to own a luxury item such as a bicycle or a radio. Recognition of the utility of manufactured products led to wage labour as long as a cash income could not be obtained from farming or fishing, and this was discouraged by Government and traders for a time. A second kind of resistance to wage labour appeared at this point. The villager had not lost his ability to fend for himself and if there was not a considerable positive advantage to be derived from wage labour he was prepared to make do with goods produced by his own household economy. As one effect of the Recruited Labour System – as well as the proto-capitalist establishments it often supplied – was to keep wages low, considerable reluctance to engage in wage labour continued, and until the 1920s created labour shortages. A man who would rather not work for wages under such disadvantageous circumstances was exploited during the tenure of his contract with a labour-recruiter.

The second matter which concerned a villager was that labour recruitment meant that he was selected by an employer who might be unknown to him. Rarely would several labour-recruiters open a market in the same village and compete in offering terms to villagers. A labour recruiter tended to monopolise the labour supply of a group of villages. Once he had experienced a labour contract and observed differences among employers in his metropolitan movements a villager tried to avoid dependence upon a single source of employment, which might not be the best available. To achieve this independence and freedom of choice he was prepared to take pot luck, migrate under his own steam, and hope he would find a suitable employer at the end of his journey. This meant that he would be away from home for a longer period than was normal under a labour recruitment contract, but it was distinctly preferable. After the Mining Companies on the Copperbelt stopped labour recruitment in 1931, there was scarcely an alternative to casual labour within Zambia, but this action was not the cause of casual labour, which had already been noticeable prior to the First World War. Casual labour was devised by peasants to overcome what they considered to be imperfections on the demand side of the labour market.

At first many casual workers were exploited and compelled to work for capitalism rather than their own social systems, but they preferred to minimise the unpleasantness of labour forced upon them by choosing where they worked. Political exploitation which drove men to work in mines and shops vanished in the 1930s when most worked for periods longer than was necessary to pay taxes. It seems an unexplained paradox of Southern Africa in general, and not of Zambia alone, that wages were sticky and barely moved in real or money terms during the half-century 1900-50. Yet in response to this constant reward, more and more labour became available – so much so that by the early 1950s an absolute shortage of labour was experienced, a shortage which could scarcely be overcome by raising the rewards of recruitment or improving the transport facilities from remote villages to the mines.

Conventional economic theory encourages the appreciation of the state of a labour market by a marginal formula such as the effect on the supply of labour of a change of one unit of the marginal price paid to it. But this fails to explain an increasing supply of labour in response to a fixed demand. What seems to have happened is that Africans substituted more and more capitalist employment for less and less non-capitalist employment. In consequence a worker might increase his annual cash income by sacrificing his contribution to the vital task of pollarding trees in *citimene* cultivation. As long as there was employment, a peasant could easily increase his cash income by working more tickets (months) on a mine every year without feeling deprived because of his low wages. When this way of increasing annual incomes could be expanded little further in the 1940s, without encroaching upon necessary holidays and rests, the worker complained about 'slave wages' and demanded that they be raised. Nevertheless he was more committed than ever to capitalist employment and in the 1950s several factories and mines reported labour turnover and absenteeism which compared favourably with Western counterparts at the time. Behind this expansion in the supply of labour was the conversion of wants for blankets, bicycles and the like into the need to live a European style of life. Once set in motion by compulsion, the worker learned new wants and eagerly sought work.

Government materially helped push Africans into employment by capitalists. As long as these were willing to discharge their workers and return them to their villages at frequent intervals, their actions earned them the privileges of recruiting licences. Tension between the Government and capitalism in Zambia developed when the capitalists discarded labour recruitment, and were happy to select a few from a throng of unemployed at their gates and unwilling to return their employees to the villages every eighteen months or so. As the employers and workers were in accord on this, Government wishes did not prevail. At best, Government was able to ameliorate the welfare of Zambia labourers but not the peasant systems whence they were drawn.

With regard to international migration, Rhodesia and the Congo competed as the major consumers of labour migrants from Zambia. When the first modern copper mine in Zambia came into production in 1929 the Congo was being eliminated from the contest and from then until the 1960s Rhodesia was the major receptacle for the one third of all male Zambians engaged in wage labour who were employed in foreign countries. Government was only successful in preventing the emigration of Zambian labour in the case of the Congo in the 1920s and the termination of the supply of Barotse to Witwatersrand in 1965, Government policy encouraged the larger employers in Zambia to prefer Zambians to alien Africans when filling labouring jobs. But many aliens, especially from Malawi, were allowed to fill more responsible posts until Zambia became independent in 1964. Since then they have been squeezed out of employment in Zambia.

Capitalism and imperialism intended that a more or less regulated labour market should be established. But neither from the outset willed the transformation of small-scale African systems and the creation of urban systems as consequences of the labour market. Though the small-scale African systems would have been altered as they were bureaucratised as designated local authorities, it is less certain that without the labour market they would all have become peasant systems dependent upon wage labour. Even the North-Western and Barotse Provinces, the most conservative of all in terms of metropolitan involvements and reluctance to let their women outmigrate, sent many men to work. And the provinces where cash-cropping is important sent more men to work and allowed more women to outmigrate than the conservative provinces. The dependence upon capitalism and the urban system has recently been most evident in two provinces: between 1963 and 1969 an absolute fall in population of 3.4 per cent occurred in the Northern Province and a corresponding fall of 5.9

per cent was recorded for the Luapula Province. This was due to outmigration. Wage labour, rather than the prodding of District Officers determined to make local government more effective, provided the catalyst for rural change. When a man gave up a job and returned to village life he recounted his metropolitan experiences, exhibited his booty and aroused the interest and envy of his fellows. But although the material possessions of wage-earners might be envied, customary ralationships were also prized by villagers. From these sources came the incentives to be peasants who owned a few of the material appurtenances of Western civilisation.

To those for whom peasant life held no appeal, outmigration to an urban system seemed a solution. Migration of this kind was mass migration in contradistinction to the circular migration of the Permanent Target-Worker. With the model of the Permanent Target-Worker in mind (largely the creation of Major Orde Browne when Labour Adviser to the Colonial Secretary) neither social scientists nor government officers recognised the presence of mass migration which included both sexes. They were aware of this as a distinct possibility rather than as reality. Hence they started making plans, which they regarded as anticipatory, sometime after the proverbial horse had bolted. These plans believed that unless specific conditions were created women would not come to the urban system in numbers great enough to help make it attain optimum productivity and a pleasanter environment for workmen. So an immense programme of environmental development tore down the Labour Camps and in their places built Towns for Africans, shortly after substantial numbers of women had arrived in the urban system during the War.

In retrospect there is reason to believe that there was considerable and undetected entry of women into the urban system which predated this change of policy. Perhaps Government was overconfident that the Native Authority and other controls on the movement of women really took effect. Just before Labour Camps began to be demolished, it was possible in 1945 for 63 per cent of the adult urban population to form equal, permanent, heterosexual relationships. This left only 37 per cent of the remaining adult population, men, without the chance of durable sexual partnerships.

In the Towns for Africans on the Copperbelt, by 1951 the proportion of possible sexual unions had risen sharply to 80 per cent; when the Towns for Africans were closed down in 1963, the figure for the whole urban system was little changed at 82 per cent. During the lifetime of Towns for Africans, the population more than doubled, and in the terminal phase the housebuilding programme slackened and had difficulty in keeping pace with the inmigrant flood. The increase in the possible number of sexual unions has been attributed to the inmigration of women to join husbands who by reason of their marriage laid claims to married quarters as soon as they obtained employment. While it is probably true that the majority of women to whom urban married quarters were an important consideration arrived in Towns for Africans, it is not equally valid to believe that this accounted for the inmigration of the majority of women. Not all inmigrant women were already married with an automatic entitlement to family housing. It is possible that in the early 1950s half of all the women in Towns for Africans were not inmigrants who had come to join their husbands. At the time of entry they were not married to urban men. Initially half the urban women were single and potential partners to two-thirds of the urban men who did not have town wives. As capitalist occupations were denied to African women they relied upon cohabitation with men for their subsistence. Thus on a one-to-one basis, though only one-third of the men in the urban system actually lived with their wives, two-thirds of the men could have had regular access to women.

As housing did not directly pull in half of the women in Towns for Africans, it must be presumed that sexual opportunities unknown in the male-starved peasant systems and subsistence were their favourite bait. Important differences in the mobility of these two categories of women appeared once they had arrived in the urban system. Undoubtedly women were in general less mobile than men, but it is also likely that the inmigrant category of single women were even less prepared to leave the Towns for Africans than the married category. The 'intertribal unions' which these 'single'women were prone to contract in the towns were disapproved of in peasant systems. When a husband to an 'intertribal marriage' decided to return to his peasant system, he probably left his wife behind seeking another partner who was prepared to remain in town.

Conditions rapidly changed in African Towns, and evoked a much more positive commitment from their inhabitants than any preceding urban system. For instance, a large number of married men in the Towns for Africans preferred their wives to remain in their peasant homes. In their minds it was probable that they would return to them, and so they sent remittances to their wives whom they visited every year or so. During the first six years of African Towns, more men decided to sink roots in the urban system and summoned their peasant families to join them. Consequently, in 1969, 89 per cent of the adults in African Towns could find partners. It now appears that most of the men who are married and resident in these towns have their wives with them – and thus few of the women who remain in the peasant systems have marital attachments to absent men. In the future this may be as important as the growing differences in economic development in pushing Zambia from a heterogeneous towards a dualistic type of societal organisation. Looking back it may be concluded, since the push factor of the peasant systems remained fairly constant in migration, that the Labour Camps were the least attractive and the African Towns the most attractive urban conditions for family life. But, as has been shown, it can no longer be assumed that there were not a fair number of women in the Labour Camps in their terminal phase.

The miserable conditions in the Labour Camps were due to doubt about the future of the copper mining industry and the desire of Government to encourage industrialisation without urbanisation. It would be a bad business if more money were spent to improve Labour Camps which might become ghost towns, as in 1931 and 1932 when miners were discharged and trudged back to their villages. After international attempts to restrict the output of copper in the 1930s, who could say that the industry was safe in Zambia, until prices and demand rose after the Second World War? For their part government officers were conscious that their mission was to fit a rural people for entry into the world of complex organisation and technology. These rural people ought to step into the modern world with the best of their customs intact and not as mere and total imitators of the West. Urban life threatened to rob them of the good in their past and to needlessly 'detribalise' their social identities. A combination of the African past and the European present was impossible if rural people were overwhelmed by European civilisation. A protectorate government must guard the protected against this danger which was inherent in an urban system.

Social control was a more tangible reason for keeping too many Africans out of the Labour Camps. Capitalist employment would not, it was believed, keep pace with their inmigration. The unhappy experience of India in this regard was cited. It would cause less bother if Africans left their peasant systems only in sufficient numbers to fill known vacancies. For this reason it must be made easy for them to return. Better communication would facilitate this but if family life was impossible in the Labour Camps and available in peasant systems, the Africans would be certain to return, the Government reasoned. Even when Towns for Africans became necessary due to the pressures of Westminster, capitalists and Europeans in Zambia, many government officers were apprehensive. The 1958 recession, with the closing down of a whole mining town, seemed to confirm their worst fears. The newest of these was that if 'detribalisation' proceeded unchecked there would be no viable peasant homes for unemployed people. As the terms of trade moved in Zambia's favour, Towns for Africans were built, when they moved against the economy the boom in housebuilding was reduced to a trickle. This was more than a matter of finance and involved the questions of whether there would be people to live in the new family units and how the unemployed might be supported by destitute urban and peasant systems. Were it not for the demands and strains created by the urban system itself, much more would have been invested by Government in the peasant economies.

One close observer of the Zambian scene has written about 'excessive migration', in the sense of overurbanisation. This he defines as 'a flow of people into towns such as will raise the level of unemployment to an unreasonable degree' (Kay 1967: 80). He points to the fact that 18 per cent of the actual wage labour force in the urban system was unemployed in 1963. But this figure assumes a dual and not a heterogeneous economy and that wages were the sole form of income available to these families. As is explained in Chapter II and Table 7, on a different set of plausible assumptions, urban unemployment in 1963 was below 4 per cent. According to this line of reasoning Zambia was not over-urbanised in 1963. Consequently, the fears of Government were a misapprehension, and here is an exception to the social science belief in over-urbanisation in the Third World. An agricultural economist with considerable experience of Zambia arrived at a similar conclusion after analysing the effects of public investment in peasant economies: funds 'might have secured a better purpose in providing increased facilities for more families to live with their absent menfolk, most of whom were making a better contribution in the national (money) economy than they would be likely to make in the unpromising (peasant) areas from which they came' (Makings 1966: 234). But it would be wrong to describe the government of migration as much ado about nothing. The issues were grave. It is almost in the nature of public policy and social science to be able to understand shortcomings in the past but to be able to predict little of the future.

APPENDIX A
TABLES

TABLE 1

GROWTH: COPPER INDUSTRY, EUROPEAN POPULATION, AFRICAN
WAGE-EARNERS, ALL AFRICANS IN MAIN TOWNS
(Index Numbers [1946:100])

Year	Copper Production Quantity Index	European Population	African Wage-Earners	Africans in Main Towns
1931	5	64	57	20
1946	100	100	100	100
1951	169	168	162	215
1956	204	305	187	290
1961	313	336	169	342
1969	412	197	232	813

SOURCES

Annual Blue Books, Livingstone and Lusaka: Government Printer.
Monthly Digest of Statistics, Salisbury and Lusaka: Central Statistical Offices.
Report of the Directors of Census Regarding the Census taken 5th May, 1931, London: Crown Agents, 1931.
Commission Appointed to Inquire into the Administration and Finances of Native Locations in Urban Areas, Lusaka: Government Printer, 1944.
Report of the 1951 Census, Lusaka: Government Printer.
Final Report of the September 1961 Census of Non-Africans and Employees, Lusaka: Central Statistical Office, 1965.
Second Report of the May/June 1963 Census of Africans, Lusaka: Ministry of Finance, 1964.
Census of Population and Housing 1969: First Report, Lusaka: Central Statistical Office, 1970.

132

TABLE 2

ESTIMATES OF NUMBERS OF AFRICANS
(*millions*)

| | Wage-Earners | | Population | |
| | *Employed in Zambia* | *Zambians employed abroad* | *Main Towns* | *Remainder of Zambia* |
Year				
1931	0.080	0.031	0.025	1.3
1946	0.141	0.064	0.123	1.5
1951	0.229	0.074	0.264	2.2
1956	0.263	0.047	0.357	2.4
1962	0.231	0.094	0.520	2.8
1969	0.327	0.040	1.000	3.0
1971	0.405	n/k		

SOURCES

Report of the Commission Appointed to Enquire into the Financial and Economic Position of Northern Rhodesia, Colonial 145, London: HMSO, 1938.
P. Deane, *Colonial Social Accounting*, London: Cambridge University Press, 1953.
Report of the Census of Population 1951, Lusaka: Government Printer, 1954.
Report of the Census of Africans in Employment taken on 8th May 1956, Salisbury: Central Statistical Office, 1957.
Second Report of the May/June 1963 Census of Africans, Lusaka: Ministry of Finance, 1964.
Census of Population and Housing 1969: First Report, Lusaka: Central Statistical Office, 1970.
Monthly Digest of Statistics, Salisbury & Lusaka: Central Statistical Office.

TABLE 3

MARITAL STATUS OF URBAN AFRICANS
(Adult Men and Women per cent)

Place *(Year)*	MEN			WIVES
	Married: accompanied by Wives	*Married: Wives in Villages*	*Single Men and Youths*	*Married: accompanied by Husbands*
	(1)	(2)	(3)	(4)
Line of Rail				
Broken Hill (1940)	40	14.4	45.6	–
Copperbelt (1951)	62.2	14.3	23.5	95.4
Livingstone (1952)	46.3	18.1	35.6	96.4
Lusaka (1957)	55.2	14.7	30.1	89.2
Eastern Hinterland				
Fort Rosebery (1959)	58	15	27	–

SOURCES

G. Wilson, *An Essay on the Economics of Detribalisation in Northern Rhodesia* 1, Rhodes-Livingstone Paper 5, Manchester: Manchester University Press, 1968, reprint of 1941 edn.

J. C. Mitchell, *African Urbanisation in Ndola and Luanshya*, Rhodes-Livingstone Communication 6, Lusaka: Rhodes-Livingstone Institute 1954.

G. Kay, *A Social & Economic Study of Fort Rosebery*, Rhodes-Livingstone Communication 21, Lusaka: Rhodes-Livingstone Institute 1960.

M. McCulloch, *A Social Survey of the African Population of Livingstone*, Rhodes-Livingstone Paper 26, Manchester: Manchester University Press 1956.

D. G. Bettison, *Numerical Data on African Dwellers in Lusaka Rhodesia*, Rhodes-Livingstone Communication 16, Lusaka, Rhodes-Livingstone Institute, 1959.

TABLE 4

MIGRATION TO BROKEN HILL 1940
(Percentage of Labour Force)

Categories	From Distant Tribes	From Nearer Tribes	Total
	(1)	(2)	(3)
Married: Wives with Them	17.6	28.2	45.8
Married: Wives in Villages	4.1	8.9	13.0
Single Men and Youths	16.7	24.5	41.2
Total	38.4	61.6	100.0

SOURCE:

G. Wilson, *An Essay on the Economics of Detribalisation in Northern Rhodesia I*, Rhodes-Livingstone Paper 5, Manchester: Manchester University Press, 1968, reprint of 1941 edn.

TABLE 5

CHARACTERISTICS OF PEASANT PROVINCES IN ZAMBIA

Peasant areas in Provinces	Persons per square mile		Sex Ratios for all adults (men per 100 women)	Estimated Contribution to National Income arising from Lands and Agriculture, 1964 (££)		
	1937	1969	1963	Subsistence	Cash Sales	All Value added output
	(1)	(2)*	(3)	(4)	(5)	(6)
WESTERN HINTERLAND						
North-Western Province	3.8	7.4	80	6	0	6
Barotseland	5.0	7.6	73	6	1	7
LINE OF RAIL						
Copperbelt Province	2.7	8.9	136	6	5	11
Central Province	3.2	8.0	103	6	12	18
Southern Province	4.9	15.4	91	7	8	15
EASTERN HINTERLAND						
Luapula Province	8.0	17	96	6	1	7
Northern Province	4.9	10	79	6	1	7
Eastern Province	11.3	19	72	6	2	8
All	5.1	10				

*Only those Districts extant in 1937 compared.

SOURCES

G. St.J. Orde Browne, *Labour Conditions in Northern Rhodesia*, Colonial No. 150, London: HMSO, 1938, p. 100.
Second Report of the May/June 1963 Census of Africans, Lusaka: Ministry of Finance, 1964, p. 40.
First National Development Plan 1966-1970, Lusaka: Office of National Development and Planning, 1966, pp. 87, 103, 121, 137, 159, 177, 193.
Census of Population and Housing 1969: First Reprint, Lusaka: Central Statistical Office, 1970, pp. A7, A8.

PEASANT–URBAN MIGRATION IN ZAMBIA

Peasant Provinces (large towns excluded)	Peasant Outmigration Adults aged 22 and over in 1963 (excluding Africans not born in Zambia), resident in Peasant Systems; Percentage of Total Sex Categories		Sex Ratios (men per 100 women)	Urban Inmigration Rate of Inmigration to Main Towns, 1960. Inmigrants Resident in Main Towns as percentage of all Persons born in Province and Resident in Zambia			Sex Ratio for all Ages in Main Towns by Province of Origin, 1960 (males per 100 females)
	Men	Women		Males	Females	Total	
	(1)	(2)	(3)	(4)	(5)	(6)	(7)
WESTERN HINTERLAND							
North Western	46	52	78	10.2	6.8	8.5	138
Barotseland	42	51	68	5.4	2.6	3.8	160
LINE OF RAIL							
Copperbelt	56	46	130	57.8	59.9	58.1	105
Central	43	44	97	20.7	19.4	20.1	106
Southern	40	42	88	5.4	3.6	4.5	143
EASTERN HINTERLAND							
Luapula	39	41	96	8.4	6.6	7.5	129
Northern	36	41	79	13.0	8.9	10.9	137
(Abercorn District)	35	42	76	–	–	–	–
Eastern	37	45	70	12.3	8.7	10.4	127
(Fort Jameson District)	41	49	72	–	–	–	–

SOURCES:

Report on Northern Rhodesia African Demographic Surveys, Salisbury: Central Statistical Office, 1961. *Second Report of the May/June 1963 Census of Africans*, Lusaka: Ministry of Finance, 1964.

TABLE 6:1

RURAL–URBAN MIGRATION IN ZAMBIA

Peasant Provinces Ranked 1 to 8 (Province of Least Outmigration = 8)

Provinces	Peasant Outmigration: Adults aged 22 and over in 1963 (excluding alien Africans) resident in Peasant Systems				Population Change 1963-9 in Peasant Systems
	Men	*Women*	*Combined*	*Rank Order*	*Percentage*
	(1)	(2)	(3)	(4)	(5)
WESTERN HINTERLAND					
North-Western Province	7	8	7	6	+10
Barotseland					
(Western Province)	5	7	6	7	+12
LINE OF RAIL					
Copperbelt Province	8	6	8	8	+26.3
Central Province	6	4	5	4	+ 6.8
Southern Province	4	3	3	4	+ 6.8
EASTERN HINTERLAND					
Luapula Province	3	1	2	1	− 5.9
Northern Province	1	1	1	2	− 3.4
Eastern Province	2	5	3	3	+ 6.3

SOURCE:
Table 6.
Census of Population & Housing 1969: First Report, Lusaka: Central Statistical Office, 1970.

TABLE 7

ESTIMATED AFRICAN WORKFORCE BALANCE SHEET FOR ZAMBIA
(in thousands)

ASSETS

Population	1963	1969	Change
Children under 15 years	44.8	46.0	+1.2
Elderly more than 44 years	11.4	13.9	+2.5
Women 15-44 years	22.7	21.7	−1.0
Men 15-44 years	21.1	18.4	−2.7
Total Percentage	100.0	100.0	
Total numbers	3,409	3,998	+589

AVAILABLE WORKFORCE

	1963	1969	Change
(a) Workers for incomes mainly in cash	31.8	36.3	+4.5
Workers for incomes mainly in kind	68.2	63.7	−4.5
Total Percentage	100.0	100.0	
Total Numbers	889	1,111	+222
(b) Urban* women	4.9	5.4	+0.5
Urban* men	21.6	22.7	+1.1
Rural† women	27.1	23.3	−3.8
Rural† men	46.4	48.6	+2.2
Total Percentage	100.0	100.0	
Total Numbers	889	1,111	+222

DEPLOYMENT IN CAPITALIST SYSTEM

Actually and Mainly Work for Cash	1963	1969	Change
Urban* women	1.5	3.9	+2.4
Urban* men	58.1	48.4	−9.7
Rural† women	1.0	3.5	+2.5
Rural† men	39.4	44.2	+4.8
Total Percentage	100.0	100.0	
Total Numbers	283	403	+120

UNEMPLOYMENT: Seeking Cash Jobs

	1963	1969	Change
Urban* women	n/k	2.8	n/k
Urban* men	3.1	3.1	±
Rural† women	n/k	13.2	n/k
Rural† men	5.2	15.1	+9.9
Total Percentage of Available Workforce	n/k	34.2	
Total Numbers	74	382	

*Main Towns

†More accurately, non-main towns plus rural.

TABLE 8

MIGRATION, MODERNISATION IN ZAMBIA

| *Stage of Modernisation* | *Social Systems* | | *Social Action Systems* | |
	Labour Markets	*Urban Systems*	*Wage-Earners*	*Women*
1. Take-off	Recruited Labour	Labour Camps	Tribal Man	Tribal Woman
ditto	ditto	ditto	Exploited Man	ditto
ditto	ditto	ditto	Permanent Target-Worker	Peasant Woman
2. Routinisation	Casual Labour	Towns for Africans	Temporary Target-Worker	Urban Woman
ditto	ditto	African Towns	Industrial Man	ditto

TABLE 9

ECONOMIC SYSTEMS OF ZAMBIA

Characteristics	Pre-Capitalist	Peasant	Capitalist
Income Source:	Slash and Burn	Wage Labour OR Cash Crops	Industry and Commerce
Form of Exchange:	Barter	Barter/Money	Money
Market Extent:	Nil	Local/National	National/International
Organisation:	Decentralised	Decentralised	Centralised
Decision Location:	Village	Village	Town
Occupational Mobility:	Nil	Low	High
Produces Loyalty to:	Tribe/Clan Descent Group	Extended Family	Diffuse Family
Orientation:	Consumption	Consumption	Consumption/ Production

TABLE 10

RESOURCES FOR PEASANT AND URBAN SYSTEMS IN ZAMBIA

Resources	Peasant Systems	Labour Camps	Towns for Africans	African Towns
Mobility	Outmigration high Immigration low	Inmigration high Outmigration high	Inmigration high Outmigration higher	Immigration high Outmigration low
Scale and Density of Settlement	Very low	Scale low Density high	Scale low Density higher	Scale higher— growth of peri-urban areas. Density lower?
Ethnic Differentiation	Nil	High	High	High
Demographic Disproportion	Shortage of Men	Acute Shortage of Women	Shortage of Women	Equality Among Young Adults
Economic Differentiation	Nil	Low	Slightly higher	Higher
Local Government	African Controlled	Total European Control	Africans Consulted	African Controlled
Welfare of Africans	Abysmal	Low	Higher	Higher

TABLE 11

DIVORCE IN ZAMBIA

System	Type	Size of Sample	Percentage Divorced*	Mode of Descent
Lamda	Peasant	285	41.8	Matrilineal
Ngoni	Peasant	427	36.9	Omnilateral
Ndemba	Peasant	347	61.4	Matrilineal
Mambwe	Peasant	220	27.9	Patrilineal
Luvale	Peasant	303	45.0	Matrilineal
Plateau Tonga	Peasant	655	38.4	Matrilineal
Gwembe Tonga	Peasant	327	26.3	Matrilineal
Cewa	Peasant	108	51.6	Matrilineal
Nkana	Urban	430	25.6	Bilateral

*Divorced at least once and possibly remarried.

SOURCES:

J. C. Mitchell, 'Aspects of African Marriage on the Copperbelt of Northern Rhodesia', *Rhodes-Livingstone Journal*, 22, 1957, 1-30.

J. C. Mitchell, 'Marriage Stability and Social Structure in Bantu Africa', *International Population Conference*, 1961, pp. 255-263.

C. N. N. White, *An outline of Luvale Social and Political Organisation*, Rhodes-Livingstone Paper 30, Manchester: Manchester University Press, 1960.

M. Marwick, *Sorcery in its Social Setting*, Manchester: Manchester University Press, 1965.

APPENDIX B

SOME LABOUR HISTORIES

by M. G. MARWICK

1. Sindikani Phili's Journey to Southern Rhodesia

The following description given to me by a boy aged about sixteen of his first journey to the distant labour centres, then still fresh in his memory, reflects some of the anxieties, frustrations and excitements of such an undertaking. Speaking in Ceŵa, Sindikani told me of his experiences, and I recorded them in mixed English and Ceŵa.

In October 1949, I began to get ready for my journey to Southern Rhodesia. My maize-flour I carried in a new towel, and a fowl I put in a pot. At Kambaua village, where I slept the first night, the fowl was stolen. I had obtained a pass from Chief Kaŵaza. I got on to a lorry at Sinda Stop [near Kambaua village] on a Sunday. We travelled through the night and arrived in Lusaka on the Monday. This part of the journey cost me twenty-three shillings. In Lusaka, they took our names to find whether anyone had been lost on the way. After that, I went to the compound where the passengers from the lorries all stay. The following day my friend and I went to the Government offices to have our passes put in order. They were unable to see us, and told us to come back next day. When this had gone on for two weeks – without our having our papers put in order – we became very worried. We therefore took the train to Livingstone, where, having been sent to the hospital to be vaccinated, we had our papers put in order without much trouble. We were in Livingstone two days. At three o'clock one afternoon, we set off on foot for the Victoria Falls. We walked because we were short of money. At the Victoria Falls the next morning they [Southern Rhodesian officials] lined us up to count us and see where we had come from; and, on the third day, we caught the train for Bulawayo. We had free passes on the train – it's 'Government' [i.e., free – part of the Southern Rhodesian scheme then operating to facilitate the entry of labour migrants]. Our free passes expired at Nyamandlovu, and we had to pay ninepence each to get to Bulawayo, where we arrived at 7 a.m. We got off the train and went to the place where people go before they have any work. The friend who had made the journey with me deserted me. I was very much afraid, as I was only a child. I knew why he had left me: he wanted to go to Johannesburg, and he said that, since I was a child, I might die on the way there. I therefore decided to go to Gwelo and get work there.

At 2 p.m. I went to the railway ticket office and bought a ticket to Gwelo for four and ninepence. I got to Gwelo at seven o'clock that evening. I slept at the station, and next morning went to seek my mother's brother, Mawano. I found him at 12 o'clock on Mr R's farm. He received me well; he went to the store to buy me sugar and bread, and he made me tea, and I drank it well. When I was drinking it, he asked me all about here at home, asking, 'Is all well at home?' I said, 'Yes.' I slept there where he was, and next morning started to go out to look for work; but my uncle stopped me, saying that I should rest for one week. I rested for a week and then on the Monday I went to look for work. Mr R. gave me a job – in the garden where I worked for three weeks. He promised me thirty-five shillings a month because I was still a child. He told me that if I worked well he would raise my wages to two pounds. He then put me in the dairy to work the cream separator and make butter in a glass churn, which I used to take to the kitchen when the butter was made. I worked at this for six months, and then left (after giving notice properly) because, as a person of work [an able-bodied person], I felt that I should be earning more. At the time of my going, we troubled each other very much, the Master and I. I cancelled my notice and then gave it again. He wanted to have me arrested, and my uncle, too, who wanted to go to another town.

Eventually I left in April 1949, and went to work in a shoe factory in Gwelo. My starting wage was two pounds a month. They told me that I would have to work for at least six months. I earned from two pounds to two pounds fifteen shillings a month, depending on the amount of overtime I worked. I gave notice in July 1951 and went to the office of the Native Commissioner to have my documents put in order for the journey home. I then got on the train, paying nine shillings and elevenpence for the journey from Gwelo to Salisbury; and four shillings and ninepence from Salisbury to Bindura. I paid half-a-crown for a lorry fare from Bindura to Mount Darwin. At Mount Darwin [from which the free transport operated at the time], I had to stay a month because there were many people waiting to go down to the Zambezi. When I eventually got to the Zambezi, I lost a basin and twenty enamel plates, altogether worth about two pounds. I left them on the lorry, and remembered about them only after the lorry had gone back to Mount Darwin. When we had crossed the Zambezi, the boy from a village near home with whom I was travelling and I got on our bicycles (which we had bought for twelve pounds each in Salisbury) and took four days to reach home. Each night we slept in villages, buying food with our money; we got it for reasonable prices.

We entered our home villages at seven or eight o'clock in the evening because this is one of our customs. There are certain people who have bad hearts, as if sorcerers, who, if they see you coming with a big bag with many blankets and nice pillows, say: 'That person has come back with many things.' If you don't give them a shirt or some money or something, they start seeking medicines with which to kill you. We do this only in our home villages. On the road there's nothing to fear.

When I was in Southern Rhodesia I earned good money, and on returning I had thirteen pounds, a bicycle and other things, such as shorts, [long] trousers, six shirts and a jacket. When I came back I was in great trouble and confusion, not knowing how to take my money and divide it among my relatives. Some I gave ten shillings; another, a pound; and another, two pounds. In July 1950, I had sent home five pounds to my mother so that my relatives could buy a beast. On my return they rejoiced, saying, 'You've done well because you have bought a "bank".'

At the end of his story, Sindikani and I had a general discussion of his experiences, which produced the following miscellaneous afterthoughts:

On the way to Southern Rhodesia, when I was in Lusaka, I had some trouble because someone stole my supply of maize-flour. When I was working in the shoe factory in Gwelo, a watchman stole three pairs of shoes, and they imprisoned him for two months. Another man stole a bath towel, and they caught him and imprisoned him for a month. At Gwelo a man was killed by dynamite. When they were making a dam, he went down after an explosion to clear away the rubble, when an unfired charge of dynamite exploded and killed him. They buried him, and the Europeans said it was an accident. In Gwelo someone had his money and blanket stolen, and they were unable to find the culprit. On 25 October 1950, there was a motor-cycle race in Gwelo. A man called B once assaulted an Indian, and they arrested him and took him to prison where he stayed for two months. When we were on our way to Southern Rhodesia, a man on the train started making tea on a pressure stove. The European guard caught him and hit him and put him in prison when we reached Bulawayo because he might have set the train on fire. At the shoe factory in Gwelo, two houses fell down in December 1950 because of the wind and rain, and one end of the tennis-shoe building collapsed. At Mr R's farm, the African foreman had a fight with one of the workers, and Mr R discharged him. In 1951 Mr R, who was very obese and could not walk well, went to hospital to have some fat removed. When I left him, he was well. I didn't want to work in Bulawayo because there are *tsotsis* [juvenile delinquents] there who kill their fellow-men. The Fort Victoria train was once derailed and took a whole week to complete its journey. On the way to Southern Rhodesia, I saw some wild animals from the train when we were near Mazabuka. I was delighted to see them. When we arrived at the Victoria Falls, I cried very much because I felt home was very far away. I was greatly depressed; but from that time onwards I stayed with the thought, 'No matter; if God keeps me, I'll see home again.' A certain prisoner went mad, and they tied him up and took him to the hospital. As I watched this, I felt great compassion for him. The grown-up son of Mr R fought with an African, and the African was badly beaten. Mr R discharged him, but didn't have to have him arrested.

2. David Mwanza's Journey

The following is my translation, slightly abridged, of an account written for me by David Mwanza. It refers to the year 1936 when he was about twelve years old.

I had been staying with my mother's sister at a village near the Mzime river for two months, when, one day, my father arrived in the company of another man and the latter's children. He said, 'What do you think? I'm going to Southern Rhodesia.' On hearing this, I rejoiced in my heart. I said, 'I'm coming with you.' My father said, 'Your mother has sent you a fowl to eat on the way to Southern Rhodesia.' We stayed in the village for a day.

On starting our journey, we were three children and two adults. After three days' journey, we slept at a village in Portuguese territory. There we met others who were going to Southern Rhodesia, and with them formed a single company. On the way we met my brother who was returning from Southern Rhodesia. Since our company was poor and without rations and without blankets, my brother took his blanket and gave it to me, and he gave me sixpence that I might eat on the way.

One day we came to a stream. As I bent down to drink, I saw a bicycle pump under the water. When we arrived at a village we found people coming home from Southern Rhodesia; and we sold it to them without any haggling for half-a-crown.

At that place we were three days' journey from the Zambezi. And our companions told us [children], 'When you see the Zambezi, you are not to exclaim because, if you do, we'll all die of disease of the belly.' We went on and we came to a small hill from which one could see the Zambezi; and we all saw it. This was when we were a day's journey from it. We went on, and, after a short distance, I exclaimed, 'Oh!' My companion asked me what I was exclaiming about. I replied, 'I was exclaiming at the size of that enormous Zambezi.' My companion reported this to the adults, who were very angry indeed and wanted to beat me.

. . . .

We went on and came to a village where we slept. The next afternoon at three o'clock we came to the Zambezi. We slept there. Next day we waited until the sun reached its nine o'clock position, when we saw many people coming from Southern Rhodesia singing songs. When they landed on our side of the river, they all went, and we got on to the ferry. The men operating the ferry went off to drink beer and returned at one o'clock. We started our crossing and went slowly because there was not much water. We reached the other bank at four o'clock. We slept there. We ate wild fruit that grows on the banks of the Zambezi.

We started off [next morning] and, after travelling a long distance, cooked some food at about four o'clock in the afternoon. Then we started to traverse a long stretch of country where there is no water anywhere for forty miles. We traversed it during the night, not knowing that there were small villages on the way at places where the Government was having wells dug. At one of these we got into trouble by trying to kill an animal which turned out to be a pig; and were saved from serious consequences by a man going in the opposite direction, who threatened to beat the people who were trying to detain us.

We went a long distance, and all became very tired. The adults said, 'Come, let's sleep.' We slept; and started off early the next morning and travelled until the sun reached its ten o'clock position, when we arrived at a place called Mkumbula, where we cooked food and where they gave us maize to roast. This was because the Government had laid down that persons going to

Southern Rhodesia should receive maize to eat. We left there, and, after a
long journey, came to a certain village. There we found women who smoked
tobacco; and, since my father had tobacco, we bought maize-flour with it.

We slept there; and next morning left and came to a hill called Makomo.
The path goes right over it. We climbed it from six o'clock until eleven
o'clock. We went on a little, and came to Mandawi [Mount Darwin?], where
people from here [Northern Rhodesia] take out documents for entry into
Southern Rhodesia. There they showed us houses for defecating in – what
Europeans call latrines – saying, 'This is yours; and that is the women's.' The
next morning they gave us the work of sweeping the yard. When we had
finished, we went to the office to await our documents. They gave us these in
the afternoon, when the doctor came to examine people for sores, rash and
venereal disease. He found many people with these, but he didn't discover my
sore thumb, which I had hurt on the way, because I had thrust it into the
sand and it was difficult to see the sore.

Then they called us to the house of the senior European where they
instructed us in the manner in which we should conduct ourselves in
Southern Rhodesia. When they had finished, they said that those who wanted
to go could go. We went that same day, and that evening slept in the bush
because there was no village nearby. There was no water there, and, on going
to find some, we found the place where cattle had been drinking; we drew
some and cooked our food with it, not caring that it was dirty.

Next morning we resumed our journey and came to [the farm of] the
European where my elder [classificatory] brother, Patisoni, was. On our
arrival he was greatly distressed at seeing that I had come. He said, 'Come, let
us go home [together] because I have much money and [with it] I shall buy
all you want.' But I would not agree [to his taking me home]. And he gave
me half-a-crown that I might eat on the way because [he saw] we really
intended to press on. And another acquaintance gave me a shilling; and
another, sixpence. We slept the night at that European's farm.

The next day we continued on our way, and, after a long journey, came to
where my 'small father', who had married my mother's sister, was. He gave
me ninepence. We pressed on. At that time I became very lame; my feet were
blistered, and I could not walk properly. I therefore asked my father to buy
me some tennis shoes. This he did . . . . . We walked a long way and came to a
certain stretch of country which resembled a large *dambo*. We went a long
way, and the sun set. There was no tree nearby, but we eventually found one,
which we cut down and used for making a fire. We slept there, but ate
nothing because there was no water. Next morning we pressed on. We came
to a stream and [after we had cooked food] I refused to eat any because I
had quarrelled with my father . . . . . . Before the food was finished, I heard
something say, 'Ku---u.' They all told me it was a train. I was greatly
frightened because this was my first experience [of a train]. And my father
told me I must eat the food; otherwise the train would strike me. In fear I ate
the food. The train went.

We slept the night on the way, but in the bush. Next morning we reached
the farm of a European where we found many Tumbuka people. We asked
them about the character of their European [master]. They gave a good

account of him; and we went to ask him for employment. He took us on civilly, and immediately gave us maize-meal [as opposed to pounded maize-flour]. He told us to go and build ourselves huts.

This was in October 1936 that we started work. At the end of a month we children received five shillings; and the adults, fifteen shillings. And seeing that, on leaving home, we had had no proper clothes, we were [now] in rags. We bought clothes. Shorts cost [me] half-a-crown; a shirt, half-a-crown; all my money was finished.

We worked four months; and in the fifth month one of our companions fell ill of the chest. And there came a certain deceitful person who said he knew how to prepare medicines for the chest. He began seeking these for our companion. He said that his price was one and sixpence, but, as we had no change, our companion gave him half-a-crown, telling him to get change at the store and bring back a shilling. But did he return? On receiving the half-crown he went, and was not seen again in spite of our searching for him.

We were greatly worried on account of the sick person. In April 1937, we realized that his illness had become very serious. Therefore my father said, 'It were well that we went home lest he should die here.' Our homeward journey began in May 1937. I had altogether two pounds, ten shillings; and my [child] companion, the same. My father had six pounds, fifteen shillings; and the sick man, five pounds, ten shillings. On leaving work, we went to buy at the store. I bought shorts, a shirt, a belt, a sweater, a hat and tennis shoes; and my friend did the same. We began our journey home . . . . . We took four weeks and arrived home in the fifth week. Everyone rejoiced exceedingly, especially my mother, who danced very much. It was in the month of June that we arrived home. I perceived that my elder [classificatory] brother, Patisoni, who had now returned home, rejoiced [at our return]; and so did my elder brother, Kadze. Seeing that I had ten shillings [of my money left], I took half-a-crown to give to my mother, but she refused it; I gave Kadze two shillings, and he bought a pair of shorts and a shirt. And with the half-crown my mother had refused I bought shorts, and with two shillings I bought two hoes, one for my mother and one for me. I gave a shilling to another [classificatory] mother, the mother of Patisoni. And half-a-crown I kept that I might give it to my other [classificatory] mothers.

There were many fowls at home. We ate as many as eighteen, and twelve remained. There was much joy because I remembered the words I had spoken when still a child, viz., 'I want, if I go to Southern Rhodesia and return, to eat many fowls.' The tennis shoes I had bought I gave to another elder brother . . . . . I stayed at home for six months, and in November there came a teacher to start school in the village. [After I had got over the fear of being laughed at for making mistakes in reading], I began school.

3. Notes of an Interview with a Man recently returned from Work, 18 December 1952

The informant said that he had been through Southern Rhodesia to Kimberley and Cape Town and 'Western Germany', which turned out to be South-West Africa. He was in Cape Town for two weeks, and found many people from Northern Rhodesia living there. (He pointed out that, in a distant labour centre, if a person comes from near your home, you are as if his brother, and make friends with him.) At this time he was out of work, but during the two weeks he found work with a canning company who sent him to Walvis Bay [South-West Africa] to work in a fish canning factory. There he earned in a week as much as he would earn in a month here, i.e., two pounds, ten shillings. Provided you were not too fond of beer and women, he added, you could put in a good deal of overtime and earn up to seven pounds a week. (This sounded an exaggeration, since he quoted the overtime rate at one and sixpence an hour.) When I asked him what he had done with his money (he worked two years, from 1949 to January 1952), he said that the bank of black people was their hands: that he had not bought any cattle, and that by the time you had bought yourself clothes, clothed your wife and had some beer, the money was gone. In reply to a question he said that he would very much like to go again, and would write to his employers in Walvis Bay for a document enabling him to go back. In reply to another question he said that it was not possible to make money locally. Some people were lucky and made it, e.g. if they had cattle. A grain-store yielded the best kind of money, although he did not think that the price of maize was good.

4. A Typical Labour History summarized

Person	Journey No. Date	Place of Work	Kind of Work	Duration	Wages (shillings) p.m.	Rations Provided?
Cuzu Phili, a man	1 c.1899	Carrying between Fort Jameson and Tete		3 years	3	Yes
born c. 1884	2 c.1906	Carrying between Fort Jameson and Ndola		8 months	5	Yes
	3 'before 1916'	Local farm	With cotton	3 weeks	4	Yes
	4 do.	Local farm	Well-digging	1 month	3	Yes
	5 do.	Local farm	With cotton	2 months	3	Yes
	6 do.	Mvuma, S.R.	In a mine	1 year	30	Yes
	7 1916	Jombo Mine, S.R.	In a mine	1 Year	60	Yes
	8 1926	Near Salisbury	On a farm	1 year	12	Yes

REFERENCES AND SOURCES

ALLAN, W., *The African Husbandman*, Edinburgh: Oliver and Boyd, 1965.

ARMOR, M., *Unauthorised Locations in Lusaka Urban District*, Lusaka: Boma, 1958.

——, *African Housing in Lusaka Urban District*, Lusaka: Boma, 1958.

——, 'Migrant Labour in the Kalabo District of Barotseland', *Bulletin of the Inter-African Labour Institute*, 9, 5-42, 1962.

BALDWIN, R. E., *Economic Development & Export Growth: A Study of Northern Rhodesia 1920-1960*, Berkeley and Los Angeles: University of California Press, 1966.

BARBER, W. J., *The Economy of British Central Africa*, London: Oxford University Press, 1961.

——, 'Urbanisation & Economic Growth: the Cases of Two White Settler Territories', *The City in Modern Africa* (ed. H. Miner), London: Pall Mall, 1967, pp. 91-126.

BARNES, J. A., *Marriage in a Changing Society*, Rhodes-Livingstone Paper 20, London: Oxford University Press, 1951.

——, *Politics in a Changing Society*, London: Oxford University Press, 1954.

——, 'The Fort Jameson Ngoni', *Seven Tribes of British Central Africa* (2nd impression, eds. E. Colson & M. Gluckman), Manchester: Manchester University Press, 1959, pp. 194-252.

BERG, E. J., 'Backward-Sloping Labor Supply Functions in Dual Economies – the Africa Case' *Quarterly Journal of Economics*, 65, 3, 1961.

BETTISON, D. G., *Numerical Data on African Dwellers in Lusaka, Northern Rhodesia*, Rhodes-Livingstone Communication 16, Lusaka: Rhodes-Livingstone Institute, 1959.

—— and RIGBY, P. J., *Patterns of Income & Expenditure Blantyre-Limbe Nyasaland* Rhodes-Livingstone Communication 20, Lusaka: Rhodes-Livingstone Institute, 1959.

BEZY, F., 'Problems of Economic Development of Congo' *Economic Development for Africa South of the Sahara* (ed. E. A. G. Robinson), London: Macmillan, pp. 71-88, 1963.

BOEKE, J. H., *Economics & Economic Policy of Dual Societies as Exemplified by Indonesia*, New York: Institute of Pacific Relations, 1953.

BOGUE, D. J., 'Techniques & Hypotheses for the Study of Differential Migration' *International Population Conference*, Paper 114, pp. 405-11, 1961.

BOHANNAN, P., *Social Anthropology*, New York: Holt, Rinehart and Winston, 1963.

BRADLEY, K., *Diary of a District Officer*, London: Harrap, 1943.

BROMWICH, E., oral communication to H. Heisler, 25.6.1966.

BUELL, R. L., *The Native Problem in Africa*, New York: Macmillan, 1928.

BURDEN, G. N., 'Labour Migration in Africa Part 1', *Corona* 3, 1951.

CALDWELL, J. C., 'Introduction' *The Population of Tropical Africa* (eds. J. C. Caldwell and C. Okonjo), London: Longmans Green, pp. 3-27, 1968.

——, *African Rural-Urban Migration: the Movement to Ghana's Towns*, Canberra: Australian National University Press, 1969.

CLAY, G. F., *Memorandum on Post War Development Planning in Northern Rhodesia*, Lusaka: Government Printer, 1945.

CHAMBER OF MINES, *Year Book*, Kitwe: Chamber of Mines, 1957, 1958, 1959.

COLSON. E., *Marriage and Family among the Plateau Tonga* Manchester: Manchester University Press, 1958.

———, The Social Organisation of the *Gwembe Tonga*, Manchester: Manchester University Press, 1960.

———, 'Trade and Wealth among the Tonga' *Markets in Africa* (eds. P. J. Bohannan and G. Dalton) Evanston, Ill.: Northwestern University Press, 1962, pp. 601-16, 1962.

———, 'Competence & Incompetence in the Context of Independence,' *Current Anthropology*, 8, 92-111, 1967.

COULTER, C. W., 'The Sociological Problem', *Modern Industry and the African* (ed. J. Merle Davis, 2nd edn. with a new intro. by R. I. Rotberg) London: Cass, pp. 31-130, 1967.

CUNNISON, I. G., *Kinship and Local Organisation on the Luapula* Rhodes-Livingstone Communication 5, Lusaka: Rhodes-Livingstone Institute, 1950.

——— *The Luapula Peoples of Northern Rhodesia*, Manchester: Manchester University Press, 1959.

DAVIS, J. Merle, *Modern Industry and the African* (2nd. edn.) London: Cass, 1967.

DAVIS, K. and GOLDEN, H., 'Urbanisation and the Development of Preindustrial Areas', *Economic Development and Cultural Change*, 3, 6-26, 1954.

DEANE, P., *Colonial Social Accounting*, London: Cambridge University Press, 1953.

DEUTSCH, K. W., *Nationalism & Social Communication* Cambridge, Mass.: M.I.T. Press, 1966.

DOOB, L. W., *Communication in Africa*, London: Yale University Press, 1961.

EAMES, E. and SCHWAB, W., 'Urban Migration in India and Africa', *Human Organisation*, 23-7, 1964.

ELIZAGA, J. C., 'Internal Migration in Latin America', *International Social Science Journal*, 17, 213-31, 1965.

EPSTEIN, A. L., *The Administration of Justice and the Urban African*, London: HMSO, 1953.

———, *Politics in an Urban African Community*, Manchester: Manchester University Press, 1958.

———, 'Urbanisation and Social Change in Africa' *Current Anthropology*, 8, 275-95, 1967.

FOSBROOKE, H., 'Effects of Economic Change on African Society', *Economic Development in Northern Rhodesia*, Study Conference 2, Lusaka: Northern Rhodesia Association, 1958.

———, 'Can Labour be Stabilised with Permanent Urbanisation and Concomitant Social Security Measures?', *Present Interrelations in Central African Rural and Urban Life*, 11th Conference of the Rhodes-Livingstone Institute, Lusaka: Rhodes-Livingstone Institute, pp. 88-94, 1958.

FURSE, R. *Aucuparius: Recollections of a Recruiting Officer*, London: Oxford University Press, 1962.

GANN, L. H., *The Birth of a Plural Society*, Manchester: Manchester University Press, 1958.

GARDINER-BROWNE, *Memorandum on Native Policy in Northern Rhodesia* Lusaka: National Archives, 1950.

GLASS, R., 'Urban Sociology in Great Britain' *Readings in Urban Sociology* (ed. R. Pahl) London: Pergamon Press, 1968, pp. 63-73.

GLUCKMAN, M., 'Kinship & Marriage among the Lozi of Northern Rhodesia and the Zulu of Natal', *African Systems of Kinship and Marriage* (eds. A. R. Radcliffe-Browne and D. Forde), London: Oxford University Press, 1950, pp. 166-206.

————, 'Anthropological Problems arising from the African Industrial Revolution', *Social Change in Modern Africa* (ed. A. Southall), London: Oxford University Press, 1961, pp. 67-82.

————, *Order & Rebellion in Tribal Africa*, London: Cohen and West, 1963.

GOODFELLOW, D. M., *Principles of Economic Sociology*, London: Routledge, 1939.

GUGLER, J., 'On the Theory of Rural-Urban Migration: the Case of Sub-Saharan Africa', *Migration*, Sociological Studies 2 (ed. J. A. Jackson), London: Cambridge University Press, 1969, pp. 134-155.

GUILLEBAUD, C. W., *Report and Award of the Arbitrator Nominated under the Industrial Conciliation Ordinance to Arbitrate in a Dispute between the Northern Rhodesia African Mineworkers Trade Union and the Copper Mining Companies*, Lusaka: Department of Labour, 1953.

HAILEY, Lord, *An African Survey*, London: Oxford University Press, 1938.

————, *Report on Native Administration in British Tropical Africa* London: HMSO, 1940-2.

————, *Note on the Bearing of Native Policy on the Proposed Amalgamation of the Rhodesias and Nyasaland*, Confidential, London: Colonial Office, 1941.

————, *An African Survey: Revised Edition 1956*, London: Oxford University Press, 1957.

HALL, B. (ed.), *Tell Me Josephine*, London: Andre Deutsch, 1964.

HANCE, W. A., *Population, Migration & Urbanisation in Africa*, New York: Columbia University Press, 1970.

HANCOCK, P. J., *Report on the Social Survey held in Ndola Main Location*, Lusaka: Institute of Social Research, 1958.

HARRIES-JONES, P., 'The Tribes in the Towns', *The Tribes of Zambia* (ed. W. V. Brelsford), Lusaka: Government Printer, rev. edn., 1965, pp. 124-46.

HAUSER, P. M., 'The Social, Economic & Technological Problems of Rapid Urbanisation' *Industrialisation and Society* (eds. B. F. Hoselitz and W. F. Moore), The Hague: Mouton-UNESCO, 1963, pp. 199-217.

HEISLER, H., 'Continuity & Change in Zambian Administration' *Journal of Local Administration Overseas*, 4, 183-93, 1965.

————, 'Class and Class Competition in a Plural Society', Cardiff: University of Wales, Ph.D. Thesis, 1970.

————, 'A Class of Target-Proletarians', *Journal of Asian & African Studies*, 5, 161-75, 1970.

————, 'The Creation of a Stabilised Urban Society in Northern Rhodesia/Zambia', *African Affairs*, 70, 125-45, 1970.

————, 'Approaches to the Study of Social Change & Zambia', *Sociologus*, 21, 2. 1971.

————, 'Two Causal Models of African Economic Conduct', *Economic Development & Cultural Change*, 21, 1, 1972.

HEUSSLER, R., *Yesterday's Rulers: the Making of the British Colonial Service*, London: Oxford University Press, 1963.

HICKMAN, A. S., *Men Who Made Rhodesia*, Salisbury: British South Africa Company, 1960.

HOLE, H. M., *The Making of Rhodesia*, London: Macmillan, 1926.

JANSEN, C., 'Some Sociological Aspects of Migration' *Migration* Sociological Studies 2 (ed. J. A. Jackson) London: Cambridge University Press, 1969, pp. 60-73.

————, 'Migration: a Sociological Problem', *Readings in the Sociology of Migration* (ed. C. Jansen) Oxford: Pergamon Press, 1970, pp. 3-26.

JOHNSON, H. M., *British Central Africa*, 3rd edn., London: Methuen, 1906.

JONES, D. A., 'Two Views of European Influence on African Behaviour' *The*

Multitribal Society Proceedings of the 16 Conference of the Rhodes-Livingstone Institute (ed. A. A. Dubb), Lusaka: Rhodes-Livingstone Institute, 1962, pp. 39-48.

———, 'Social Networks of Farmers among the Plateau Tonga of Zambia', *The New Elites of Tropical Africa* (ed. P. C. Lloyd), London: Oxford University Press, 1966, pp. 272-85.

JONES, R. J. D., *The Welfare of African Workers* Johannesburg: Anglo American Corporation of South Africa Ltd., 1957.

———, 'The Effects of Urbanisation in South and Central Africa' *African Affairs*, 52, 37-44, 1953.

KAY, G., *A Social and Economic Study of Fort Rosebery*, Rhodes-Livingstone Communication 21, Lusaka: Rhodes-Livingstone Institute, 1960.

———, *Maps of the Distribution and Density of African Population in Zambia*, Institute of Social Research Communication 2, Lusaka: University of Zambia, 1967.

———, *Changing Patterns of Settlement and Land Use in the Eastern Province of Northern Rhodesia*, Occasional Papers in Geography 2, Hull: University of Hull Publications, 1967.

———, Social Aspects of Village Regrouping in Zambia, Department of Geography Misc. Series 7, Hull: University of Hull, 1967.

KIEWIET, C. W. de, *A History of South Africa: Social and Economic*, London: Oxford University Press, 1941.

KUCZYNSKI, R. R., *Demographic Survey of the British Empire II*, London: Oxford University Press, 1949.

LEE, J. M., *Colonial Development and Good Government*, London: Oxford University Press, 1967.

LEHMANN, D., 'Marriage, Divorce & Prostitution of African Women in a Changing Society', *Marriage and the Family*, Lusaka: Government Printer for Northern Rhodesia Council of Social Service, 1961, pp. 27-35.

LENIN, V. I., *Imperialism: the Highest Stage of Capitalism*, Moscow: Progress Publishers, 1968.

LEWIN, C. J., *Agricultural & Forestry Development Plans for Ten Years*, Lusaka: Government Printer, 1945.

LEWIS, W. A., *The Theory of Economic Growth*, London: Allen and Unwin, 1955.

LONG, N., *Social Change & the Individual*, Manchester: Manchester University Press, 1968.

LORIMER, F., BRASS, W., van der WALLE, E., 'Demography', *The African World: Survey of Social Research*, ed. R. A. Lystad, London: Pall Mall, 1965.

LUGARD, Lord, *The Dual Mandate in British Tropical Africa* 5th edn., London: Frank Cass, 1965.

MAKINGS, S. M., 'Agricultural Change in Northern Rhodesia/Zambia: 1945-1965', *Food Research Institute Studies*, 6, 1966, 195-247.

MARWICK, M., *Sorcery in its Social Setting*, Manchester: Manchester University Press, 1965.

McCULLOCH, M., 'Survey of Recent and Current Field Studies on the Social Effects of Economic Development in Inter-Tropical Africa', *Social Implications of Industrialisation & Urbanisation in Africa South of the Sahara* (ed. D. Forde), Paris: UNESCO, 1956, pp. 52-225.

———, *A Social Survey of the African Population of Livingstone*, Rhodes-Livingstone Paper 26, Manchester: Manchester University Press, 1956.

MIRACLE, M. P., and FETTER, B., 'Backward Sloping Labour Supply

Functions and African Economic Behaviour', *Economic Development & Cultural Change* 18, 240-251, 1970.

MITCHELL, J. C., 'The Tribes in the Towns', *The Tribes of Northern Rhodesia* (ed. W. V. Brelsford), Lusaka: Government Printer, 1956, pp. 109-121.

——, 'Aspects of African Marriage on the Copperbelt of Northern Rhodesia', *Rhodes-Livingstone Journal*, 22, 1-30, 1957.

——, 'Labour Migration in Africa South of the Sahara: the Causes of Labour Migration', *Bulletin of the Inter-African Labour Institute*, 6, 12-46, 1959.

——, 'Wage Labour & African Population Movements in Central Africa', *Essays on African Population* (eds. K. M. Barbour and R. M. Prothero), London: Routledge and Kegan Paul, 1961(*a*), pp. 193-248.

——, 'Social Change and the Stability of African Marriage in Northern Rhodesia', *Social Change in Modern Africa* (ed. A. Southall), London: Oxford University Press, 1961(*b*), pp. 316-30.

——, 'Marriage Stability and Social Structure in Bantu Africa' *International Population Conference*, 1961(*c*), pp. 255-63.

——, 'Labour and Population Movements in Central Africa', *Essays on African Population* (eds. K. M. Barbour and R. M. Prothero), London: Routledge and Kegan Paul, 1961(*d*), pp. 193-248.

——, 'Urbanisation, Detribalisation, Stabilisation & Urban Commitment in Southern Africa: a Problem of Definition & Measurement: 1968', *Urbanism, Urbanisation and Change: Comparative Perspectives* (eds. P. Meadows and E. H. Mizruchi), Reading, Mass.: Addison-Wesley Publishing Co., 1969.

MITCHELL, M., *Basic Information on the Structure of Local Government in Northern Rhodesia at 31 December 1962*, Salisbury: Department of Government, University College of Rhodesia and Nyasaland, 1963.

MOORE, W. E., 'The Adaption of African Labour Systems to Social Change', *Economic Transition in Africa* (eds. M. J. Herskovits and M. Harwitz), London: Routledge and Kegan Paul, 1964, pp. 277-98.

MULFORD, D. C., *The Politics of Independence 1957-1964*, London: Oxford University Press, 1967.

MUNGER, E. S., *African Field Reports 1952-1961*, Cape Town: C. Struik, 1961.

NATIVE COURTS ADVISER, 'A Note on African Marriage & Divorce', *Marriage and the Family*, Lusaka: Government Printer for Northern Rhodesia Council of Social Service, 1961, pp. 6-14.

NIDDRIE, D., 'The Road to Work: Survey of the Influence of Transport on Migrant Labour in Central Africa', *Rhodes-Livingstone Journal*, 15, 31-42, 1954.

ORDE BROWNE, G. St. J., *Labour Conditions in Northern Rhodesia* Colonial 150, London: HMSO, 1938.

PETERS, D. U., *Land Usage in Serenje District*, Rhodes-Livingstone Paper 19, London: Oxford University Press, 1950.

PHILPOTT, R., 'The Mulobezi-Mongu Labour Route', *Rhodes-Livingstone Journal*, 3, 50-54, 1945.

PRAIN, R. L., 'The Stabilisation of Labour in the Northern Rhodesian Copperbelt', *African Affairs*, 55, 1956, 305-17.

——, *Selected Papers Vol. III*, London: Roan Selection Trust Group 1964.

PRIESTLEY, J. S. W. and GREENING, P., *Ngoni Land Utilisation Survey 1954-1955*, Lusaka: Government Printer, 1956.

PROTHERO, R. M., 'Migration in Tropical Africa', *The Population of Tropical Africa* (eds. J. C. Caldwell and C. Okonjo), London: Longmans Green, 1968, pp. 250-63.

RAVENSTEIN, E., 'The Laws of Migration', *Journal of the Royal Statistical Society*, 52, 1889, 241-305.

READ, M., 'Migrant Labour in Africa & its Effects on Tribal Life', *International Labour Review*, XLV, 1942, 605-31.

RICHARDS, A., *Land, Labour and Diet in Northern Rhodesia*, London: Oxford University Press, 1939.

———, 'Some Types of Family Structure among the Central Bantu' *African Systems of Kinship and Marriage* (eds. A. R. Radcliffe-Browne and D. Forde), London: Oxford University Press, 1950, pp. 207-51.

———, 'A Changing Pattern of Agriculture in East Africa: the Bemba of Northern Rhodesia', *Geographical Journal*, 124, 1958, 302-314.

———, 'Multi-Tribalism in African Urban Areas', *Urbanisation in African Social Change*, Edinburgh: Centre of African Studies, University of Edinburgh, 1963, pp. 43-51.

RICHARDSON, E. E., *Aushi Village Structure in the Fort Rosebery District of Northern Rhodesia*, Rhodes-Livingstone Communication 13, Lusaka: Rhodes-Livingstone Institute, 1959.

RICHMOND, A. H., *Post-War Immigrants in Canada*, Toronto: University of Toronto Press, 1967.

RIDLEY, H. C. N., 'Early History of Road Transport in Northern Rhodesia' *Northern Rhodesia Journal* 2, 5, 1955, 16-23.

ROACH, J. C., 'A Theory of Lower-Class Behaviour', *Sociological Theory & Paradigms* (ed. L. Gross), New York: Harper, 1967, 294-314.

ROBINSON, E. A. G., 'The Economic Problem', *Modern Industry and the African* (2nd edn., J. Merle Davis), London: Cass, 1967, pp. 131-226.

ROCKETT, E. T., *Industrial Injury Insurance in Britain and its Relevance to the Further Development of Social Policy in Zambia* Lusaka: Ministry of Labour and Social Development, 1966.

ROTBERG, R. I., 'Rural Rhodesian Markets', *Markets in Africa* (eds. P. J. Bohannan and G. Dalton), Evanston, Ill.; Northwestern University Press, 1962, pp. 581-600.

ROTH, R. and WITTICH, C., eds., *Max Weber: Economy and Society*, New York: Bedminster Press, 1968.

SADIE, J. L., 'The Social Anthropology of Economic Underdevelopment', *Economic Journal*, 70, 1960, 294-303.

SAFFERY, A. L., *A Report on Some Aspects of African Living Conditions on the Copperbelt of Northern Rhodesia*, Lusaka: Government Printer, 1943.

ST. JOHN-WOOD, A. H., 'Administration and Myth in Central Africa; *Myth in Modern Africa*, 14th Conference Proceedings of the Rhodes-Livingstone Institute for Social Research (ed. A. A. Dubb), Lusaka: Rhodes-Livingstone Institute, pp. 38-49, 1960.

SCOTT, P., 'The Role of Northern Rhodesia in African Labour Migration', *Geographical Review*, XLIV, 1954, 432-4.

SKINNER, E. P., 'Labour Migration among the Mossi of the Upper Volta' *Urbanisation and Migration in Africa* (ed. H. Kuper) Berkeley and Los Angeles: University of California Press, 1965, pp. 60-84.

SJOBERG, G., 'Rural-Urban Balance & Models of Economic Development' *Social Structure & Mobility in Economic Development* (eds. N. J. Smelser and S. M. Lipset), London: Routledge and Kegan Paul, 1966, pp. 235-61.

SMITH, E. W. and DALE, A. M., *The Ila-Speaking Peoples of Northern Rhodesia*, reprint of 1922 edn., New York: University Books, 1968.

SOUTHALL, A., 'Population Movements in East Africa', *Essays in African*

Population (eds. K. M. Barbour and R. M. Prothero), London: Routledge and Kegan Paul, 1961, pp. 157-92.
――――, 'Introduction', *Social Change in Modern Africa*, London: Oxford University Press, 1961, pp. 1-66.
SPEARPOINT, F., 'The African Native & the Rhodesian Copper Mines', Supplement to the *Journal of the Royal African Society*, 36, 1937.
STOOKE, G. BERESFORD, *Memorandum on African Development in Northern Rhodesia*, Lusaka: Government Printer, 1943.
TAYLOR, J. C. and LEHMANN, D., *Christians of the Copperbelt*, London: SCM Press, 1960.
TAYLOR, W. L., 'Problems of Economic Development of the Federation of Rhodesia and Nyasaland', *Economic Development of Africa South of the Sahara* (ed. E. A. G. Robinson), London: Macmillan, 1963, pp. 222-45.
THOMAS, B., *Migration and Economic Growth*, London: Cambridge University Press, 1954.
THOMSON MOFFAT, *The Native Affairs Conference held at Victoria Falls*, Lusaka: National Archives, 1933.
TRAPNELL, C. G., *The Soils, Vegetation and Agriculture of North-Eastern Rhodesia*, Lusaka: Government Printer, 1943.
―――― and CLOTHIER, J. N., *The Soils, Vegetation & Agricultural Systems of North-Western Rhodesia*, Lusaka: Government Printer, 1937.
TURNER, V. W., *Schism and Continuity in an African Society*, Manchester: Manchester University Press, 1957.
UNECA, 'Size & Growth of Urban Population in Africa' *The City in Newly Developing Countries* (ed. G. Breese), Englewood Cliffs, N.J.: Prentice-Hall, 1969, pp. 128-45.
VELSEN, J. van, 'Labour Migration as a Positive Factor in the Continuity of Tonga Tribal Society', *Social Change in Modern Africa* (ed. A. Southall), London: Oxford University Press, 1961, pp. 230-41.
WATSON, W., *Tribal Cohesion in a Money Economy*, Manchester: Manchester University Press, 1958.
――――, 'Labour Migration in Africa South of the Sahara: Migrant Labour & Detribalisation', *Bulletin of the Inter-African Labour Institute*, 6, 2, 1959, 8-32.
WILSON, G., *An Essay on the Economics of Detribalisation I* Rhodes-Livingstone Paper 5, Livingstone: Rhodes-Livingstone Institute, 1941.
――――, *An Essay on the Economics of Detribalisation in Northern Rhodesia Part II*, Rhodes-Livingstone Paper 6, Manchester: Manchester University Press (reprint 1968), 1942.
WILSON, G. and M., *The Analysis of Social Change*, Cambridge University Press, 1945.
WINTERBOTTOM, J. M., 'The Ecology of Man & Plants in Northern Rhodesia', *Rhodes-Livingstone Journal*, 3, 1945.
WHITE, C. M. N., *A Preliminary Survey of Luvale Rural Economy*, Rhodes-Livingstone Paper 29, Manchester: Manchester University Press, 1959.
――――, *An Outline of Luvale Social & Political Organisation*, Rhodes-Livingstone Paper 30, Manchester: Manchester University Press, 1960.
――――, 'Social Change & Community Development', *Social Research & Community Development* 15 Conference of the Rhodes-Livingstone Institute for Social Research (ed. R. Apthorpe), Lusaka: Rhodes-Livingstone Institute, 1961, pp. 100-7.

————, 'Factors Determining the Content of African Land-Tenure Systems in Northern Rhodesia', *African Agarian Systems* (ed. D. Biebuyck), London: Oxford University Press, 1963, pp. 364-73.

WRONG, D., "The Oversocialised Conception of Man in Modern Sociology', *American Sociological Review*, 26, 1961, 183-193.

ZACHARIAH, K. C., 'Bombay Migration Study: a Pilot Analysis of Migration to an Asian Metropolis', *Demography*, 3, 1966, 378-92.

(1926) District Circular 15.

(1927) District Circular 8.

(1929) *Report of the Commission on Closer Union of the Dependencies in Eastern & Central Africa*, Cmnd. 3234, London: HMSO.

(1930) District Circular 14.

(1931) District Circular 9.

(1932) *Report of the Finance Commission*, Livingstone: Government Printer.

(1935) *Report of the Commission Appointed to Inquire into the Disturbances in the Copperbelt*, Lusaka: Government Printer.

(1935) *Report of the Commission Appointed to Inquire into the Disturbances on the Copperbelt, Northern Rhodesia, Evidence Vol. I.*, Lusaka: Northern Government Printer.

(1935) *Minutes of the Provincial Commissioners Conference 1935*, Lusaka: National Archives.

(1935) *The Recruiting of Labour in Colonies and Other Territories with Analogous Labour Conditions Report IV*, 19 Session, Geneva: International Labour Office.

(15.6.1936) File SEC/FIN/23, Lusaka: National Archives.

(1936) *Minutes of the Conference of Provincial Commissioners*, Lusaka: National Archives.

(1936) *Report of the Chairman of the Native Industrial Labour Advisory Board, November-December 1935*, Lusaka: Government Printer.

(1936) *Report of the Inquiry into Emigrant Labour*, Zomba: Government Printer.

(1938) *The Minutes of the Proceedings of the First and Second Meetings of the Native Development Board with Appendices*, Lusaka: Government Printer.

(1938) *Report of the Commission Appointed to Consider and Advise on Questions relating to the Supply and Welfare of Native Labour in Tanganyika Territory*, Dar-es-Salaam: Government Printer.

(1938) *Minutes of the Provincial Commissioners Conference*, Lusaka: National Archives.

(23.6.1938) File SEC/H/4, Lusaka: National Archives.

(1938) *Report of the Commission Appointed to Enquire into the Financial and Economic Position of Northern Rhodesia*, Colonial 145, London: HMSO.

(1939) District Circular 3.

(1939) *Minutes of the Provincial Commissioners Conference 1939*, Lusaka: National Archives.

(1939) District Circular 39.

(Feb. 1940) File SEC/NAT/92, Lusaka: National Archives.

(1940) *Northern Rhodesia 1938*, Colonial Reports, Annual No. 1935, London: HMSO.

(1941) *Report of Commission Appointed to Enquire into the Disturbances on the Copperbelt, Northern Rhodesia*, July 1940 Lusaka: Government Printer.

(December 1942) File SEC/NAT/351, Lusaka: National Archives.

(February 1942) File SEC/DEV/1, Lusaka: National Archives.

(1942) *International Labour Review* 45.

(1942) *International Labour Review* 46.

(1943) Circular Minute NAT/K2 28 July, Lusaka: National Archives.

(1943) *Minutes of the Provincial Commissioners Conference*, Lusaka: National Archives.

(1943) *International Labour Review,* 48.

(25.1.1944) File SEC/LAB/71, Lusaka: National Archives.

(Sept. 1944) File SEC/LAB/34, Lusaka: National Archives.

(1944) *Report of the Commission Appointed to Inquire into the Administration & Finances of Native Locations in Urban Areas*, Lusaka: Government Printer.

(2.1.1945) File SEC/LAB/27, Lusaka: National Archives.

(23.7.1945) File SEC/LAB/27/63, Lusaka: National Archives.

(5.9.1945) File SEC/LAB/27/79, Lusaka: National Archives.

(1945) *Minutes of the Conference of Provincial Commissioners and Heads of Social Service Departments*, Lusaka: National Archives.

(1945) District Circular 6.

(13.2.1946) File SEC/LG/1, Lusaka: National Archives.

(1946) District Circular 5, Lusaka: National Archives.

(1947) *Interim Report of the Commission of Inquiry into the Cost of Living*, Lusaka: Government Printer.

(1947) *International Labour Review* 55.

(1947) *Interim Report of the Commission of Inquiry into the Cost of Living*, Lusaka: Government Printer.

(1948) *Financial Report 1947*, Lusaka: Government Printer.

(1948) *Review of the Ten-Year Development Plan of Northern Rhodesia*, Lusaka: Government Printer.

(1948) *Minutes of the Conference of Provincial Commissioners and Heads of Social Service Departments*, Lusaka: Government Printer.

(November 1948), File SEC/LAB/34, Lusaka: National Archives.

(1949) *Report of the Financial Relationship Committee*, Lusaka: Government Printer.

(1949) *Minutes of the Administrative Conference for Provincial Commissioners & Heads of Social Service Departments*, Lusaka: Government Printer.

(1949) *Report of the Financial Relationship Committee*, Lusaka: Government Printer.

(Feb. & March 1950), File SEC/LG/49, Lusaka: National Archives.

(1950) *Reports of Secretaries & Members to accompany His Excellency The Governor's Address to the Legislative Council at the Opening of the Third Session of the Ninth Council 1950*, Lusaka: Government Printer.

(1950) *Final Report of the Commission of Inquiry into the Cost of Living*, Lusaka: Government Printer.

(1951) *Central African Territories: Comparative Survey of Native Policy* Cmnd. 8235, London: HMSO.

(2.8.1952) Circular Minute N/0082/1.

(8.10.1953) Circular Minute 102/4.

(August 1957) Commissioner of Police, Lusaka.

(1958) 'Urban Problems in East and Central Africa', *Journal of African Administration*, 10, 182-251.

(1958) *Report of the Urban African Affairs Commission 1958*, Salisbury: Government Printer.

(1960) *Survey of Developments Since 1953*, Cmnd. 1149, London: HMSO.

(1961) *Report on Northern Rhodesia African Demographic Surveys 1960*, Salisbury: Central Statistical Office.

(1961) *Report of the Rural Economic Development Working Party*, Lusaka: Government Printer.

(1962) *Draft Development Plan for the Period 1 July 1961 to 30 June 1965*, Lusaka: Government Printer.

(1962) *Symposium on Unemployed Youth* Publication 89, Dar es Salaam: CCTA.

(1963) *1963 Report on the World Social Situation*, New York: UN.

(1964) *Report of the UN/ECA/FAO Survey Mission*, Lusaka:Government Printer.

(1964) *Second Report of the May/June 1963 Census of Africans*, Lusaka: Ministry of Finance.

(1965) *First Report on Urban African Budget Surveys held in Northern Rhodesia May to August 1960*, reprint, Lusaka: Central Statistical Office.

(1965) *An Outline of the Transitional Development Plan*, Lusaka: Central Statistical Office.

(1965a) *Final Report of the September 1961 Census of Employees*, Salisbury: Central Statistical Office.

(1965b) *Final Report of the September 1961 Censuses of Non-Africans & Employees*, Lusaka: Central Statistical Office.

(1966) *Housing & Social Services: Evidence to the Commission of Enquiry into the Mining Industry by Copper Mining Companies*, Lusaka: Copper Mining Companies.

(1966) *First National Development Plan 1966-1970*, Lusaka: Office of National Development and Planning.

(1967) *Annual Report of the Department of Labour 1965*, Lusaka: Government Printer.

(1968) *Education in Transition: Report of the Administrative Working Party Appointed to Examine Certain Aspects of the Teaching Service*, Lusaka: Ministry of Education.

(1970) *Statistical Yearbook 1969*, Lusaka: Central Statistical Office.

(1970) *Census of Population & Housing 1969*, First Report, Lusaka: Central Statistical Office.

INDEX